About the Author

A domestic violence survivor, Rosie Malezer was born in 1971 in Queensland, Australia. She is a profoundly Deaf, legally blind, Indigenous Australian author, writer, Copy-Editor, Proof-Reader, Translator and Professional Book Reviewer, and is a proud member of the Gubbi Gubbi tribe. Gubbi Gubbi Country is situated on the Sunshine Coast in Queensland. She studied AUSLAN (Australian Sign Language) in her youth, and used it in her employment, with the Queensland government, to translate conversations between Deaf customers and police. When Rosie lost her hearing *completely* in 2014, she studied ASL (American Sign Language) extensively, under the guided tutelage of Dr Bill Vicars.

Rosie's father – a retired police officer of the Royal Australian Navy – trained her in the usage and safety of various guns at a very early age. Although she enjoys target shooting, Rosie is strictly against the idea of hunting for fun; her belief being that unless you need to hunt an animal for food and clothing, in order to survive, animals should be treated with respect, and left to live in peace.

Rosie is now a housewife with a wonderful and supportive husband – a hearing man who learned ASL just so he could communicate with her. She dedicates all of her spare time promoting awareness of issues relating to domestic violence, the vilification of her own people in her home country, as well as standing up for Deaf rights. When not writing, she spends her time doing everything she can to remove the communication barriers between the Deaf and Hearing people of the world.

Dedication

The internet became a big game changer for me. Without it, I would not have met three very important people from across the globe. These people have not only helped me survive, they also helped me to thrive.

~ To Tommi ~

You protected me, and gave me hope, from the other side of the globe. Because of you, I survived... and discovered the beauty of Finland.

~ To Marko ~

You married me, and rolled with all the punches and speed bumps that came with these damaged goods. When I lost my hearing, you didn't even flinch at learning a new language and embraced our new journey, without sound.

~ To Dr Bill Vicars ~

You selflessly gave your free time, in order to tutor me and my husband, giving us a new way to communicate when I became profoundly Deaf. As a result, my marriage is stronger than it has ever been.

I thank you all from the bottom of my heart and soul.

Rosie Malezer

CHANGE YOUR NAME AND DISAPPEAR

A terrifying true tale of survival

Copyright © Rosie Malezer (2017)

The right of Rosie Malezer to be identified as author of this work has been asserted by her in accordance with section 77 and 78 of the Copyright, Designs and Patents Act 1988.

All rights reserved. No part of this publication may be reproduced, stored in a retrieval system, or transmitted in any form or by any means, electronic, mechanical, photocopying, recording, or otherwise, without the prior permission of the publishers.

Any person who commits any unauthorized act in relation to this publication may be liable to criminal prosecution and civil claims for damages.

A CIP catalogue record for this title is available from the British Library.

Cover Illustration "Blood Roses" © Charli Siebert

ISBN 9781785548741 (Paperback)
ISBN 9781785548758 (Hardback)
ISBN 9781785548765 (eBook)

www.austinmacauley.com

First Published (2017)
Austin Macauley Publishers Ltd.
25 Canada Square
Canary Wharf
London
E14 5LQ

Acknowledgments

I would like to thank my mum who, regardless of her torment, was forthcoming with the full details of Steve's pestering, in order that the details in this book were accurate. Both of my parents have pointed out that it was never a case of my family not ringing or contacting me, but rather a case of Steve answering the phone, saying I wasn't home and hanging up. This was something I never knew until I started writing this book.

Thank you, also, to my Finnish family. Marko held me through all of my tears and calmed me down through each panic attack I suffered, while writing these pages. Sirpa, my amazing mother-in-law, helped me to keep my head on straight, and motivated me to continue writing until the book was complete, and Tommi, who picked up the shattered pieces from the floor, each time I remembered something new to include in the book.

NOTE TO READERS

Within these pages is a part of my life which still haunts me to this very day. While many memories are lost to me forever, due to the injuries received, I have written what I could, in the hopes that other women do not follow the same path.

While all places and incidents detailed within these pages are real, people's names have been changed to protect their identity.

Readers' discretion is advised, as some of the contents are of an extremely graphic nature.

"It's ironic that it was not until I lost my hearing that I finally found my voice. Sign language saved my soul."

- Rosie Malezer (2015)

Chapter 1

A college graduate, Tammy had landed her dream job in the legal field. Shortly afterwards, a brand new martial arts studio opened its doors in the building directly behind the one where she worked in Fortitude Valley. Having studied both Judo and Karate as a child, Tammy had decided to sign up. She had always loved martial arts. Although this school specialised in Kung Fu, it was situated in such a convenient location and would teach her the necessary skills to defend herself from attackers. She was happy and confident. With no interest in anything except for her job and keeping fit, Tammy was excited to be able to practise her newly acquired martial arts skills as often as she wanted.

Tammy's job allowed her to constantly meet and interact with some amazing people. Most days would end on a high. At the end of each day, she changed into her martial arts uniform, took her training weapons from her locker and walked down the secret "staff only" staircase which led directly to the doors of the Kung Fu studio. Having already graduated to her second belt just six months after signing up, she was very excited as she had memorised the drill for the Chinese Knife over the past few weeks, practising it until she had it perfect. Tonight it was her turn to shine in front of the class. If only the instructor would pick her.

Training was always fun. Tammy was a regular at the martial arts studio, training at least five or six days of the week, enjoying the sweat and the hard work. She stood in line and waited. Steve, the instructor of her class, tried to psyche the class out, advising that he would be making each and every one of them perform the Chinese Knife drill in front of the whole school. A slight tingle of butterflies stirred in her stomach. The school was big and she did not anticipate performing the drill in front of so many people. But Tammy decided she had nothing to fear. She would impress them all.

Steve asked the class who wanted to go first. Tammy's hand shot up in an instant. She looked around and saw that nobody else had volunteered. Regardless, her hand shot up even higher and her face beamed with excitement. With a smile, Steve asked Tammy to approach the front of the class. He then used his booming voice to get the attention of all other students training that night. Quickly and obediently, they formed three lines, similar to that seen during military drills, and stood at ease. Steve announced to the students and instructors that Tammy had volunteered to perform her Chinese Knife drill for their viewing pleasure. This was it. It was her chance to shine and to demonstrate what she had learned.

Masterfully and so gracefully, she showed how well she could wield her weapon. Every step was exactly as she had been taught. Her mind was no longer on the students or instructors, but solely on the Chinese Knife. Her full focus and concentration were on her arm movements, her feet, the positioning of the knife. Tammy swung the weapon so elegantly, picturing that she and blade were one. She wanted to be the best, and she wanted her class and teachers to know that she knew her routine down to the very last detail. What surprised her at the end of the drill, however, was the silence. Still standing in the final position of the practised routine and facing the students, Tammy's mind left her place of peace and returned to those who had watched. It was then that she noticed their mouths agape; eyes open wide. Then one word was uttered from the instructor's mouth: "*Wow*" Students of the school then started to applaud. Tammy could not stop smiling. She looked at her instructor with pride and Steve told her that he was impressed. Those words meant the world to her. She looked up to him so much and his approval made her heart swell.

A few weeks after her success with the Chinese Knife, Tammy was now hard at work trying to master *two* new weapons, which would be no easy feat. The Double Daggers were weapons she could wear on her belt, while the Chinese Staff was a long stick of bamboo which could double as a whip. She started with the Staff, getting into a schedule of practising each and every day after work. At first, twirling the Staff in a figure eight in front of her had led to her hitting herself in the nose, the eye, the ear. At one stage, Tammy had hit her head so hard with the Staff that she fell over sideways, landing with a thud on the floor. *Dammit,* she thought to herself. She needed to keep practising. Not only did Tammy want to do well in front of the school, but she wanted to once again impress Steve. She practised day and night.

A couple of months after Tammy had started practising her new weapons drills, Steve advised her that the school's Christmas party was fast approaching and asked if she would like to attend. She was not too sure. Although Tammy trained with most of these people, her focus was always on the fighting. She had never tried to get to know any of them in a social setting. Tammy asked Steve if he would be attending. He nodded, advising her that *all* of the teachers would be attending. Steve said that although attendance was not mandatory for students, it would be in every student's best interest to be there, as awards would be presented and it would be a great way to get to know your fellow students and teachers in a social setting. Tammy took a deep breath, forced a smile, and assured her instructor that she would be there.

The following morning, Tammy approached her boss, seeking permission to work a half-day on the date of her martial arts school's Christmas party. She had so much overtime up her sleeve that her boss quickly gave the okay. When the date of the Christmas party finally arrived, Tammy spent the morning typing up letters to the Courts, to Police, to Defendants, while keeping a close eye on the clock. The very second the clock hit twelve, she grabbed her bag and jacket and was out the door in a flash. No time for pleasantries or goodbyes; there was a lot to do that afternoon and she could not afford to waste any time.

Although not one for wearing skirts or dresses, Tammy hunted through her entire wardrobe looking for the most feminine, eye-catching outfit that she could find. She was after something that was not too revealing, but definitely not a "Nanna dress". This was her school's night of nights and she wanted to do them proud, social setting or not. Tammy spotted just what she was looking for. The blue dress she pulled out of her wardrobe matched her eyes beautifully and hugged her curves in all the right places. She then spent an hour on hair, make-up and matching jewellery. With high heels on and ready to leave, Tammy stood in front of the full-length mirror in her bedroom and said out loud... "*Damn* girl, you look good!"

She drove into the heart of the city in her little Mazda 626, her mind racing, filled with so many insecure thoughts. *What if I can't find the place? What if there are too many people? What if nobody knows me?* Tammy knew that if Steve had not been the one to ask her attendance, she would most likely have not considered going to the event that night. All she could think about was that she might not be able to find the restaurant listed on the invitation. Eventually finding a car park close to the address of the restaurant, Tammy locked the car and started walking. The entrance to the restaurant was so well hidden that if you had blinked while walking past the doorway, you would have missed it. Luckily, she didn't blink. Tammy entered through the tiny door, walked up the stairs, and found the most stunningly elegant Chinese restaurant she had ever seen! When she looked around, she noticed that not many people had arrived as yet and she was not sure where to sit. Sure enough, Steve stood up from his table and walked over to greet her. He escorted Tammy back to his table and sat her down beside him. Suddenly, she felt a lot more nervous than she had been, just moments before. Although she could not at all understand why,

Tammy felt like she and her martial arts instructor were the only two people in the room. Seated beside him, she truly felt like a queen.

They both watched as the other guests arrived. Steve stood up to greet each and every one of them with a smile, advising that they could sit wherever they wished. Within half an hour, the restaurant was completely full and everybody was talking amongst themselves. Well, everybody except for Tammy and Steve. Until that night, Tammy had thought she was a confident person, but actually being able to get her mouth to form even the most basic of intelligent words, while sitting next to Steve, proved impossible. Tammy literally had no idea what to say. Luckily, the talking and noise in the restaurant subsided as the Grand Master of the school stood at the front podium, commanding the utmost of respect.

Throughout the evening, many awards were given to people who had voluntarily helped clean the school on a regular basis, who'd volunteered their time and hard work to move everything from inside the old school building into the new school building when the martial arts school changed address, as well as people who'd kept their muscles working overtime in their spare time, by keeping all of the school trophies polished and shiny at all times. Then awards were given to students who'd shown their dedication through hard work and training in both fighting and Chinese language skills at the school during exams. The awards tonight were for students of the school who had excelled constantly. Tammy almost fell off her chair when her name was called. She received three awards that night for her hard work, dedication and focus during training. Discipline had never felt so good.

At the end of the evening, Tammy collected her jacket and advised Steve that she would be heading home. He offered to walk her to her car, advising that it was not a very safe world out there. Although Tammy was quite sure that she could take care of herself, a little voice inside her told her not to argue. Nobody had ever walked her to her car before. It was almost romantic, although she knew that any kind of romance between teachers and students was strictly forbidden at the school. Besides, she did not think of Steve in that way. He was her martial arts instructor and nothing more… *right?* Steve was just walking a student to her car. How very responsible of him.

They did not say much during the walk but, with each step, her heart was pounding and her skin was tingling. She told herself it was from the cold. She had no interest in relationships in any way. There was no time for romance when her job and her martial arts studies took top billing in her life. When they arrived at the car, she opened the door, got in – all the while, smiling at Steve – and then wondered where her steering wheel had gone. Horrified, she realised she had just gotten into the wrong side of the car and was now sitting in the passenger's seat! *Oh my God, I did not just do that!* Tammy had no idea how to get out of this without looking like a total fool. *Shit! I wish the Earth would just swallow me up!* Steve stifled a giggle and winked at her. He walked around and opened the passenger side door, so she could get out of the car, before escorting her to the driver's door. Tammy was so embarrassed that she was shaking like a leaf, almost in tears, but she managed a very red-faced smile. She thanked Steve for being such a gentleman before she got into the car and drove home. When Tammy got there, she cried her eyes out, ever so angry at herself and wondering how she would ever be able to face her martial arts teacher *again*, after such a humiliation.

Chapter 2

Tammy did not attend martial arts class for the next week. She put every bit of focus into her job, pushing out as much legal correspondence and typing up as many summonses as she could handle, sometimes working until after midnight. She simply wanted to *forget* what had happened and figure out if she would ever gather the courage to return to her martial arts training. Tammy missed the adrenaline rush which had come with pushing her muscles to the absolute limit, wielding her weapons, avoiding a hit and knocking her opponent to the ground before they could see it coming. It was an addiction, and after a full week of being away from it, she decided that it was time to pull up her big girl panties and face her fears. *Besides, surely Steve has too much other stuff going on in his life to even remember me making an idiot of myself last week.* Tammy did all she could to try and forget about it.

She decided that Friday night training would be the best time to return. That was the night when all students and instructors fought against each other, regardless of belt colour, sex or skill. It was also a night when instructors could kick the ass of any student they pleased, or for students to try and kick the ass of any *instructor*, should they be silly enough to try. Friday nights were for the diehards who were not afraid of pain. Tammy arrived at the training studio early, so she could take her frustrations out on the sand bags and steel bars along the walls for an hour or two, before being forced to come face-to-face with her martial arts instructor again. Her arms were as hard as steel and any new bruising that formed on her arms or hands would quickly heal. She just needed to burn off all of that built-up embarrassment before training began.

When Steve walked through the door, Tammy was suited up in her uniform and already dripping in sweat, from head to toe. She was out of breath, but the pre-training seemed to do the trick. She bowed to and saluted her martial arts instructor when he entered the studio and paid her respects. He reciprocated, before going to the locker room to change into his uniform. Around Tammy's waist was her satin black belt. Around Steve's waist was his satin black belt, accompanied by a satin fourth Dan red belt. She pitied the poor bastard who would have their butt kicked by him that day. Well, she did until he came directly towards *her*. Her only immediate thought: *Yikes!* Tammy was ready for many things tonight, but she was not ready for *that*. When he stood in front of her, he told her that he would like her to stay behind after training, as he needed to have a word with her about a few things. *Well that's just great. So much for beating the crap out of the steel bars earlier. There is just no escaping the shame of that night!* She was, once again, a bundle of nerves.

For the next four hours, training was absolutely brutal. Although she could not avoid Steve's hits, grabs and elbows to the stomach, chest and face, Tammy was also able to get a few of her own right back at him. She was not sure if he'd simply let her connect with her punching, elbowing, eye-gouging, kneeing or kicking, but none of it seemed to worry him. He had a look of sheer intensity for most of the evening, when they sparred, but he also smiled at her, occasionally, when she was going at it, full throttle. It gave her confidence a much-needed lift. With only a few new bruises at the end of the night, Tammy was proud that Steve had not winded her. She had seen other students winded, when somebody landed one hard in their stomach, before they'd had the chance to tighten their stomach muscles and prepare for the blow. It was not a pretty sight – their red faces, their tears and their inability to breathe.

At the end of the Friday night training session, Tammy went back to the locker room, showered and changed. She remembered that Steve wanted to have a word with her. She was not sure if he wanted to talk to her about something she had done wrong in her training, if he wanted to recommend extra training to her, or even if he just wanted to have a bit of a giggle (at her expense) over what had happened, the evening of the Christmas party. Her head was going in circles but still, she waited.

When Steve came from the locker room, freshly showered and wearing jeans and sleeveless black shirt, Tammy's breath stopped. Besides the night of the Christmas party, she had never before seen him out of uniform. This was also the first time she had seen him freshly showered. Thoughts entered her head that should not be there. *Stop with the drooling! He's your teacher, dammit!* She managed to shake off any improper thoughts, before trying to figure out why he would want to speak with her after class. He had never wanted to speak to her outside of training-time before, and she was panicking. What was up? Steve said he will *again* walk her to her car. Tammy's unimpressed look instantly made him aware that she thought he was being sarcastic and trying to rub the humiliation that she felt into her face. He quickly said he really would like to talk to her and just wanted to go for a walk. Reluctantly, she agreed.

While slowly walking up the long ramp to her work building's private car park, they both enjoyed the gentle breeze outside. Four hours of sweating was met with nature's reward during their walk, and he told her how impressed he was, tonight, with her fighting. Steve told Tammy that he had been worried she would never return to the martial arts studio, and if she had not returned to training by Monday, he would have called her, requesting her presence at the next training session. Now that Tammy had returned to the school, she had saved him that trouble. A slight grin appeared on her face and her mood lightened. She did not think that she would be missed at all, yet here Steve was, telling her that her absence in class was most definitely noted. She also liked the recognition he was giving her for all of her hard work during training.

They finally arrived at her car. Before she opened the door, Steve took her hand and stopped her. She turned around, feeling like a thousand butterflies were having seizures inside her stomach. He told her that he'd had a wonderful night, a week ago, and even enjoyed the little piece of amusement that she had provided, after he had walked her to the car that night. Steve pointed out that he was glad she had found the driver's door on the *first* attempt this time.

Once again, Tammy looked unimpressed and hurt by his comment. He quickly apologised.

"I'm sorry. I don't mean to sound like some kind of asshole. But it is really hard to *speak* to you sometimes. You make me nervous," Steve said to her, with a slightly embarrassed look on his face.

Tammy was dumbfounded. What on Earth did such an amazing man have to be nervous about? Steve then asked Tammy, if she was not doing anything next Saturday night, would she do him the honour of being his date for the night. *An actual date? Like, a romantic dinner?* Tammy's mouth dropped open. This is not, at all, what she expected. Was he serious? He wanted to go on a *date* with her? For about a minute, she did not answer. Her mind's gears were in overdrive. *Is this a test? What if I get into trouble? He is not even my age! Will he be mad if I say no?* Besides, she did not think of him romantically. He was just her martial arts teacher. None of this was right. And yet it all felt so amazingly perfect. Finally, she answered with a smile. *Of course* she would be his date for the evening. And she knew that it would be the start of something truly wonderful.

Chapter 3

Steve showed up at the security door of her Coorparoo apartment at precisely 6:00 in the evening, that Saturday, and pressed the buzzer for Tammy's apartment number. She was dressed to the absolute nines, wanting to make the best possible impression on their very first official date. When she opened the door, she was amazed at what greeted her. Starting from the top and working her way down, she saw a black cowboy hat, a giant bunch of different coloured Carnations – her absolute *favourite* flower – and a large heart-shaped box of chocolates. Below the flowers and chocolate were two legs wearing blue jeans, and at the very bottom, a pair of dirty work boots. She had never seen a bunch of flowers so big in her life.

Tammy knew who was standing behind the flowers and chocolate but, in an attempt at humour, she asked "Yes, can I help you?"

Steve giggled and said that he hoped he had the right door, since he couldn't see too well over the flowers. Tammy was definitely impressed. *Not a bad start at all*, she thought. After being handed the bouquet of flowers and the chocolate, Tammy saw nothing but 'eye-candy' before her. Steve was wearing a black suit jacket, white shirt, blue jeans, and a black cowboy hat. It was not what she expected, when she pictured them out on tonight's date, but she most certainly had no complaints. He certainly knew how to *look* good.

Tammy invited Steve into the apartment, found a crystal vase for the flowers and placed them on the dining- room table in some water. She could not stop smiling. After putting the chocolates into the refrigerator, she grabbed her purse and her wrap as they left the apartment. Tammy had never before seen Steve's car until that night. A clean, well-looked-after, brown Holden Kingswood was parked on the street, at the front of the apartment complex. The only other time she had heard of somebody actually *owning* a Holden Kingswood was on a television show called *Kingswood Country* – an Australian show about a foul-mouthed husband called Ted Bullpitt, his mild-mannered wife, his three obnoxious kids and their spouses who called him "Mr Bullshit" – but the star of the show was the Holden Kingswood. Only in Australia, would such a bizarre show stay on the air for so long, with such a dedicated following. But here was Tammy's chance to ride in one of these famous chariots in real life. Steve opened the passenger-side door for her and told her that this time she can sit in the passenger's side *without* being too embarrassed. Not wanting to ruin the evening, she just smiled and let the comment slide.

They went to a local Vietnamese restaurant, not far from her home. He got out of the car and opened the door for her. He was being such a gentleman and she felt truly special in his company. After a magical evening of great food and soft music, Steve asked

Tammy if she would like to go back to his place for a night cap. Out of sheer curiosity of what his home looked like, she agreed.

Steve drove Tammy to his home in Woodridge – a small house which was fairly run-down, but she did not care. She was with a man who'd sent an amazing feeling right through her – a feeling that told the whole world that pure gold was worth far less than she was – and she was enjoying the moment. When they arrived at his home, he once again stepped out and opened the car door for her. They stood at the front door of his house while he searched his pocket for his house key. Tammy noticed two sadly-neglected gardens, and her heart sank a little. If this relationship went anywhere, she would make it her mission to turn both of those gardens into wonderfully blooming masterpieces, which would bring smiles to the faces of all who laid eyes on them.

Steve took the house keys from his jeans pocket and opened the front door. Tammy's mouth dropped open. Newspapers and rubbish were on the floors – floors which had no carpets and were bare, paint-stained concrete. It seemed obvious to Tammy that Steve had tried to do a little bit of self-renovation on his home. There was a very large pile of unopened mail on the table. His home life seemed to be the complete polar-opposite of his life at the martial arts studio, and Tammy wondered if a woman's touch would help. She did not offer this out loud, however. If life had taught her anything so far, she knew never to give unsolicited advice, especially in circumstances such as this.

Steve cleared off some of the newspapers from the couch and asked her if she would like to have a cup of tea and watch a movie with him. Worried that she might offend him by declining, she took a seat and said she would be happy to. He put the kettle on and then picked out a film from his vast VHS video collection that would be suitable. The film he picked, much to Tammy's horror, was a movie called *IT* – based on a novel by Stephen King. She was not a fan of horror at all and, reluctantly, told him that she actually would prefer to watch a romance or a comedy. Steve picked out another film called *When Harry Met Sally* and they both sat and watched the movie. Tammy was glad she had made the choice to come to his home, after the restaurant. Steve was a complete gentleman and, at the end of the evening, he drove her home and planted a kiss on her lips that sent tingles right through her, from head to toe.

The next martial arts training session arrived and, throughout the lesson, Steve seemed to pay Tammy absolutely no attention at all. He was fully focussed on training his students and, although she admired his dedication to martial arts and to teaching, she could not help but wonder if she had maybe done something wrong during their date, which might have pissed him off. Regardless, she managed to put her fears aside and gave her all that night, just as she had done every other lesson. When the night's training was over, she looked at him, her face showing every bit of doubt that she was feeling. He looked up at her, smiled and winked. He then asked her, again, to wait behind for him... and she did.

While walking Tammy to her car once more, he asked if she would consider moving in with him. Steve told her that he knew his home needed a woman's touch, and it would also give him the opportunity to see her every single day. Another bonus is that she would no longer have to pay any rent at her apartment, so she would be able to save up for anything special that she wanted to buy. *Bloody hell, you want me to move in with you? But we have only ever been on one date! Dammit, Steve!* Tammy said that she would need to think about it. It was fast... *and* it was a very big step. He looked disappointed, but accepted her decision.

Three weeks had passed and, being the naive lovebird that she was, Tammy had found somebody to take over her lease at Coorparoo. She packed all of her belongings into the removals truck her mother had hired to take Tammy's things to her new home. Her mum, Janine, was the driver of the truck and Tammy's oldest sister, Lisa, had also decided to lend some muscle-power to the big move. It was quite a surprise to Tammy's entire family, that she was moving (so fast) into this relationship, with somebody they had never even *met*. But her family had always trusted her instincts and supported her decisions.

Tammy was extremely grateful to her mum and sister for all the help they were selflessly giving, so that she would not have to organise this big move all by herself. She was also most eager for her entire family to meet the love of her life. Lisa had the knack of getting along with everybody she met and knew how to make light of just about any situation. Tammy was therefore taken by surprise, when Lisa was helping unload the refrigerator from the removals truck, only to rip her finger open on one of the spikes on the back grill of the refrigerator.

Instead of offering any concern or assistance, whatsoever, Steve immediately laughed at Lisa and said "Wow, what a prick!" His callousness was met with an icy glare from Lisa and, for the very first time, Tammy felt an uncomfortable twinge inside her stomach. Something was not right. But then again, maybe Lisa was just having a bad day. Tammy's mother did not say much while the move was taking place, but it was a big job and Tammy was just grateful that her family were so wonderful, in their willingness to help.

When the hugs between Tammy, Lisa and Janine were over, and the truck pulled away, there was just one thing left to do. Time to find a place for everything and clean up the mess! As Tammy set to picking up all the dirty dishes and used newspapers off the concrete floor, Steve tackled her onto the couch, pinned her down and kissed her, like she had never been kissed before. It sent tingles throughout her entire body, and all doubts which had come to surface, an hour earlier, completely disappeared. She could do this. Her knight in shining armour (and his palace) were her next step in life. This was meant to be.

After a solid, five-minute, *passionate* kiss, Steve then got to his feet, advising that he had to go out for a while. He told Tammy to make herself at home. After all, this was *her* home now, too. He said to do whatever makes her happy and he will be back later. Looking at her watch, it was almost 3 o'clock in the afternoon. She asked if he will be home for dinner and he replied he didn't know. Tammy said not to worry about a thing. She would keep herself busy while he was away on his errands. After one more kiss on the lips, Steve was out the door. She heard the Kingswood pull out of the drive and then looked around. She seriously hated mess. Every place she had ever lived had been all shiny and clean. A clean home always gave her pride, so she pulled her sleeves up, put on some gloves and got to work.

Floors cleaned and mopped, dishes washed, dried and put away, trash packed up and put to the wheelie bin outside, beds made, bathroom scrubbed clean, house dusted… it truly was a big job. But she didn't mind cracking a sweat. The one thing that kept her spirits lifted, while scrubbing and cleaning, was picturing the look of joy all of her hard work would bring to Steve's face, when he walked through the door of his newly-cleaned home. No more mess. Everything had found its place. It was 8 o'clock at night, already, and he was still not home, so she opened up his clothes cupboards to see if anything might need ironing. Tammy was not a great fan of ironing, but she hadn't figured that she would be looking for something to do on her first night at her new address, which did not include Steve. She had pictured romance, romance and more romance. Instead she received a shock, when she realised that not even *one* of his buttoned shirts even had a hanger. Each shirt was all scrunched up and at the bottom of his wardrobe. So tomorrow, she would need to go shopping for clothes hangers. At 8:15pm, Tammy found herself bored and miserable. Where was her Steve?

By 8:30pm, Tammy was sitting on the front porch and breathing in the fresh air. She looked, again, at the neglected gardens and tried to picture, in her mind, what she could do to make them look happy and cared for. She tried not to worry about where her boyfriend was or even if he was okay. At 10:00pm, she came back inside and decided to ring his pager. When she got to the phone in the living room, her worry was replaced by a frown. Steve had locked the phone, so she was unable to ring out – not even to her parents. That was strange. Why would he have a lock on his phone, when she was the only other person living there?

Hungry and alone, Tammy made herself a sandwich and turned on the television. A late night show came on, which she had not heard of before – *Late Night with Conan O'Brien* – and, since the only other shows on television at that time of night were *horror* movies, she decided to watch the late night show. Before long, she was smiling, even laughing out loud, at the humour projecting from the television screen. The show went for an hour, finishing at 11:30pm, which was about two minutes before the front door opened and a very *drunk* Steve came in with a carton of beer (minus a few beers) and a hot chicken. All humour left her. She could not find anything to smile about now. Yes, she was relieved that he had come home in one piece, but all she could feel now, beyond that, was disgust. She did not see her Steve before her. Instead she saw a *pig of a drunk driver*, who could barely stand, and who did not give a crap about her. After he handed Tammy the beer and the chicken, he threw up on the floor and went to bed. Tears streamed down her face. She was angry. This was not what she'd signed up for. And this was not the man who'd taken her out on a romantic date, trying to win her heart. Something was wrong. Was it her? Did she do something to upset him and not realise it? She put the beer and chicken into the fridge and cleaned up the vomit from the floor, before deciding it would be best if, tonight, she slept on the couch.

This was definitely not the first evening's welcome which she had anticipated it would be. Hopefully, tomorrow would be better.

Chapter 4

The next morning, when Steve woke, he still stank of beer from head to toe. He had vomited in the bed, and his hair was *matted* with it. He was also rather confused as to why Tammy had slept on the couch. Steve gently woke her and asked if she was alright. She looked up at him but did not respond. All she could smell was beer and vomit coming from his clothes. After a few minutes, she suggested that he should, perhaps, go and take a shower while she washed his clothes. Steve responded with a face, full of regret, and nodded. He went to the shower, and Tammy felt stiff and sore from sleeping on such a lumpy couch. *When Steve comes out of the shower all clean and refreshed, we definitely need to talk.* Although this was his house, it was their *relationship*. She had agreed to live with him, but they needed a few ground rules, for this to work.

Tammy got up from the couch and went to the bedroom, to see if there were any other messes which needed to be attended to. She almost puked at the smell of the room and when she saw vomit on his pillow. She knew that all of it would need to be washed, hosed, and aired out. *Good grief, what on Earth got into him last night?* She stripped the bed sheets and pillow cases from the bed and tossed them onto the back porch, before going back into the bedroom to open the windows. Steve came out of the shower, dripping wet and naked, complaining that he didn't have any clean towels. She closed her eyes, shook her head, and mentally added *towels* to the things she needed to buy. *How on Earth has he actually managed to survive until now?* Tammy went to the hallway cupboard and pulled out a very old, raggedy beach towel which smelled like moth balls. She handed it to him and asked him to dry off, get dressed and meet her in the lounge room. They were in serious need of a talk.

Steve finally came out of the bathroom, dried and fully dressed. He sat next to Tammy on the couch and looked at her, like a sad, lost puppy. Suddenly, Tammy felt her heart go out to him. She should be absolutely *furious* with him right now, but he looked so miserable and troubled. Maybe she should not express her anger right now. After all, she still had no idea what had happened last night. So, she decided the best way to approach it was simply to ask.

"Steve, what happened last night? Why did you just disappear, like that, on my first night here?" she asked.

He looked at his feet and mumbled something that she could not understand. *Okay, maybe a new tactic is needed.*

She said to him "Do you realise how *alone* I felt? I thought you wanted me here?"

Steve looked up at her and started to cry. This was definitely not the response she was prepared for, and she asked him what had happened. Steve said, "I don't know. I think I just got scared. I don't know why."

Tammy asked him if he would prefer she move out again, if her being here was too much. Sudden shock came over his face and he insisted that was not what he meant. He had just been alone for so long, and he just needed time to adjust. She was confused. After all, *he* was the one who had asked *her* to move in. She was the one who had ended her lease, uprooting her entire life to move in with him so they could start something new and wonderful. Was he now regretting his decision?

Steve started to cry again, and all she could think to do was hug him. He hugged her right back and, for the very first time, she heard those magical words come from his lips. "I love you," he said with a smile. "You're my *bubba*, you know?" And regardless of the past eighteen hours, Tammy realised that maybe, she loved him too.

Before leaving to do some much needed shopping for essential home items, Tammy decided it would be best to get a few loads of washing done first, and hang them up to dry while they were away. She hooked up her old washing machine in the laundry and got the first load done, while they both sat down to have breakfast. While eating her cereal, Tammy, again, noted the large pile of unopened mail on the table. She asked Steve what he would like her to do with it.

Steve replied, "I don't know."

Tammy asked if they were bills, letters, legal items or what? He vaguely replied that he had no idea what they were. He hadn't opened them.

She asked him if he would like her to go through them and he said, "Sure, whatever."

One by one, Tammy opened each envelope. Many were filled with correspondences, invitations to attend events, bills, his Will (which she very quickly and carefully stuffed back into the envelope and handed to him), and a Death Notification from his father, advising that his mother had died. She slid that one across the table, slowly, and with a lump in her throat, asked if he had known about this. Steve looked blankly at the paper and shrugged. Tammy figured he did not want to talk about it, so she asked if he would be paying the bills any time soon. Steve again shrugged. Tammy wondered how yet another communication breakdown could possibly occur so soon, when she had been living there with him for less than twenty-four hours.

She slammed a hand down on the table and said *"Dammit, talk to me!* What is going *on* with you?"

Steve responded with a very red face. "I just... I can't read."

Tammy sat in stunned silence. She wondered if he was serious or joking. He worked in construction. He also worked as a martial arts instructor. How could he not know how to read? Steve told her that in construction, he just needed to know how to work numbers, know how to measure, know where to cut. In martial arts, the only thing he ever had to sign was a document, when he had joined the martial arts school. It was a *long* document, which he had to read before he signed. He had not told those in charge of the school that he could not read it. After all, he could speak. He could scribble a name. And he could fight. Steve figured he did not *need* reading, since his father had pulled him out of school long before he was fifteen. His attendance record was almost zero, but in such a small country town in those days, nobody really cared. It was that same small country town that had issued him with a driver's licence when he was eighteen. All he had to do, back then, was pass the driving test itself, which he had done just fine. He was now thirty-seven years old and he could not read. Tammy was the first person he had ever confided in about this. She asked him if he would like her to teach him. He warily looked at her and said he didn't think he could ever learn, but he would give it a try. Finally, Tammy had a mission. She would teach Steve how to read. She would also now go shopping, and get him some coat hangers and towels for his hallway cupboard. Steve grabbed his car keys as they walked out the door together, starting the latter part of the morning on a happy high.

While driving to the shops, Steve said there was probably something else she needed to know about. Tammy started to panic. Was this when he would tell her he went out screwing last night, got drunk, and screwed some more before coming home? She asked what was on his mind. Steve told her that now they were officially together, Tammy would need to leave the martial arts school as a student, or he would risk losing his job as an instructor. Her stomach knotted. She loved Kung Fu. She loved her school, and she didn't want to leave. But she also did not want him to lose his job, so she reluctantly agreed not to return to the martial arts school, in any capacity.

Steve smiled, took her hand, and said, "Thank you."

For the very first time, his hand on hers did not have the magic touch that it always had. She felt sad. She felt alone in the world. Her martial arts training was such a big part of her life, and now she had to give it all up... because they lived together. Had she known that this would be the price of moving in, she would never have broken her lease. But now, it was too late to go back to the way things were. Her martial arts days were over. She looked out from the car window, as a single tear slid down her cheek.

Chapter 5

The following six months were rather uneventful for Tammy. Her life seemed to lose a lot of its direction, due to the fact that she was no longer permitted to study martial arts. Each night while Steve was at training, however, she would slip out into the back yard and practise her weapons drills briefly, just to keep herself from going insane from withdrawals. She would only allow herself 10-15 minutes of practise each time, for fear of getting caught. Although disappointed, Tammy did not want to murky the waters at home between her and Steve. Martial arts had been such a big part of her life, and now it was gone.

Each night, when Steve came home after training, as well as every single weekend when there was time to spare, Tammy would sit down with Steve and read with him. She had purchased books which could be read to very young children at bed time. That way, he would be able to form pictures in his head when he read the words, just like she had always done. For Tammy, seeing pictures when hearing or reading words, which formed a story, was what psychologists had told her was a special type of sensitivity that could sometimes be rather debilitating. It would also happen to her when she was driving with the radio on. Listening to music on the radio was fine but, the moment the news broadcast began, she would have to quickly turn off the radio or the pictures would take over from what she was supposed to be seeing, in front of her, while driving. It was definitely not a risk she was ever willing to take. As a passenger, listening to the news would bring images of violence, planes crashing, people getting murdered. This is something she would rather live without, but to her it was a normal part of her life – a part of who she was.

Before too long, Steve was able to identify the letters of the alphabet and the sounds they made in smaller words. Within a year, he was able to understand the words on some of the bills and correspondence which he had received. Until then, Tammy had used all of her savings to pay the many debt notices that Steve had incurred, during his time of illiteracy. He reasoned with her that he had saved her ample amounts of money in rent and in student fees at the martial arts school – money which could now go towards his bills and help him get into much better financial shape. Feeling sympathetic, she decided it probably made sense. Within six months, Steve's bills were all up-to-date, with Tammy having not a single cent of savings left to her name. She knew a pay increment was coming soon, but had decided not to tell Steve that she would be receiving an extra $20 per week in her pay packet. Somehow, she needed to try and rebuild her savings, whether for herself or for them both, in case of an emergency.

When Steve's birthday arrived in August, Tammy was excited and left work early, so she could come home and make sure everything was perfect. She wanted to get some washing done, dust and clean the house before surprising Steve with a great meal to celebrate his special day. She even wanted to bake him a cake, because *everybody* deserved to feel special on their birthday – especially her Steve. It was quite foggy outside, that afternoon, and she had her car headlights on – not because she couldn't see too well, but because she had been taught that when driving in foggy or rainy weather during the day, turning on your headlights would enable other cars and pedestrians to see you. If there was anything that Tammy could still pride herself on, it was that she was a good driver. She knew the road rules and she stuck to them, no matter what.

When she arrived home at 2:30 in the afternoon, Tammy was a little surprised (and her heart sunk a little) to see the Holden Kingswood parked in the driveway. It was odd, because usually Steve worked until 5:30 or 6:00 in the evening. Tammy parked on the road in front of the house, turning to grab her handbag and coat from the passenger's seat of the car. When she turned around to open the car door, Tammy was startled, and her heart skipped a beat, to find that Steve was standing beside her car, staring at her through the driver's window. The look on his face was one of pure fury. Tammy felt her face go red. She did not know if she had pissed him off somehow or if, perhaps, somebody else had caused his anger and he was simply waiting to tell her about it. Unfortunately, there was only one way to find out.

She opened the car door and slowly stood up. "What is it, hon? What's happened?" Tammy asked.

He walked towards her until she was leaning back against her car; they were standing nose to nose. Steve's temper then exploded in her face. "Why the *fuck* are your lights on during the *day?*" he demanded.

She was stunned. Anybody with a driver's licence knows, when you are driving in Australia, vision between you and others is paramount. After all, it is on the driving test and... *oh*. She remembered that he had not been able to read a word of his driving test when he was a teenager. Tammy was at a loss for words. She did not want him to get any angrier than he obviously already was. "Steve, let's go inside and talk about what is going on, okay? The neighbours do not need to know our business," she suggested. This was not the afternoon birthday surprise she'd planned for.

When they were indoors and the front door had closed, he shoved her so hard, she fell to the ground. "Use your lights at *night* like a normal person. Where is your brain? Are you stupid? What the fuck is *wrong* with you?!" Steve yelled at her.

Tammy had tears in her eyes and, for the first time in as long as she could remember, she was actually scared. She did not try to get up. Instead, she backed up from him, sat on the floor with her back against the wall and stared at him, eyes wide.

"ANSWER ME!" he screamed at the top of his lungs.

She started crying and quietly told him that if it is raining or foggy in the day time, the law says that you must have your headlights on.

Steve kneeled down and again got up close to her. "Tell me why you need your lights on in the day time! Are you suddenly blind? I can see outside. You can't?" he said in a low, growling voice which sent a wave of terror right through her.

"It's the law, Steve. It is so *other* people can see *you*. I promise you, it is the *law*. It is what you learn on your driving exam," she softly answered, tears streaming down her face.

He flinched, almost as if he had just been slapped, and realised that he hadn't known this before. After all, he hadn't had to do a written exam for his driving licence. He just had to know how to operate a car and his driving licence was handed to him, no questions asked. Besides, the testing officer had been one of his best mates.

Steve apologised to Tammy as he stood up. He extended his hand to help her up, but refused to take it. Her trust level in him was suddenly a big, fat zero. He had never before been violent with her, and she didn't know how to react. When he apologised again, with "I'm sorry, Bubba," she just nodded and stayed where she was, waiting for him to leave the house before she got up. When he did, she cleaned herself up and had a good cry.

When the insanity of what had happened, that afternoon, had started processing itself inside her mind, Tammy went to the kitchen and sat at the table. She had been so excited about today, wanting to make this a perfect birthday for him. All of those thoughts were now gone. She didn't care what Steve wanted to do today. She needed to get out of here for a while. Janine did not live too far from where she now lived. Maybe she could call her mum and see if she was home? Tammy stood up and walked to the phone, only to find that it was, once again, locked. *Screw it, no harm in showing up unannounced. Mum won't mind*, she thought. She was not sure if her mother would be at home, at this time of day, or if she would be still working. Tammy leaned down and picked her handbag up off the floor, before reaching inside for the keys. They were not there. She searched and searched, even turning the handbag upside down and emptying out the contents on the table. Her car keys and her wallet were gone. Steve had not only taken away her ability to *ring* somebody, but he also wanted to make sure she didn't leave the house while he was gone. It was at that moment, she decided that he did not deserve *anything* special on his birthday, or any other day. He was some crazy, misogynistic asshole... *and* a bully. Tammy's heart ached. She felt so angry at herself for ending up in this situation. She was almost twenty years old and felt like she was sixty already, with the world on her shoulders. Without keys to re-enter the house, she knew she could not even go next door and meet her neighbours for the first time, before asking to use their telephone. Instead, she made herself a sandwich and grabbed a book to read – the words, taking her into a world without pain – until she fell asleep.

At 2:00 in the morning, Steve roughly shook her awake. He was drunk and, once again, stunk of beer. The smell of it made her gag. She also noticed that he had a freshly-swollen, bruised eye and a split lip. Obviously he had been in a fight. *And got his ass kicked. Good!* She quickly got out of bed and asked him to come into the bathroom, so she could clean up his face a little bit. Steve shook his head. He was not interested in cleaning anything up. As far as he was concerned, it was his *birthday*. He wanted sex, and as long as she lived under his roof, she was his *property*. Sadly for the birthday boy, the one thing that Tammy could assure him of, was that sex was most definitely *not* on the menu tonight. Thoughts of her being anywhere near Steve, when he threw up the contents of his stomach, almost made her puke. She asked where her wallet and keys had disappeared to.

Steve slurred his words in response. "They're both on the kitchen sink, exactly where you left them."

Tammy knew they had not been there earlier, and she looked at him with accusing eyes. He shrugged his shoulders at her, as he fell into bed in his stinky bloodied clothes, and started snoring.

"Oh, thank you, God!" she whispered quietly, as he snored. And she meant it. Although she knew she would have to clean all of the sheets and pillow cases when he woke up the next day, Tammy was relieved that she would not have to sleep in the same bed as this man.

She grabbed her pillow, went out to the living room, lay on the couch and stared up at the ceiling, wondering what to do about this mess that she'd found herself in. Maybe she could leave him, but she had only managed to save up a very small amount of money, after paying off all his debts. She had many friends she could camp with, for a few nights. Well, that might have *once* been true, but not anymore. She had not contacted any of these friends in almost two years. Tammy doubted that showing up on their doorstep, out of the blue, and saying "Do you mind if I *live* with you for a while?" would go over very well.

She could also ask her mum, but that would all but admit that she had made some majorly stupid decisions, and that she was a complete fuck-up in life. Yes, her own decisions had led to this. Tammy had nobody else to blame, but herself. She had not been afraid, at all, to go into this relationship so fast, regardless of age difference. Steve was eighteen years older than she was, but her own parents were twelve years apart in age when they had been married, so this had not bothered her at all. Besides, Steve used to be so sweet. Maybe she could find a way to bring all that sweetness back into their relationship. She had to find a way to change this man back into the wonderful person she knew he could be – the man she had fallen in love with. Everything was so perfect, back then. Yet now, every time he was stressed, he would go out and get drunk. This was the first time he had come home looking like somebody's *punching-bag*, though. She knew Steve could fight well, so she wondered how on Earth somebody else could get the better of him, the way they had. Maybe a bunch of guys had held him down? Perhaps he had been sucker-punched? *Maybe he was just so drunk that he'd tripped over his own two feet and had taken a header into the gutter?* Although he'd acted like an asshole, it was his birthday, and he didn't deserve to have the crap beaten out of him. Tammy's mind would not switch off and, before she realised it, the sun had started to break over the horizon and shone through the living room window, onto the facing wall.

Steve would usually be awake by now, eaten his breakfast and gotten ready for work. Only weeks ago, his boss had promoted him to "Leading Hand" at the work site, so he was now in a supervisory role. He had told her it was basically doing the same job he had been doing for years, except that now he got to tell a few of the *others* what to do. He didn't like the fact that some of them took so many cigarette and coffee breaks, while he had always worked so hard to keep things running smoothly.

Tammy went into the bedroom to wake Steve up, and the very second that she'd touched him, she was met with a fist in the chest. She went down hard, unable to breathe. She reached up and grabbed him by the arm, almost ripping his skin off with her fingernails, thinking she was about to die. Not a single bit of oxygen would enter her lungs.

Suddenly, Steve was sitting up on the bed with his hand on her back, telling her "*Breathe*, Bubba. Just take it easy, relax and breathe."

He helped her up onto the bed and she cautiously sat beside him, tears running down her face, once more, this time due to oxygen deprivation. Slowly, she was able to get a little bit of air into her lungs with each breath. Steve gently rubbed her back and continued telling her to breathe.

He then told her, with regret "I'm sorry. I am really, really sorry. Oh, Bubba, I'm sorry. Please, I am sorry."

Tammy did not care how sorry he was. Right now he could fall, head-first, into a flaming volcano and she would not lose any sleep over it. If she was physically able to stand up right now, she would walk out the door and be gone. This was just too much. She did not know this man anymore.

Chapter 6

Today was supposed to be a full day *away* from work for Tammy. It was known as a Recreation Day, or "Rec Day" for short, which was a day that an employee could take from work, here and there, with full pay, if they had accrued enough overtime. These days, she had overtime in abundance. Her chest was hurting in a big way, and breathing was still somewhat of a chore, but *anything* was better than being at home with Steve today.

Before Tammy left for work that morning, Steve had decided his head hurt too much to go to work, so he unlocked the phone and forced her to call to his boss, saying that Steve had some 24-hour stomach bug.

Rather than suffer a full day at home with a hungover bully, Tammy had chosen to, instead, enjoy the feeling of being physically nowhere near him. She needed to get busy and take her mind off everything. When Tammy arrived at her work building, she went into the boss's office and asked him if she could rescind her day off and take it some other time.

She lied and said, "There is just so much work here to get out, and I am here to help make sure that it gets done."

The boss smiled, impressed by her dedication to the job, and he put her to work immediately. Relieved, Tammy had decided that today would be one of those extra-long work days, where she would *not* be hurrying home.

After typing up over one hundred summonses, without taking a lunch break, while being asked *constantly* by her co-workers if everything was okay (and Tammy insisting that everything was just fine and dandy), she finally shut off her computer at 10:00 that night, and headed home. She was hoping that Steve would be either out getting drunk with his loser mates and had passed out in a gutter somewhere, in which case she could watch some more of her new favourite show, *Late Night with Conan O'Brien,* to help her mood, or maybe Steve had gone to bed already. His martial arts training would have ended at 9:00 so she pictured him, possibly, coming home exhausted and dreaming his insane, unpredictable, violent self into the lair of the Sandman. If he was asleep, she would not dare wake him. Even if the house was *on fire*, she would let him sleep. Yes, Tammy was still *that* angry. When she arrived home and saw that the lights were on in the living room, her heart sunk. She did not want to go inside, preferring to just stay in the car for an hour or two, but that would just be delaying the inevitable. She parked the car in the driveway and went to the front door, taking a deep breath before she put the key into the lock. Tammy was fully on her guard.

What she saw, before her eyes, when the door opened, took her completely by surprise. Steve was dressed up nice in jeans and his black sleeveless shirt. Freshly shaven and with his hair brushed, he smiled at her, looking like butter would not melt in his mouth. He stood up, walked over to her and asked if he could hug her.

Tammy was not sure if she was awake or not and was tempted to pinch herself. Instead, she whispered, "Sure." She trembled in fear as he opened his arms and embraced her; a dull pain still thumping in her chest, where he had hit her that morning.

Steve gently said, "Bubba, I'm so very sorry. I didn't mean it. I don't know what happened, or even *why* I did it. I didn't think it was *you* there. I am sorry. Please don't leave me."

She was speechless, not to mention, very on-edge. Tammy wondered what the catch was. *What unpredictable, messed-up thing is about to come next?* she thought to herself, not trusting a single word he'd said.

Steve let go of her and gently took her hand. He led her into the kitchen and there, sitting on the kitchen table was the biggest white teddy-bear she had ever seen in her life. Surrounding the giant teddy-bear – a teddy-bear which was at least one metre tall – were Carnation flowers in every colour imaginable. Her heart melted. *Maybe he really is sorry?* He asked Tammy if they could sit and talk. He also assured her that the teddy-bear was for her, as were the multitude of flowers... and his heart-felt apology. She half-smiled and hugged him. She also agreed with what he had said. It was definitely time for a talk.

The first thing Tammy asked was what had happened to him last night, when he'd left the house. *Why does it look like his face collided with a runaway train?* Steve said he couldn't actually *remember* what happened. He didn't even remember coming home.

He said, "You know, in my family, it is tradition, on a person's birthday, that they go out with their friends and they enjoy the moment. We don't know how many birthdays we are going to *get*, right?"

It suddenly reminded her of the Death Notice that Steve's father had sent to him. She asked him, "Steve, did you read what was in the envelope that your dad sent to you, a couple of years back?"

He nodded. Steve then smiled a cruel smile, and said his mother had it coming. "That bitch was nothing but a fucking *slut!*"

The words that had, so coldly, come out of Steve's mouth left Tammy's jaw open. She had never, in her life, heard anybody speak about their mother like that. She was going to ask, but then decided that she did not even *want* to know what had gone on in that relationship. She was still recovering from the morning's bruises and did not want any fresh ones.

Steve's next question also took her by surprise. "Are you close with *your* mother?" he asked.

She frowned, wondering where this line of questioning was going. Tammy said that he had already *met* her mother and that he *knew* they got along great.

"But your dad raised you, didn't he?" Steve continued.

"Yeah, Dad raised me. My dad is my hero. My best friend. Strict, tough as nails, and takes absolutely no shit from anybody.

Former military police officer. Weapons specialist. Tough guy. I love my dad to bits," she replied with a smile.

He looked at her, curiously, and she started to feel uncomfortable. Tammy had absolutely no idea where this conversation was going. She thought he had wanted to talk about *their* relationship and where things were going wrong. Instead they were talking about her *mother*? She wondered what devious thoughts were going through his mind.

Steve then asked, "You obviously didn't *always* get along with her. I saw your face when you talked about your dad. It lit up. But you were *frowning* when you talked about your mum. So what did she *do* to you?" he asked.

What the fuck is he up to, trying to start shit with my mum now? She frowned, when his "let's talk" suggestion was suddenly about her mother, instead of about their own problems. Tammy shrugged, and said that, long before she ever met Steve, she briefly had a boyfriend (with a very big emphasis on the fact that it was a *very* long time ago). She had been fresh out of high school and, being her first love, this boy had been her whole world – for about two whole months – before deciding to break up with her. Tammy told Steve that when her ex-boyfriend broke her heart, he had told her that he had a crush on her mum. For a long time, she wrongly put the blame on her mother, not even realising, back then, that her mum knew absolutely *nothing* about it. She told Steve that she had been very young, very stupid, and could find no fault with a moron who had decided to use her and then break her heart.

Steve simply responded with, "*Uh-huh.*"

Tammy was grateful that the interrogation about her upbringing and her parents had finally come to an end. She didn't know where the questions came from, in his mind, but was glad that the conversation over.

The following weekend, Steve decided to put his building skills to work while at home. Steve and Tammy had very little cupboard space to store dishes, so Steve bought a large wall cabinet from a garage sale. All he had to do was mount it on the wall in the kitchen. Tammy had no idea how he was going to do that, since the walls were so thin and would not support much weight. Her father had taught her a lot about building, tiling, wallpapering and painting when she was a child, since her dad was very much a do-it-yourself kind of guy. But when Steve held the wall cabinet up and asked Tammy to hold it still, she stayed quiet. Steve was the expert in building and carpentry. It was not her place to speak up, even when she doubted that he wasn't doing something right.

Tammy used all of her strength to hold it in the air, making sure it did not move as he put the first nail into the back of the cabinet, to hold it to the wall. The hollow noise had Tammy doubting that Steve had managed to secure the nail to a piece of the house's framework inside the wall. Steve then put the spirit level up to make sure the wall cabinet was perfectly horizontal before putting the next nail in.

Steve removed the front vertical support of the cabinet to give him better access to the back, allowing him to hammer the next nail in. With the second nail now in place, Steve told Tammy to let go of the cabinet and step back as he replaced the front, vertical support to the wall cabinet. She did as he said, and stood behind him in the kitchen doorway. Steve held the support in place, making sure the nail was going to go straight into the centre of the shelf. He then swung the hammer... *hard*.

Steve screamed in agony. At first, Tammy thought he had simply hit his thumb, but when he'd turned around, the support was attached to his face after having spun around, when the hammer hit, sending the nail straight into his eye. Trying not to faint from the blood pouring down Steve's cheek, Tammy did her best to keep a level head. She grabbed her keys from the table, not worrying about her handbag or anything else, and put Steve's arm around her shoulders, so that she could guide him.

"Just walk with me, Steve. One step in front of the other. Try not to panic. Close your eyes. Don't move them at all or look at anything. Trust that I won't let anything happen to you. Just walk with me, hon," Tammy said, gently, as she slowly led Steve to her car.

With that, she drove straight to Logan Health Centre, at the other end of their street. When he walked into the waiting room – Tammy still guiding his steps and telling him to keep his eyes closed and not move them – several of the patients freaked out. The nurses at the front desk immediately called a doctor to the desk and both Tammy and Steve were led to a room at the back of the clinic. The doctor vanished from the room, momentarily, and when he returned, he asked Tammy to wait outside. The next time she saw him, the nail had been removed, and Steve's eye had a cloth patch taped over it. He was instructed to completely rest and take the medication that the doctor had prescribed.

A couple of months had passed since the nail accident and Steve's eye was almost healed. Tammy and Steve had been together now for over two years, and he decided that it was time for her to meet his father. His dad lived in a tiny, southern New South Wales town in the Australian outback, with a population of fifteen or so. His house was made of fibro and he shared it with his tiny Chihuahua, which was absolutely adorable.

It took about twelve hours to drive there, and when they arrived, both Steve and Tammy were exhausted. It was the middle of summer and the Australian heat was nobody's friend during the summer months, especially when you drove a Kingswood that didn't have an air conditioner. When Steve knocked, the front door opened. Steve's dad gave him a hug and then picked up the little dog.

Steve introduced his father, Alan, and his father's dog, Snowflake, to Tammy. She smiled at them both, and said, "So very nice to meet you both."

Alan looked at Tammy with suspicion in his eyes and nodded, before telling Steve and Tammy, "So get your asses inside and shut the bloody door or the air conditioner will blow up."

Alan served up some cucumber sandwiches and a glass of water. He did not talk too much, except to tell Steve that his brother and "that fucking cow bitch of his" had dropped by for a visit, the previous week. Tammy stayed silent, not knowing at all how to participate in such a bizarre conversation. Steve rolled his eyes and said that he and Tammy were going to go for a walk through the main street of town to get some groceries. Alan gave Steve $20 and told him to buy a carton of beer, while he was there.

Walking out the front door, Steve decided that he might also pick up a *second* carton of beer for himself. Tammy asked him – *begged* him – not to drink beer during this trip. They were only going to be there for a few days so she suggested that, perhaps, Steve should just have one or two of the beers from the carton that he would be buying for his dad.

Steve laughed. "You're *joking*, right?" he said, while shooting her a look that told her, silently, not to argue the point.

They ended up climbing into the Kingswood, instead of walking, and they drove into town. After all, two cartons of beer and groceries would not be easy to carry, after such a long drive. The first stop was the drive-thru of the local boozer. *Of course this would be the first stop. He wouldn't want to risk that they run out of beer!* She was *not* loving this plan of his one little bit. Surprisingly, however, Steve only bought one carton of beer.

He smiled at Tammy and said, "Yeah, I guess we might need the extra money for petrol to get home. Good thinking, Bubba."

She breathed a sigh of relief. Steve and beer were always a bad combination. Hopefully his father could hold his alcohol a lot better than Steve could.

That night, while Tammy and Steve were both sleeping on an air mattress in the living room, they were both awoken by incoherent screaming, which seemed to come from both Steve's father and little Snowflake, at the same time. Panic shot right through her, but instead of jumping up to go and assist his father, Steve grabbed Tammy and dragged her back behind one of the couches, telling her to be very quiet. He crouched down next to her with a serious look on his face and shook his head, while putting his hand over her mouth, telling her not to make a single noise. The screaming continued and, even with Steve's hand over her mouth, Tammy managed to sneak a peek to see what on Earth was going on. She was left absolutely horrified when she saw the Chihuahua run through the living room and out again, chased by Steve's father who was screaming at the dog while wielding a very large kitchen knife.

Oh my God, oh my God, oh my God, this is not happening, PLEASE this is not happening! Tears started streaming down her face and she wanted to run out, grab Snowflake and save him from the maniac chasing him, but Steve held her down, tight. He told Tammy to shut her mouth and stay where she was.

About twenty minutes had passed before the screaming stopped. She wondered if the dog was still alive. Suddenly, Tammy put two and two together. *The apple does not fall far from the tree. Like father, like son.* Now she knew where Steve had inherited his insane behaviour from, while drunk. A few minutes more had passed, and Tammy could hear loud snoring. She and Steve slowly got up from behind the couch, only to find Alan sitting on a chair at the kitchen table, slumped over and passed out.

Tammy guessed that Alan had run out of breath. *I guess, chasing and trying to kill your dog, while being a drunken turd, must really take it out of you, hey, asshole?* Tammy thought, and she told Steve that, regardless of what he chose to do, she would *not* be staying. She packed up their things, folded the bedding, checked that the dog was okay (the poor little thing was hiding in the bathroom, shaking like a leaf, but unharmed), and they left. Steve had refused to allow Tammy take the dog with them, so she decided that she would be calling the RSPCA, the moment they got back home.

The trip back to Queensland was a long, hot and unpleasant one. Tammy was glad that Steve decided to make it a two-day journey, so they could take advantage of some hotel air conditioning. They did not speak a word to each other for several hours. She wanted to ring RSPCA from the hotel, but Steve decided that the bar across the road would be a perfect way for them both to spend the evening. With her options forcibly removed, Steve pocketed the hotel room key and they crossed the road to the bar. Tammy hated being at these places. They stunk of beer, were always filled with morons who wanted to pick a fight with each other, over *ridiculously* random things, but, at least they had served up a decent meal that night, before she and Steve decided to engage in a two-hour billiards session. By the time they returned to the hotel room, Tammy was utterly exhausted and fell asleep, the moment her head hit the pillow.

The following morning they continued their long drive back home. On the final leg of the journey, Steve told Tammy that he rang his dad, the previous night, to see how he was doing. Alan had told him there had been an accident – perhaps a break-in – and that he had found his dog – *dead* – in the living room.

Suddenly, feeling a pain in her chest and sobbing uncontrollably, Tammy knew there had been no break-in. She needed to report what she had seen that night to authorities. *We should have taken the dog with us. That poor baby deserved a hell of a lot better life than being with that piece of shit son-of-a-bitch!* "Damn him!" she screamed out loud. through her sobs. Steve ignored her outburst and kept driving, with not a single bit of emotion showing on his face.

The moment Steve pulled into the driveway of their Woodridge home, Tammy got out of the car and marched inside – straight to the locked telephone. She was furious.

Steve followed shortly after and, once inside, saw her standing by the phone. "What do you think you are doing?" he asked.

"He cannot get away with this! I *know* what he did. I *saw* it! I saw his insane behaviour, Steve. I am ringing RSPCA. He needs to be reported for what he did, so unlock the fucking phone – *now!*" she screamed through angry tears.

Instantly he grabbed her by the throat. His thumb and first two fingers formed a claw – a deadly move she had also learned in martial arts training – and he pushed his fingers hard on either side of her windpipe, pulling it forwards. She could not breathe.

He held Tammy against the wall, and leaned over to her ear, whispering, ever-so-calmly, "If you ever *think* of bringing embarrassment to me, or my family, I will snap your neck. Do you understand me?" She felt her lips tingle with numbness. Darkness was threatening to take her. She felt dizzy and weak. Tammy stared at him, eyes wide, scared that she was about to die. She was unable to answer. She was unable to breathe. "DO YOU UNDERSTAND ME?!" he screamed, at the top of his voice. Tammy managed a faint nod and he finally let go of her neck. She dropped to the floor, completely devoid of any strength or energy. She could not move, nor did she want to. Right now, she blamed herself for the death of Steve's father's dog and for that, she wished herself dead.

Chapter 7

It had been two months since Tammy and Steve had returned home from their trip, to visit his dad. Tammy found that she could not focus on anything at all. She had used up ten days of sick leave during the past two months, without telling Steve. Those ten days, she simply could not face being at work and she spent the whole day in bed, crying. Every part of her body was numb. The guilt she felt at not taking Snowflake with them, or reporting Steve's dad for his crimes, was eating her alive. Not being able to report what happened, unable to be the voice for that poor pup or even to talk about it to her friends and family, was certainly taking its toll. Tammy needed help. She may not have been allowed to speak to authorities or family, but she needed an outlet. She needed friends – people she could talk to, without fear of being judged. The *last* thing she needed was some know-it-all stranger, dishing out unsolicited advice. Advice from strangers never did sit well with Tammy. She did not do that to other people, and expected the same in return.

When Thursday's local newspaper arrived in the letterbox, she decided to look through the columns at the back to see if there were any meetings or support groups she could attend. After all, she felt like she was losing her sanity, being so secluded from the world, and she needed somebody to talk to. Besides, Steve was training almost every night these days, it seemed. Rather than sitting around the house, feeling numb, being useless, and crying all the time, she could be doing something proactive. She read the columns in the paper, finding listings for jobs, for garage sales, for escort services (*umm, definitely no thanks*), and then came the column for support meetings. Alcoholics Anonymous was the first on the list, and she immediately wished that Steve would attend a few of those meetings. She continued reading. Domestic Abuse support group... no, she would never dare attend one of those. Steve would *kill* her. Her eyes then stopped at a local meeting for LGBT and friends. It was not a support group as such, but rather a group where members of the Lesbian, Gay, Bisexual and Trans-sexual community would get together and have a chat, a few laughs, and plan get-togethers at pubs, surprise parties. Tammy decided she would like to go to one of these meetings. She was bisexual, yes, but most *certainly* not on the market, nor was she interested in hooking up with anybody. She just needed to socialise with people she could relate to and trust. There was a phone number listed in the advertisement, but she had no way to ring the number. Luckily, the building's address, where the meeting took place, was also listed. It was right across the road from Woodridge Railway Station, which was less than three blocks from their home. The meetings ran from 6:00 to 8:00 in the evenings, on Tuesdays and Thursdays, each week. Steve trained every single week on those two days, and was never home before 9:00, so it was perfect.

The next Tuesday afternoon at 5:30, Tammy decided to go for a walk. There was no point in using petrol when the meetings were so close. Besides, the walk would do her good. She really needed to think about things in her life, and figure out a way to make them better. Right now, however, all she could think about was the night she'd heard a small dog screaming, while being chased by a drunken madman with a big knife. The terror and the pain that little dog must have gone through, she could not even begin to imagine. She found herself in tears, once more. Tammy stopped walking, closed her eyes, took a few very deep breaths and told herself to relax. Focus. *Get through this evening, woman. That is all you have to do. And don't forget to make sure you get your ugly ass back home before Steve finds out you were gone.* Tammy was determined to remove herself from the isolated bubble of a world Steve had created for her. This was her only chance to do just *that*.

She found the building's address, which had been listed in the newspaper, but nobody was around. There was a bench not far from the entrance, so she decided to sit. It wasn't the best of places in the neighbourhood to be, at this time of night. Woodridge Railway Station was famous for drugs and violence, but she knew how to protect herself.

"*Bullshit, you are a weak piece of shit!*" Steve's voice sounded, inside her head. It startled her and, before Tammy knew it, that one statement had started to lessen her resolve. *Maybe I should start heading home? What if he is not training tonight? What if nobody even shows up at this meeting? What if...*

"Hi there! Are you here for the meeting?" A woman's voice snapped her out of a panic attack, which had started to build.

Tammy took a deep breath and apologised to the stranger for not ringing beforehand. She told the stranger, she had seen a listing for the LGBT meeting in the local paper. Tammy then crossed her fingers and hoped it would be alright if she could attend.

The stranger smiled at her, and said, "Of course. Welcome. I'm Gay."

Tammy replied, "Oh, I'm bi."

The woman laughed – a warm and friendly laugh – and said, "My *name* is Gay, but I like what you *did* there. May I ask your name?"

Feeling a little stupid, yet also feeling like she had already made a new friend, she said "I'm Tammy, and sometimes I'm an idiot. Pleased to meet you, Gay." They both giggled and headed inside the building. The feeling of being so alone had already started to fade.

Inside the building, Tammy saw a large room with double doors open. Within the room was a circle of chairs. Almost every chair was filled with adults of different ages and a lump formed in her throat. Being alone, in a room with so many strangers, was never a good thing. She looked up, and could swear that she saw her confidence grow wings and fly out of the nearest window.

Suddenly, she was lost for words. Everybody in the room seemed to know each other well and they were all laughing, telling stories about their weekend and talking about their plans for next weekend.

Gay then asked for everybody's attention as she introduced a very shy, red-faced Tammy to the group. Every single face in the room turned to her and smiled, waved and gave a very hearty welcome to their newest member. Before long, Tammy was also smiling. She did not talk much at the first meeting, but she did listen carefully to all that was said and was fascinated by the tales that were shared with the group that night – tales of discrimination at home or at work they had received that past week, which were not so fun, as well as some absolutely hilarious tales of the funny reactions they'd received when they had entered a room. Listening to these people bonding, and the laughter they shared, was so heart-warming.

Before leaving, at the end of the meeting, Tammy had been invited to three different "pub crawls" and Gay, the leader of the group, handed Tammy a business card with her phone number, just in case she ever needed to talk about anything. The business card stated that Gay was a health and social worker who worked with the LGBT community. Reality suddenly set back in. She could not ring because the phone at home was always locked, and attending a pub crawl was out of the question. The smell of beer made her want to vomit. But even though she had obstacles, with regards to socialising, at least she had these meetings, not to mention the brand new friends she had made that night. It was uplifting, and she looked forward to next Thursday's meeting, so she could do it all over again.

At 8:00 that night, she started walking home. The breeze on her face felt wonderful. Tammy felt kissed by Mother Nature, with every bit of cool that brushed her cheeks. But while the wind and the happy memories of the evening gave her a reason to smile, it all faded in an instant when she reached the front of her neighbour's house and found Steve's car in the driveway of their home. A thousand terrifying thoughts started racing through her head, all at once. She had to figure out what to tell him. If he suspected, even for a moment, that she had been out with people or had gone to a support group – if he thought, even for a second, that she had told anybody what had happened to his dad's dog – there was no helping her. Again, she closed her eyes and took a very deep breath, followed by another.

She felt her panic ease, just a little, before she arrived at the front door. When she finally opened the door and went inside, Steve appeared from the hallway with a strange look on his face.

Tammy forced a smile and calmly said, "Hey, hon," before walking through to the kitchen and putting her handbag on the table. "How was training tonight?" she asked.

Steve's response was not at all unexpected. "You're finally home. Where were you?" he asked. Tammy detected worry in his voice – something she had not heard in a very long time.

"It was hot inside so I went for a walk. No biggie. Are you okay?" Tammy asked.

Steve didn't answer. Instead, he pulled her into a hug. She did not expect his strange reaction, but was not about to question it, either. It almost felt like old times, and took her back to the days when she actually felt like he *cared* about her. She put her arms around him and hugged him back.

"I love you," Steve whispered in her ear. Tammy smiled. Tonight was a good night.

When she woke, the next morning, Tammy was surprised to see that the Kingswood was still parked in front of the house. She sniffed the air and smelled something delicious, cooking. Quickly slipping her glasses onto her face and her feet into her slippers, she tottered out to the kitchen to see if, maybe, they had guests. Steve was still in his pyjamas. She then remembered that the long weekend had arrived – no work today. But while that explained the *Kingswood* being outside and Steve being at home, it did not tell her the reason he'd cooked bacon, eggs and fried tomato on toast for them both, for breakfast. She smiled and sat down at the table.

"Are we expecting visitors?" Tammy asked.

Steve looked at her with the biggest smile on his face and said, "No, my bubba, we are not expecting any visitors. This is just a special breakfast for us!"

His good mood kept her smiling. She had her old Steve back. This was something she'd dreamed of for a very long time, and she sat, patiently, at the table while he served breakfast, poured her a cup of tea, put a single red rose in front of her in a small crystal vase, and said to her, "For my bubba."

Tammy giggled and thanked him. Steve then brought his own plate over to the table with his cup of coffee, and sat down next to her. They both ate, silently, while occasionally glancing up from their plates to stare into each other's eyes. This was love. Love had returned into their lives and she was so happy that she wanted to jump up onto the table to dance and sing. She had wanted this feeling to return for so very long.

When they had both finished eating, Steve cleared away the plates and asked her not to go away anywhere. Tammy complied. She wondered what comes next. Did he have more flowers and chocolates? She was filled with anticipation, waiting for Steve to clear away the table and come back to her. He quickly disappeared into the bedroom and then came back, a look of pure innocence and happiness on his face.

Before she could ask what he was up to, Steve dropped down on one knee in front of her. Tammy's jaw dropped. Steve held up a small red ring box in front of her, and slowly opened it. If Tammy's jaw had dropped any further, it would be residing somewhere in China by now. A beautiful diamond ring stared at her, from the box.

Steve said, "I know we have had some bad times, but we have also had a lot of amazingly good times. I am not perfect in any way, but I do know that I love you and that you make me a better man. Will you marry me?"

Silence filled the room. Tammy was shaking like a leaf, mostly because she was suddenly scared of what would happen if she gave the wrong answer to such an emotionally charged question.

Before she could say something stupid and ruin the moment, she looked into his eyes, a tear rolling down her cheek, and whispered, "Yes."

Steve stood up and cheered, almost as if he had just found a winning lottery ticket, and he started laughing and dancing. Tammy had never seen him so happy. He then leaned down and gently slid the ring onto her ring finger, before kissing her passionately. Laughing once again, Steve danced his way down the hallway and to the bedroom, so he could get dressed. Looking at her watch, Tammy figured it was probably time she did the same.

They decided to eat out today, for lunch. A new store had opened in Springwood called "Subway" and they both decided they would check it out. Tammy's favourite food was Chinese, but apparently this special day called for something new. When they entered the food outlet, Steve had problems understanding how Subway worked. Tammy was equally baffled. There were no tables and chairs. No menus for customers at all – just a large board up on the wall with too much writing for him to take in. Tammy explained the different food items they offered.

Steve seemed to be deep in thought, before saying "Nah!" and walking out.

Tammy was going to tell him that was possibly a little bit rude, but did not want to ruin the high he seemed to be on. Instead, Steve took her to Hungry Jacks for a burger and fries. *Oh, how very romantic. What better way to celebrate this special day*, Tammy thought with sarcasm. But she stayed silent. Steve ordered for them both, and they ate in silence. On arriving home, each with an overly-full stomach, the phone rang. Steve answered, just as he did with every *other* phone call that came when he was at home.

He looked at Tammy with caution and said, "Your dad is on the phone."

She raced to the phone, so very excited. It was so rare to receive phone calls from any of her family. "Hi, Dad! How are you? Oh? Umm, sure, I think that will be okay. Hang on just a second," she said. Tammy looked at Steve, who was now sitting on the lounge chair, watching her – a concerned look on his face. She covered the ear piece of the phone with her hand and said, "Dad is coming down to Brisbane for a couple of days, and he has asked if he could stay with us while he is here. I have not seen him in forever. It's not a problem if he stays with us, is it?" Tammy caught a glimpse of what looked like *fear* in Steve's eyes, but then it vanished.

Steve smiled and said, "Of *course,* he is welcome to stay here! He's your dad, and fathers are *everything*, right?"

Yes, Tammy understood, loud and clear, what Steve had just said to her. She would not say a word about what had happened, and Steve knew that his message had been understood. Returning to the phone, Tammy told her dad that he was welcome to come and stay with them. She gave her father the address, with basic directions as to the easiest way to find the house. Her dad would be arriving the following Friday morning and Tammy couldn't wait for him to meet her new fiancé.

Chapter 8

That week went by quickly. Tammy attended both LGBT meetings that week with her new friends, while Steve attended his martial arts training. Before she knew it, the big day had arrived. Tammy's dad would arrive at approximately 8:00 in the morning. Steve had left for work before 6:00, so there would be no distractions at all while Tammy cleaned the house, did the washing, swept the floors and the front and back porch, vacuumed, mopped and dusted. When she had finished, not a single thing was out of place. She wanted to make her father proud of *"Daddy's little girl"* the very moment that he walked through the door. Then the phone rang. Tammy answered, worried that her father had ended up lost somewhere on the Gateway Motorway, but instead, the voice at the other end of the phone was Steve. He wanted her to know that he would be having a very short day at work, and that he would be home *well before* the usual time.

"Make sure that you are there when I come home, please. No going out of the house until I am there." Steve wanted to keep an eye on her, and Tammy assured him that she would be at home when he arrived. She could not wait for her dad to meet him.

Tammy's father pulled up in front of the house in his shiny, new, silver utility truck a couple of minutes after 8:00, and her smile was so wide that she felt like her face was going to burst. It had been literally *years* since she had last seen or talked to her dad.

Before he even had a chance to knock, Tammy opened the door and greeted her dad with a big hug. "I MISSED YOU!" she smiled, as she hugged her father tight.

"I missed you too, Tam," her dad said, affectionately. "Can you help me bring a few things in from the car? I had a little bit of a problem finding the place. Bloody streets, everywhere and *none* of the bastards make any sense. I had to pull over for a bit and check the map."

Tammy asked her Dad to first come inside and sit. She knew it had been a long drive for him, and felt that a cup of tea was definitely in order, before any unpacking took place. With the kettle boiling, Tammy put two large mugs on the counter, each with a teabag, before she sat down with her dad. She was excited to be catching up on what had been going on, over the past few years, at the farm where she'd grown up. After finishing their cups of tea over a chat, Tammy and her dad went out to the truck and brought in a bag, with his clothes and his medication, as well as a bag of groceries he'd picked up at the store, two blocks away.

As she was getting an air mattress sorted out for her father, the front door opened and Steve walked in, with his work clothes covered in sawdust, and wearing his cowboy hat. Obviously, the cowboy hat was to try and impress Tammy's dad.

She rolled her eyes, giving Steve the slightest grin. "Steve, this is my Dad, Ralph. Dad, this is Steve, my fiancé." Steve and Ralph shook hands.

"Nice to finally meet you, Ralph," Steve said.

"Yep, same here, mate. *Steve*, is it?" Ralph responded. Steve nodded.

Tammy then continued setting up the air mattress, while her dad and her fiancé got better acquainted. She listened carefully to their conversation, not wanting to miss a single word that her father said. It felt so good to see him again!

Tammy's dad asked Steve about his fighting and Steve said that all was well on the martial arts front. Steve then told Ralph that Tammy had "*decided*" to drop out a few years back.

"Wow, that's too bad. She always loved her martial arts," said Ralph, flashing Tammy a curious look. Tammy looked away, her face red, and Steve quickly changed the subject, asking Ralph about his days in the Australian Navy. That started a decent conversation, with Tammy's father reminiscing about the best days of his life as a navy cop. After sharing a few amusing, yet awesome, anecdotes, Ralph asked Steve what type of weaponry he was proficient with. A list of martial arts weapons started to come out of his mouth – Chinese Knife, Double Daggers, Staff…

Tammy's father interrupted, "I am not talking about all that *namby pamby GOOK* crap. I am asking about *real* weapons. Guns. Artillery. Rocket launchers. Grenades. What rifles or hand guns do you specialise in? Do you have any favourites?"

Steve went red with anger, and told Ralph that he'd never signed up for the military. "I just stick with martial arts. Kung Fu is the only way to fight like a *real* man."

Oh Steve, you silly little boy. Close your mouth and stop talking... NOW. Tammy stopped fussing with the air mattress and turned to look at her father. Ralph's face showed what almost looked like amusement, and Tammy nearly burst out laughing, nervously wondering whether her father would also laugh, or if a fight was about to break out between them both.

Disrespecting Ralph was never a good thing. He had served for many years in the military, with partial duties of a naval copper, had fought in several conflicts and was proud of every achievement he had ever made, taking special care of his bars and medals. Respect for life was something that he had brought with him from the military when he had finally retired. He was also as tough as nails, having raised Tammy on his own, teaching her good manners, good morals, good judgement, respect and high standards.

Ralph was most likely going to crush Steve's little "brain fart" of a statement about how to fight like a man, if not challenge it, and it most definitely would not be a challenge of words. *Bloody hell. This is already turning into a crazy weekend, and Dad's only just arrived!*

Tammy spent the entire weekend trying to keep the peace between Ralph and Steve, by going on walks with them, making sure that both were fed, well-taken-care-of and happy, the entire weekend. She even sat and watched *war movies* with her dad on television, in the afternoons. It did not matter at all, that she did not like watching war movies, but her dad loved them, and she knew it would keep him happy.

She already noted that her father was not a fan of Steve. Tammy's dad had stood behind her choices, throughout her life. He had been a very strict dad, but he always made sure that she knew she was loved, and that he was there for her, if ever she needed him to be. Tammy's biggest fear, however, was that Steve and her father would, one day, come to blows. She knew that if that day ever came – if her dad ever found out that Steve had been *violent* with her – she would lose her dad. Either Steve would take some blind-siding cheap shot, taking her father's life without any regret, or Ralph would hunt Steve down with one of his impressive gun collection, and shoot Steve, dead. She did not fancy her dad in jail, or worse, and would do *anything* to make sure there was no friction between them, during the visit.

Way too soon, Monday morning had arrived. Ralph was awake at 4:00, packing things up and getting ready to make his journey back home. Steve was out of bed as well, getting ready for work. Tammy woke early and made them both a hot breakfast and cup of tea. While they ate, she packed Steve's lunch.

"Geez, mate, she really *does* take good care of you, doesn't she?" Ralph said.

"Yeah, she's my bubba," Steve replied, with a grin.

"Your what? What the fuck is a bubba?" Ralph asked. Tammy quickly explained to her dad that "Bubba" was Steve's pet name for her. She further went on, further, to say that, although she had no idea what it meant, she thought it was cute. *I will do anything to keep the peace between you two. Just please, stop with the arguing already!* Tammy smiled at her dad.

Ralph shrugged, and said, "Cute? Yeah, okay. Whatever floats your boat, I guess. Anyway, I have to go, so I can beat all that bloody early morning traffic. Love you, Tam. Was great seeing you, kiddo." Ralph kissed his youngest daughter and they hugged tight, before Tammy quickly grabbed a few apples out of the fridge and put them into her father's hands.

"You can nibble on these on the way home, if you get hungry. I love you, Dad. Drive safe, okay?" Tammy said, as she walked her father to the car, while helping to carry some of his bags.

Steve did not walk Ralph to the door as he was leaving, nor did he go outside to say goodbye or wish him a safe journey. Tammy stood out on the street and waved, as the truck drove away. She already missed her dad, and knew it would be a long time before she saw him again.

When she turned around and went back inside, she looked down at her watch. It was 6:00 already and Steve was late for work. She walked quickly into the kitchen to hurry him up, so he would not be in trouble with the boss, only to be met with a sharp slap across the face. Tammy saw stars, the second his hand connected with her face, and she was left grabbing the kitchen sink for support so she would not fall.

"I *warned* you about embarrassing me," Steve growled at her. He then grabbed his lunch and left for work.

Tammy stood in the kitchen with her hand on her face, wanting to scream the house down. *WHAT NOW, DAMMIT? FUCK!!* She clenched her fist, pushing her nails into the palm of her hand, tight, so that she could try to manage some of the pain in her face. She had absolutely no idea what she had done, or said, to upset him. Through tears, she cleared away the dirty dishes on the table, then washed, dried and put them into their rightful places in the cupboard, before getting herself ready for work. While getting showered and dressed, she could feel her heart beating through her cheek as her eye throbbed.

Arriving at work ten minutes late, she approached her supervisor as soon as she walked through the door, and apologised for her tardiness. Tammy offered to make the time up at lunch, or after work. Her supervisor, Stacey, told Tammy it was *her* choice if she wanted to take the ten minutes from her lunch hour or after work. As long as it showed on her time sheet that those ten minutes had been worked, it would be fine. Tammy quietly walked to her desk, sat down and removed her sunglasses so she could better see her computer screen.

Throughout the day, her colleagues asked about her new shiner. She had tried to cover it with make-up but, apparently, had failed, miserably. Trying to joke her way through it, Tammy advised them, simply, that she would not apologise. "If you have a problem with this face, take it up with my parents. This is *their* DNA you are looking at!" she joked. This brought about a few giggles, as her work mates returned to their desks and stopped bothering her.

She then received a phone call from the other end of the office. Her dearest friend, Patrick, said he had heard a rumour. Tammy asked what rumour he was talking about. He said he was coming to her desk now to see her. Patrick walked from the other end of the office and seated himself on Tammy's desk. He looked at her eye and he was *not* smiling.

"Are you okay?" he quietly asked. Tears started to form in her eyes, but she was *determined* not to cry. Not here. Not now. It was humiliating enough that she could not even explain to Patrick what had happened, especially since she had no idea *why* it had happened. Tammy nodded and said she will live.

Patrick whispered, "He is a filthy, rotten bastard." *You don't know the half of it, my friend.* Tammy silently looked up at Patrick with agreement in her eyes. He then said, a little bit louder, "I have a hell of a lot of letters for you to get through for me, today, young lady. Don't let me down!"

Appreciating the change of topic, Tammy smiled and boomed, loudly, right back at him, "Bring it on, mister!"

Patrick wasn't kidding. She must have counted at least 200 Penalty Notices and letters in the folder he'd brought down. There was a whole lot of badness going on, by drivers who could not obey the traffic rules. And there was a whole lot of typing to be done, in return. All of this work would most definitely keep her busy, and she silently thanked all of the morons who could not drive without an overloaded truck, or the fools who drove unregistered vehicles, or vehicles with stolen registration plates. She did not thank the drunk drivers, however. They could all run themselves into a tree and *die,* for all she cared.

Somehow, Tammy managed to get through every single piece of paperwork Patrick had sent down to her desk, as well as making up the ten minutes that she had lost in the morning. And now, like it or not, it was time to go home.

With nothing but pure fear and adrenaline coursing through her veins, she opened the front door and let herself into the house. Steve was sitting in the living room, watching a western movie and eating a pizza that he'd ordered for himself. He had also ordered a pizza for her, which was now in the refrigerator. When she walked through the door, he turned and looked at her. His eyes widened in shock when he saw her face.

Steve turned off the television, stood up and said, "Fuck. Love, did *I* do that?" *Is this a trick question, asshole?* Tammy wondered if maybe, she'd accidentally walked into a moving truck before coming home, and forgot. If Steve could seriously *not* remember hitting her that morning, something was definitely wrong with his brain.

"Don't worry about it. I'm fine," she lied. "I will live. Just leave me alone, okay?" Tammy did not want to talk, and turned to go straight to the bedroom to get changed.

Steve grabbed her by the arm and said, "No, no, no. Not okay. Sit." *Woof, woof to you, you prick. My next trick will neither be rolling over nor begging.* Knowing that it would be pointless to argue, Tammy sat on the couch, silently, waiting for whatever nonsense, which was about to come out of his mouth, to be over with.

"What religion are you?" Steve asked.

Tammy's eyebrows suddenly rose, to match her surprise at such an unexpected question. "I am Christian. Why do you ask?" she replied.

Steve frowned at her. He already knew she was Christian and was frustrated that she had not understood the question he'd just asked. "Yeah, I *know* that," he said, "but are you Lutheran, Baptist, Catholic, or *what*?"

Her mind started running around in circles, wondering if there was some kind of answer that he would feel was right. She decided just to go with the truth. "My great grandpa and my grandpa were Salvos and my dad is a Salvo. You know... *Salvation Army*? But when I was little, my religious lessons on Sundays were at a Baptist church at the top of our street. Why does it matter? Why are you asking?" Tammy replied.

Steve told her that his whole family were Catholics, and now that they were engaged, it was time she learned to be a good Catholic, too. It was essential before the wedding. *Oh yeah. The wedding. God help me. Weird that he considers himself to be a good ANYTHING!* Tammy tried not to cringe at the thought of their upcoming nuptials, regardless that a date had not yet been set.

Although Steve had been serious about his request, Tammy did not mind, so much, about changing religions. After all, Christian was *Christian*, right? Besides, she liked the Pope. In her opinion,

Pope John Paul II was kinda awesome. *Isn't the Pope friends with Princess Diana?* Tammy absolutely *adored* Princess Diana. *Nobody is as lucky as Princess Di,* she thought.

Tammy had also attended the wedding of one of her co-workers in a Catholic church, and it was absolutely mind-blowing. The church was incredibly fancy inside, with people getting a free feed and free drink afterwards, while waiting in a queue on the carpet, down the middle of the church. Sure, there were worse things in life than becoming a Catholic. Tammy told Steve she had no problems at all with changing over and becoming Catholic. Steve absolutely beamed at the news.

"I knew you would love it! There is a Cathedral not too far from here, and the priest is a friend of mine. He is expecting you for lessons," Steve told her.

"*Lessons*? What lessons? You mean I can't just change *over*?" Tammy looked puzzled.

Steve looked her in the eyes and said, "Catholicism lessons. They start tomorrow, and will be three days per week, until you are confirmed."

Oh no. Please don't be on Tuesday or Thursday nights. Please? Tammy should have seen it coming, but the news blind-sided her and hit her hard. She almost started to wonder if, perhaps, Steve had somehow *found out* about her LGBT meetings and her new friends.

"Your lessons will be on Tuesday, Thursday and Saturday afternoons. Each lesson will be three hours long. And you *will* attend every lesson, understood?" Steve said, as he continued to stare at her.

"Yeah, I'll be there," she replied, knowing that she really didn't have a choice. *Steve and a priest being best friends? Good grief!* Tammy would not be surprised if the very same priest went home to *his* wife, stinking of beer and vomit, on the same nights that Steve came home, smelling that way.

Chapter 9

Three months had passed since Tammy started attending her compulsory lessons, in order to become Catholic. Steve wanted her to become a "good Catholic," but if that is how he saw *himself*, she decided that she would rather sit naked on a huge pile of thumbtacks, than follow in his footsteps. Regardless, Tammy would go straight from work to the Springwood Catholic Church, three times per week. When she arrived home at 8:30 on those nights, she would immediately get dinner started and go to freshen up, before Steve arrived home.

The past two months had left her feeling a little queasy, and she thought she was coming down with the flu. But when the feeling persisted, and she had no other symptoms except for a spinning room and some of her favourite foods putting her off ever wanting to eat again, she decided to head down to the Logan Health Centre. The news she received from the doctor absolutely *floored* her.

That night, she cooked up Steve's absolute favourite meal – a hearty beef casserole with a side of mash – and she decided to get dressed up, even though it was just dinner at home. She was so excited. Tammy kept looking at her watch, then looking at the door, fidgeting and wishing that time would hurry up. She could not wait to tell Steve the news.

At 10:00 that night, she had started to panic. Hopefully, he had not gone out again to get drunk. *Not tonight. I really need this night to be special.*

A little bit after 10:15, Steve walked in the door. He looked tired and sweaty. Sniffing the air, he smiled and knew that something special had been cooking. Tammy smiled, when she saw his reaction to the food. It was definitely a good sign. She walked over to him and kissed him on his smiling lips.

"I have a surprise for you," Tammy smiled, affectionately, and looked into his eyes.

"I love surprises, Bubba. Lead the way," he said, a glint in his eye. When he saw what was cooked up and ready in the pot, his stomach growled with hunger. Steve quickly went to the bathroom to wash his face and hands, before returning to the table, grinning from ear to ear. He sat down and anxiously awaited the serving up of his favourite food.

While they ate, Tammy had soft music playing in the background. She wanted this night to be one that he would never forget. Although they no longer "dated," as such, this would be a special night, which she would remember as their first date at home.

With food finished, Tammy cleared off the table and rinsed off the dishes. She would return to those later. Leading Steve into the living room, she slowly started to dance with him. Steve lovingly looked into her eyes. She knew the perfect moment had arrived.

"Steve, we are going to have a baby. I am pregnant," Tammy beamed, as she told him the most wonderful thing happening in her world.

Steve stopped dancing. He also stopped smiling. Looking at Tammy with a confused look, he said, "What?"

"It was confirmed today, down at the health centre. We are pregnant!" Tammy was so excited.

Steve was silent. He stared at her for a moment, before turning, as if to walk away. He then thrust his elbow backwards, as hard as he possibly could, into her stomach. When Tammy dropped to the ground and screamed in pain, he kicked her in the stomach three or four times... or maybe more. She could not remember. What she did know was that the pain going through her felt like somebody had sharpened and heated a pitchfork in hot coals before shoving it into her abdomen. Tammy vomited up everything she had just eaten, no longer screaming, as she was barely able to breathe.

"You fucking slut! You filthy cunt! Who did you fuck? You disgusting, piece of shit, cheating *slut*! Tell me who he is!" he screamed at her, as she lay on the ground, gasping for air. He leaned down, grabbed her hair and pulled her head back. Steve rubbed Tammy's face in the vomit on the floor. He whispered to her, "Fuck you, cunt!" before grabbing his keys and walking out the door, leaving her gasping for air. Unable to move due to the searing pain, Tammy wished that death would claim her right then and there. She had never experienced so much pain in her life. She needed the pain to stop.

Tammy had no idea how long she'd been on the floor. Breathing was a very hard task. The pain had not lessened and she felt like she had wet her pants. Somehow, she had to clean this mess before he got home. As she continued to lie there, she forcibly slid her arm under the side of her chest and tried to lever herself, with her elbow, into a sitting position, even just a little. The pain was excruciating. She inched herself, very slowly, towards the bathroom. When she looked down, she realised she had not wet her pants. She was bleeding and she needed a doctor... *fast*. Without even looking, she knew the phone was locked. She continued to inch herself, slowly, across the floor, coming to a stop in the laundry, before passing out.

Muffled voices Tammy could not understand had stirred her from her slumber. She was floating. Was she inside a cloud? She closed her eyes.

There they were again. Those voices. *Somebody is inside this cloud with me.* Tammy did not call out. She felt weak and couldn't seem to form any thoughts that made sense. Closing her eyes again, the voices were a little bit less muffled. People were arguing. *Why would anybody want to fight in such a pretty cloud?* The arguing became much louder.

"She needs to be in a hospital, dammit!" yelled a voice that she did not recognise.

"No fucking hospitals. Just *fix* her. Do your job and make her okay," a voice growled.

This second voice was one she knew well. When she heard Steve talk, she flinched, as a sudden, dull pain shot through her stomach. Tammy opened her eyes slowly and looked around. She appeared to be in a doctor's office. Too weak to sit up, she closed her eyes and continued to listen. Tammy was unable to follow the rest of the conversation which was taking place. It almost sounded like it was being whispered behind closed doors. But she was tired and needed to sleep.

When Tammy woke, a doctor was sitting by her side. A nurse was in the room with him. She looked around, but could not see Steve. Had he gone home?

The nurse took Tammy's pulse and blood pressure before the doctor started talking. As the doctor introduced himself and held her hand, sadness filled Tammy's heart. She had already forgotten the doctor's name, as she listened to him tell her that she had lost her baby. The doctor went on to tell her to rest, and if she feels any sharp pains or discomfort, she was to call an ambulance immediately. He wrote a prescription for pain, and gave her a note for her boss to cover her from work absence for the next two weeks. Tammy could not speak. If she spoke, she would start screaming. Instead, tears filled her eyes as emptiness filled her soul.

Steve entered the room. He had been crying, but she refused to comfort him. He had taken away every bit of joy she had ever known. She had no room in her heart to feel pity for him.

"Let's go home," Steve whispered in her ear. She was too weak to fight him. He shook the doctor's hand and thought she saw money change hands at the same moment. Steve then put the prescription and doctor's note in his pocket. He turned around, gently lifting Tammy off the bed, before carrying her to the car.

"We will get through this," he said. With that, he pulled out of the car park and they headed home.

Once home, Steve lifted her from the car and carried her inside. He gently put her on the bed before going back outside to lock the car up. When he returned to the bedroom, he sat on the edge of the bed and put his hand on her stomach. She flinched from his touch and the pain it caused. Steve started to cry.

"I didn't mean to do it," Steve said, through his tears. "I got angry. My last girlfriend cheated on me with my best friend. Two babies, they had. And my mum cheated on my dad." He paused and looked into her eyes. "My brain just…. I thought you had… I am sorry. Bubba, I am *so* sorry. We are both hurting from this right now. I am sorry. I swear to you that it will never happen again."

Tammy took his hand off her stomach, before slowly rolling over to face the wall. She turned her back on Steve, and did not want him anywhere near her. After he finally stood up and left the room, her pillow, already wet from tears, kept her company, as she cried herself to sleep.

Over the next two weeks, Steve brought a glass of water to her, twice per day, along with the medication which the doctor had prescribed – pain killers, sedatives and a medication which was to prevent any infection. When Tammy's medical certificate had almost expired, Steve suggested to her that it was, maybe, time to quit her job. *It's time to quit many things, including you.* Tammy did not believe, for a second, that he would not hurt her again. She also did not want to leave a job that she truly enjoyed.

"When you are feeling better, we will discuss it more. Just rest and get better, okay?" Steve said to her.

He turned Tammy's face to look at him, when she'd refused to. She saw his face and looked into his eyes. She knew he probably loved her in his own sick, twisted kind of way. But his love was selective. Just like selective-hearing, Steve suffered a bad case of selective-love. *He* decided which times were best to show how much he cared. Right now, Tammy felt love and concern (*and guilt*) radiating off him in waves.

On the Friday before she was due to return to work, she waited until she heard the front door close, and listened, quietly, as the Kingswood pulled out of the driveway. Although still not quite feeling normal, possibly from the sedatives and who-knows-what-else Steve had given her, over the past fortnight, she slowly sat up in bed, slipped her feet into her slippers, and went for a walk. She had been bedridden for far too long. It was time to try and get back into things again.

As she walked through the house, she was hit by a whole cocktail of emotions – pain, frustration, shame, anger and disgust, just to name a few. Everything was such a mess. Dirty dishes were piled up in the sink, on the stove, on the cupboard, as well as some on the table. *More* dirty dishes were found on the floor of the living room. Dirty clothes filled the laundry and bathroom. Her eyes then landed on a trail of dried blood, which led from the laundry, all the way to the living room. A pile of dried vomit was on the floor, next to where the blood trail had ended in the living room. Tammy put her hand on her stomach and closed her eyes, vaguely remembering the events of that night.

Ensuring that she did not overdo it, Tammy slowly started to collect the dirty dishes from the living room floor and took them into the kitchen. She would wash those a little bit later. She then got a bucket from outside, filled it with hot water and antiseptic, and used a mop to clean up the mess of blood and vomit that she had made, two weeks ago. It took some time, but soon enough, all traces of that night were gone. She glanced over at the telephone. It was, once again, locked. Tammy sat on the couch in the living room and looked around. She closed her eyes and shook her head, as fast as she could, trying to force herself properly awake. Her face felt numb.

She walked back into the kitchen and started to stack the dishes onto the sink and stove, getting them ready for washing. All of the cups went into the sink, which she filled with hot water and detergent, so they could soak for ten minutes or so. Next, she walked down the hall to the laundry and sorted out the dirty clothes. Tammy found more dirty clothes in the living room, next to the couch, as well as on the bedroom floor (tucked under Steve's side of the bed) and even in the garage. The first thing to wash were the towels and dish cloths, since she saw that not a single clean towel was left in the cupboard. She lived with a pig. *Perhaps I should just go out back and build a pig pen, filled with water and mud? He would be right at home there and I would not have to clean up all his shit right now.* Tammy seriously wondered how *anybody*, with even an ounce of self-respect, could make so much mess.

While the towels were in the washing machine, Tammy returned to the kitchen and started to wash the cups. Each time the dish strainer was completely full, she would get a tea towel and dry each cup, before putting it away. With the cups all cleaned and in the cupboard, she started on the plates. Just as she had run some fresh water into the sink and put the first lot of plates in, the front door opened and Steve walked in. He got to the kitchen and stopped. He frowned at her and stared. *Go ahead, asshole. I dare you to hit me again. Seriously!* All of the kitchen cutlery, including the sharp knives, were next in line to be washed, after the plates were done. Those sharp knives were neatly stacked on the sink, right beside her. Tammy kept that thought right at the front of her mind, as she stared back at Steve.

An uneasy silence filled the room for about a minute. Steve then said, "I was going to wash those. You didn't have to do it."

Tammy simply nodded in response before turning back to the sink. She continued washing the dishes. Steve would never have lifted a finger to clean the place, even if she had been comatose for a month, and she knew it. Once she'd finished washing all of the dishes and had put them away, Tammy wiped down the stove, table and cupboards. It was then, that she noticed some muck, which looked like a handprint of dirt or blood, on the wall near the hallway. She grabbed a scrubbing brush and the tea towel and scrubbed hard, making sure every bit of it was gone, before returning to the laundry.

Although it hurt to lean into the washing machine, Tammy managed to remove the wet towels and put them into the clothes trolley, ready to hang on the line to dry. That is when she heard the television switch on. *Yep, Steve really is concerned about me cleaning all this mess, obviously!* Before heading out to hang up the towels, Tammy filled the washing machine with the next load of clothes. After this, she would need to lie down for a while. Already, she was exhausted.

Chapter 10

Monday morning arrived and Steve had already left for work. Tammy grabbed the first thing her hand touched in the wardrobe and put it on. She pulled out a pair of black tracksuit pants and one of her many Def Leppard t-shirts. *I guess there won't be any fashion parades, today at work.* She was grateful to be alone in the house, that morning, but not so grateful for yet another mess of dishes and dirty clothes, which Steve had left in his wake. Tammy did not have the time or the motivation, that morning, to clean his mess. She climbed into the shower, washed her hair, got dressed into her not-so-sexy, chosen ensemble, and made herself a piece of toast and cup of tea for breakfast. After brushing her teeth, Tammy then checked that her wallet and keys were in her purse before she left the house and drove to work.

As soon as she walked through the door, her supervisor told her that the boss wanted to see her, pronto. *Good morning to you too, Stacey.* Tammy put her bag on her desk, hung her jacket over the back of the chair at her desk and went straight to the boss's office. She wondered if she was about to be fired for being away so long. The boss told her to come in and take a seat.

"Is there a problem? Have I done something wrong?" Tammy asked, unsure of why she was summoned to the boss's office.

"No problem, no. Are you over the flu yet or are you still feeling crook?" he asked.

THE FLU?? "Umm, yeah, I am over it. Still not feeling so great, though. If I am still crook later, I might head home early, if that's okay with you?" Tammy could not believe that Steve had told her boss she'd had the flu.

"Lots of work to do, but if you aren't feeling good, let me know and you can go home. But that is not why I called you in here. There is a new group starting up in the Department – some anti-discrimination awareness thing. Have you heard about it?" her boss asked.

"No, didn't know. What's it got to do with me?" Tammy knew that she had not discriminated against anybody. Had somebody made a complaint?

"Well, it deals with your sort. People like *you*, you know?" her boss continued.

"People like me?" Tammy still wasn't sure what was going on.

"You know. Coloured people. Abbos!"

Tammy was absolutely floored. "*ABBOS*? Are you *kidding* me?" Tammy exclaimed. She stared at her boss, right in the eye, wondering what racist bullshit would come out of his mouth next.

"What? You *are* a black, aren't you?" her boss asked.

"So let me get this straight. You want me to be on a panel of people who will be specialising in anti-discrimination… and you want me to be on that panel because I am a *BLACK COLOURED ABBO*? Have I got that right?" Tammy yelled.

Her boss simply replied, "Yeah."

"Indeed, please sign me up. I would love to be a part of that group. Now I have to get to a meeting. I'll be back shortly. Thanks for thinking of me," Tammy said, sarcastically.

She then headed out to the elevator and rode it to the top floor, walking straight up to the Secretary of the Director General, and said, "I need to see the big man. *Urgently*. Thanks. And yes, I will wait." Tammy then sat down and waited. She may be helpless at *home*, when it came to bullshit, but she sure as hell was *not* going to put up with it at work.

Within five minutes, Tammy was seated in the office of the Director General. She said she would like to lodge an official complaint of discrimination against her manager, before explaining, in detail, what had happened, that morning.

"So you are an Australian Aboriginal, is that correct?" the Director General asked.

"Yes, Sir, I am. I proudly identify as Australian Aboriginal of Gubbi Gubbi tribe. I also do not tolerate racism of any kind, and when my own manager calls me a 'Black coloured abbo,' I look forward to seeing what you will *do* about it," Tammy said, staring him straight in the eye. She was angry, and on the verge of tears, but managed to hold herself together.

"Thank you for bringing this to my attention, Tammy. Leave it with me, and it will be investigated. Please know, however, that I will not be able to divulge to you, the outcome of the investigation," the Director General said.

Tammy thanked him and left his office. When she had caught the elevator back to her own floor, she went to her desk and sat down. There was a folder in her tray from Patrick. She opened the folder, which was filled with many letters to be typed. On top of the letters was a handwritten note, which simply said "Welcome back. If you need to talk, you know my number." She was grateful for his note and his concern. But she knew that, this time, she could not take him up on his offer.

It was lunch time already before Tammy took a break. She felt that she could continue for the rest of the day, although she had not packed a lunch for herself. She went downstairs to Brunswick Street Station's indoor mall, and bought herself a can of Coke and a Beef Croquette. It wasn't much, but Tammy was not feeling too hungry these days, and just needed enough sustenance to get her through to the end of the day. She took her lunch back upstairs to her desk and played Mah-jongg on her computer, until she'd finished eating. When she had finished her lunch, she got straight back to work.

At 2:00 that afternoon, her boss walked out of his office – a rare thing to see – and he bragged loudly to all of the staff in the office that he was off to see the Director General. Tammy had a knowing look in her eye and quickly glanced at him as he left. She then resumed what she had been doing. All of these letters were *not* going to type themselves and she wanted to keep herself as busy as she could. An hour later, a not so happy, racist boss walked through the door. Walking right up to Tammy's desk, he turned around to face everybody else in the office, before shouting "FUCKING ABBOS!" He then went to his office and slammed the door. Tammy guessed he would be attending one of the very *first* anti-discrimination lectures that would be given.

That was the last day he served as manager. Not only was he instructed to attend anti-discrimination classes, he was also demoted and transferred. For the first time in a very long time, Tammy felt like she'd done something proactive. Not everything in her life was controlled by Steve… or was it? Within a month, word had spread that Tammy was the reason their manager had been "fired," and she was now regarded as a troublemaker. Not wanting to deal with all the bullshit of rumour mongering, she instead decided to tender her resignation and left the job that she'd loved, for so many years.

Tammy immediately started looking for a new job. She had told Steve she'd resigned, and was hopefully going to be able to find something local so the commute to work would not be so long, and she could maybe even walk to work.

"I am proud of you, Bubba. You listened to me and quit your job. It shows how much you love me," said Steve.

Tammy nearly choked on her cup of tea. She almost laughed and wanted to tell him that her leaving had absolutely nothing, whatsoever, to do with him, but she'd held her tongue. Instead, she said, "I might go out and get a newspaper on Wednesday morning. Lots of jobs are listed there, as well as local jobs which will be listed in Thursday's local rag." She was determined to find a new job.

There was nothing in Wednesday's paper that a brain surgeon or rocket scientist couldn't apply for. But Tammy was just an Administration Officer – a lowly, level three, government worker. She knew that she would, most likely, have to find something at base level, if she was to start working for a new company. Thursday's paper, however, had a job listed which was right at the end of their street, in real estate. Pay was base level (plus commission), and you would receive a petrol bonus, as well as your own pager and… a mobile phone? *Whoa!* Tammy had never even *heard* of those. Very swanky, indeed!

Her first day on the job was the following Monday. She had attended the interview on Friday, and had done really well. The manager, Robert, was impressed with her work experience, and duties performed in her previous job. When he asked why she had left, Tammy said it had just been time for her to try something new, as she had been passed over for promotion, too many times. While it was not entirely a lie – she had indeed been passed over for promotion many times and had been told by her former manager that the reason was "because you are so good at training other people to become better" – she decided the full truth would not be wise. She really wanted this job. Tammy figured that coming right out and telling them *"because my boss was a racist piece of shit"* was not really going to do it.

Monday morning, she showed up, bright and early at opening time, was introduced to the receptionist (Pamela), the Rental Manager (Kathy), the Sales Manager (Selina) and a few Sales Consultants. Tammy's job would be fairly simple – keep the rental list up to date, help applicants fill out rental application forms for properties they were interested in renting, and perform rental inspections.

After her duties were explained to her, she was handed a pager and a mobile phone. She had seen pagers *many* times before. Steve carried one everywhere. But this was the very first time she had ever laid eyes on a mobile phone. Just a few days ago, she hadn't even heard of one! They presented her with the box, and she carefully pulled out the phone. It was a Motorola flip phone... and it was *hers*! No locks. No restrictions... or so she thought. Kathy advised Tammy that if she is out of the office and a customer walks in, she will be paged to contact the office immediately. She was to use the phone to contact Kathy, explaining why she was not in the office. *Oh great. This lot sounds like a barrel of fun, already!* Tammy loved the sound of the job, but almost felt claustrophobic when the strict phone policy had been explained to her. Regardless of their phone policy, however, she needed this job.

The mobile phone barely fit into her pocket. She could not carry it in her blouse pocket or it would look like one of her boobs was a size FFF, so she decided that she would simply take her handbag with her, everywhere she went – even to the toilet – just so she could keep her mobile phone tucked away and out of sight.

Within two weeks of starting the job with the real estate firm, Tammy had witnessed Robert fly into many inexplicable rages, having had several heated exchanges with Pamela (who, it turns out, was the Robert's long-term girlfriend) and, unfortunately for Tammy's eyes, those two were not afraid to kiss passionately at the reception desk, afterwards. At the end of the first week, Robert stormed out of the office, screaming curse words that made Tammy blush – and she thought she'd heard them all. He returned, not long afterwards, with his hand bandaged (in, what was obviously, a self-bandage job) and sought comfort from Pamela, because he had just been in a fist-fight with some *nobody* from who-knows-where. While extremely entertaining to the rest of the staff in the office, Tammy excused herself and said she had a meeting with a client. She then went home. *What a ridiculous little soap opera those two are!*

Sadly, the second week was almost an exact repeat of the first, with Robert and Pamela seemingly giving a *Days of Our Lives* rendition for all of the staff, as well as any customers, unfortunate enough to be within viewing and listening distance. Kathy told Tammy it was time to get out of their insane little setting to go do some *real* work. They drove to a few properties while Tammy listened to stomach-churning tales of soft porn, which, apparently, occurred on a regular basis, inside the real estate office. According to Kathy, Robert *quite often* made all of his bad decisions with his penis, and was laughing stock of all others within Queensland's real estate industry. This news did not surprise Tammy at all.

While continuing to listen to even *more* not-so-delightful anecdotes from her supervisor, she reached into her handbag for her new mobile phone. She was still excited that she had one – her very own portable phone, without a cord, that worked almost *anywhere*. She smiled until she suddenly realised that the phone was not there. *Oh shit!* Tammy felt around everywhere and looked inside her handbag, only to realise that her wallet was also missing. Suddenly, she felt dizzy. She told Kathy she did not feel so good, and asked if they could return to the office. She needed to go home. Kathy offered to drop her there, but Tammy's car was at the office. She told Kathy that the car would also be going home.

Back at the office, the two lovebirds were at it again. Robert and Pamela were engaged in a facial suck-fest which nearly made Tammy taste her own bile. She made her excuses, quickly searched her desk, just in case the mobile phone was in a drawer, and then left. She already knew, in her gut, that he had been through her bag. Steve had her mobile phone. He had her wallet. And she knew that she was about to face his wrath.

It was only mid-afternoon when Tammy walked through the door. She was home alone but she was trembling. She quickly looked around, turning up couch cushions, checking drawers in the kitchen, inside the bed covers, even in the bathroom cupboard under the sink while praying for a miracle, that she had simply misplaced the mobile phone. When she went back into the kitchen, she saw both her mobile phone and wallet on the sink. Tammy knew it hadn't been there when she'd come home, and the feeling of dread inside of her had slipped into overdrive. She picked up the mobile phone and wallet and turned slowly around. Steve was standing at the kitchen entry way with his hands in his pockets.

"Please take a seat, Bubba, and explain to me what you have in your hands, right now," he calmly said.

Tammy sat at the kitchen table and put the wallet and the mobile phone in front of her, on the table. "The people at the real estate office said I need to have this. It belongs to *them* and is what you call a 'tool of the trade'. Just like your nails and hammers where you work…"

"And who have you been ringing?" Steve interrupted.

"I haven't rung anybody except for my boss. Not allowed to use it for private stuff," she explained. "I swear it."

"Tomorrow you return it to them. You do not need fancy shit like that," Steve said, calmly.

She had been honest with him and he'd *believed* her? Seriously? That was most definitely a *first* for her. Not that Tammy wasn't *relieved* or anything. Her heart was beating at what felt like a million times per second. She had expected insanity. She was fully prepared for…. *something*. But luckily for her, that something never came.

The next day, Tammy took the phone into Robert's office as soon as she arrived at her job. He told her to sit. She sat at his desk, while he screamed and shouted at Pamela on the phone. The obscenities coming out of his mouth reminded her of days gone by with Steve – days that were hopefully gone forever. While she continued to listen to her manager's verbal abuse towards his girlfriend, Tammy made a decision right then and there.

"I know you are busy, and all, with your phone call, but… I quit. Thank you," she said, looking Robert straight in the eyes – eyes that were now wide while his big, gaping, open mouth. "It's been fun." Tammy then put the mobile phone and pager on his desk and walked out with her head held high. She got into her car, drove home and spent the rest of the day relaxing.

When Tammy told Steve that she had quit her job and that she no longer had a mobile phone or pager, his only response to her was, "Good. I'm hungry. Please go and cook me something to eat." So she went into the kitchen with a smile and did just that.

Chapter 11

The next few months passed without incident. Steve had kept his promise not to hurt her again. The house was once again running smoothly. Tammy was keeping everything clean, while making sure his breakfast had been served and his lunch packed each morning, before he left for work. He was also happy that Tammy was focussing hard on her Catholicism lessons and taking his religion seriously. But she had never had a problem with God. Tammy and God had always been good mates, she thought, and she had always been a good person, as far as she knew. Her bonding closer with God was no punishment, by any means.

Steve's bills had started piling up again and, not wanting Steve to get back into debt, Tammy rang the Personnel Section of her former government employer. She registered her name for any temporary assignments that might come up. When people within the government would go on holidays, extended sick leave or maternity leave, their job needed to be temporarily filled by somebody who knew what they are doing, or who was easily trained.

Within a week of registering for temporary work, she received an urgent request to fill a one month temporary assignment with the office of the Director General. The secretary was going on holidays, and Tammy was needed to fill in as her replacement while she was away. Ecstatic at such an offer, she told Steve, the moment he got home from work, that she would be working full-time, starting on Monday. Steve was surprised that such a great offer had come so fast. He decided to take Tammy's car for a drive and get it fuelled up for next week.

When Steve returned home, he said to Tammy, "Your little car drives like a constipated piece of shit. It's too slow and has no power. Tomorrow, we trade it in and get a car with *real* power."

But I love my car, dammit! Regardless of Tammy's insistence that she did not need, nor did she *want* a new car, Steve told her to go and clean out everything from inside the car – under the seats, in the boot, the glove compartment – and told her to vacuum the inside while he washed the outside.

The next morning, they drove her beloved Mazda 626 (which Tammy affectionately referred to as "Maxine") to a local car yard and exchanged it for a much more powerful Holden VK Commodore. While driving it home, she realised that every single time she hit the slightest bump on the road, the car would swerve onto the other side of the road. She had no control over it. Steve quickly made her turn the car around, returning it to the car yard. He persuaded the manager of the car company to have the car serviced, while also having the steering looked at and fixed – definitely a tall order for a Saturday. Tammy and Steve then *both* waited the whole day, while the steering column and bush were replaced. At the end of their wasted Saturday, they, once again, took the new car home but, this time, it drove like a dream. Tammy was happy, and it was a direct exchange, not costing her a single cent.

On her arrival at work on Monday morning, Tammy was greeted *personally* by the Director General, whose office was situated at her former work building. He was a very friendly man and remembered her from their one and only meeting. He introduced her to one of the Administration Officers, before returning to his duties. Tammy's task was to look over their multi-million dollar departmental budget. There was a two cent discrepancy and they were unable to find it. She was advised that she would receive no interruptions or distractions.

Tammy went through all of the figures with a fine tooth comb and in the middle of that first day, she had found the two cent discrepancy and the budget was now fully balanced.

"Bloody hell, woman. *Great job!*" exclaimed the Administration Officer.

They advised the Director General that the problem had been found and fixed, all within one day. He was pleased, not to mention *completely* surprised, and said that there were letters to type up, but he had not yet dictated any of them because he thought the budget job would take at least a week.

"I am very good with numbers, Sir. If you like, I can get some filing or other tasks done to fill up the rest of the day?" Tammy offered.

Instead, she was given the rest of the day off with full pay. *Now THIS is what a real job feels like. Damn, I miss it.* Tammy was very excited about coming to work, the next day.

Before she knew it, that month had come to an end and the Secretary of the Director General was due to return. When Tammy was called into the Director General's office, he asked her if she had any other temporary assignments lined up for Monday.

"I hadn't really planned that far ahead, Sir. You have kept me pretty busy. Not complaining, though. I have really loved working here with you," Tammy smiled.

"Well, what if I asked you to consider coming back to work for the Department on a full-time basis? There is currently a vacancy at…."

"I would love that!" Tammy interrupted. *Oops! My bad.*

The Director General did not seem to mind Tammy's interruption or, if he did, he certainly did not show it. He went on to tell her that a vacancy had become available in one of his city offices, at Mineral House. Although there would be no parking spaces available, she would *easily* be able to drive to the nearest railway station and catch a train, or she could drive into the city and then catch the shuttle bus each morning from the building she was currently standing in.

"Will you arrange the interview or would you like me to call them?" Tammy asked.

"What interview? This whole month, you have *passed* the interview with flying colours. I don't plan on letting you go so *easily* this time. You really do have a good eye for detail and I *like* that," The Director General replied, with a smile. "You start next week. Report to 25th floor of Mineral House at 9:00 sharp. Oh, and Tammy? Welcome back!"

Tammy almost floated to the car park, she was so happy. Her work life was back on track, and she was now 'in-demand' by higher offices within the government. Her home life actually started feeling normal, and she was happy.

The following Monday morning, Tammy reported to her new boss. When she stepped out from the elevator, her jaw dropped. She had never seen such a fancy office floor before. This entire floor consisted of just five employees – Tammy being one of them – and they each had their own office. Tammy could swear that her office was bigger than the home she shared with Steve. Almost bursting with joy, she sat down at her brand new office desk and wanted to pinch herself. Tammy reported to one person only – the big boss, Max. The other two senior staff shared one assistant. It was one of the weirdest setups she'd ever seen but, then again, Tammy had never before set foot in an office which was just one level down from the Minister himself. At the front of her office was a bullet-proof, glass wall with a small area to speak to any visitors, although visitors, as it turned out, were as rare as hens' teeth. She was now, *officially,* a glorified, overpaid receptionist, and she would not give this job up for anything in the world.

Three months into her new job, Tammy started to feel sick. She had her suspicions of what was ailing her, and part of her was hoping she was wrong. Tammy asked Max if she could go and see the doctor. There was one near the Health Building just two streets away. She promised that she would be quick. Max gave the okay and she headed out, wanting to vomit with every step. She had to walk past a café to get to the doctor's surgery and as soon as she did, she puked on the street. The smell of coffee was just too much for her to stomach. *Dammit!* Tammy quickly apologised to the patrons, who'd suddenly decided *not* to eat at the café, before she continued her walk and arrived at the surgery.

"I need to see a doctor urgently, please," Tammy told the receptionist.

"Have you been here before?" the receptionist asked, in a snobby tone.

"No, this is the first time. Please, where is your toilet?" Tammy asked.

Holding out a clipboard and pen, the receptionist said, "If you have not been here before, you will need to complete this with all of your details, as well as y...."

Tammy threw up on the floor, while holding her stomach. She started crying. A doctor quickly came out and led her into the surgery, while the receptionist, looking none-too-happy, cleaned up the mess that Tammy had left behind. The doctor took her temperature, her blood pressure, checked her ears, her eyes and her balance before quickly having to show her to the toilet. While she was throwing up in the doctor's private toilet, he took a small, plastic cup, with a lid, in to her. The doctor asked her to pee into the cup, when she was ready. He then left her in privacy.

The doctor wrote a prescription for Tammy to fill immediately, in order to control the nausea. Tammy left the doctor's office with a look of absolute horror on her face. She was pregnant. Even after all of the *good* things that had happened over the past six months, her thoughts were dragged right back to the *last* time she was pregnant – the night she broke the wonderful news to Steve, followed by his insane reaction. It had also been the night Steve had broken her, both physically and emotionally. A lot of time had passed since that day, but the memory was still as fresh as if it had happened just yesterday.

Tammy slowly walked up the hill from the doctor's office and decided to take a detour, down Elvis Lane – a place where her and her friends had hung out on Friday nights, when she was a teenager. From the street, it looked like an abandoned alley, but it opened up at the other end to a beautiful grassy lawn with trees and seats, right next to Education House. She sat on one of the seats and silently cried. *What do I do? What do I do? I don't know what to do!* After a while, she figured that the *best* thing to do, at that moment, was to get her butt back to the office. She would have to figure this out indoors, while getting her paperwork done. She would figure it out somehow.

Tammy filled the doctor's prescription on the way back to the office. The medication he'd prescribed seemed to help, as long as she was nowhere near food. If she could not see or smell food, and especially if she could not smell coffee – a drink that she seriously could not stand the smell or taste of, throughout her entire life – then she would be fine. That evening, when she arrived home, she had made her decision. Tammy was not going to say a word to Steve. Not now. Not yet. Her job was still relatively new and, although she had done nothing wrong, she wanted to make sure that she did not jeopardise her dream job in any way.

Her colleagues kept mainly to themselves, except to bring in work for her to do. Tammy felt "safe" in her little bullet-proof shell, and the views overlooking the Botanical Gardens were *breathtaking*. Sometimes, she would quietly crack a window in her office during her lunch hour, and breathe in the fresh air. Next to the Botanical Gardens, she could see Parliament House and Queensland University. Life really was perfect.

Six months had passed since her first day on the job. Three months had passed since the doctor told her that she was pregnant. She had returned to the same doctor *twice,* since that day, for a check-up, as well as renewing her anti-nausea prescription. Taking the detoured route via Elvis Lane, each time, was a great way to avoid the patrons of the café, which she'd passed by, three months ago. The doctor asked if Tammy would bring her husband to the office the next time, so they could have a combined visit. When she told the doctor that her fiancé was still clueless about the pregnancy, his look was that of concern.

"I have my reasons, doc. I can't tell him," she said.

"Tell him *soon*," was the only advice the doctor gave, before it was time for his next patient.

That night, she went home and sat at the table. She did not make dinner. She did not plan any fancy big surprises. She just sat quietly and waited. The doctor was right. Steve needed to know. Tammy started to picture herself in four more months standing all fat and waddly at the kitchen sink while washing dishes or peeling potatoes, when suddenly a baby falls out. It reminded her of the Monty Python movie, *The Meaning of Life,* and before she could stop herself, she started singing "Every sperm is sacred" in her head. *Good grief.*

She jumped, when the front door opened. Tammy's skin went numb from head to toe. She was absolutely terrified to do this, but she had to do it. She moved herself, quickly, into the chair at the end of the table so that she would be as far away from Steve as possible, when she told him the news. When he walked into the kitchen, he was *filthy* from his job, but smiled, when he saw that she was home. His smile was quickly replaced by a look of concern, when he saw how upset Tammy was. She asked him to take a seat. He first went into the bathroom to wash his hands and face, before returning to the table, and sat down.

"Something's happened. I can see it in your face," Steve said.

"Yeah, it has. And I would like you to sit at the other end of the table, please. I don't feel well and I don't want you getting sick," she said. Well it wasn't completely a lie. She was sick.

"Do you remember when you hurt me? I know it was a long time ago, but do you *remember* what you did?" Tammy asked.

Steve's face was filled with shame. He still felt guilty. "I remember," he whispered.

"Do you remember what you promised to me, after it happened? Because I am scared, right now, to tell you what I have to tell you. I am worried th...."

"HOLY FUCK!" Steve yelled. "Are you *pregnant*? Are *we* pregnant?" he asked, with a huge smile, eyes wide. "I thought you were just getting *fat*! Are we having a baby?"

"Yes," Tammy responded, half smiling. While not appreciating the "fat" comment, she was pleased to still be in one piece, and was enjoying what she was seeing before her. The last time she'd seen Steve *this* happy was the night he'd proposed. With a wave of utter relief flowing right through her, a happy tear rolled down her cheek. Life really *was* perfect!

Chapter 12

Tammy had just had the most blissful weekend of her entire life, with the exception of the occasional bout of nausea. Steve had actually *helped out* around the house, insisting that Tammy put her feet up and relax. He mowed the grass (she *loved* the smell of freshly cut grass) and he offered to prepare each meal. As she had previously tasted his cooking, however, she thanked him and told him to sit and take a load off while *she* cooks. Cooking and cleaning were a *passion* to Tammy. She had been diagnosed with Obsessive Compulsive Disorder in the past, but nobody had ever complained about the fact that she loved to clean and cook. She was told, throughout most of her life, however, that she was *insane* for enjoying such domestic chores.

When Monday arrived, Tammy decided to get to work early, so she could leave early in the afternoon. The commute to and from the city was not so fun during peak hour, so she avoided those heavy travel times, as much as she could.

At 7:20 that morning, she arrived at Mineral House. The guard on duty, at the front desk, buzzed her in and greeted her with a smile. Tammy knew that this was how life was meant to be. She felt sorry for all the people in the world, who were jammed tight, inside a crowded train, in the middle of summer.

While she waited for the elevator, another girl, whom she'd never seen before, entered the building. She was also buzzed in, and greeted by the guard at the entrance. They both waited in silence for the elevator to arrive. Tammy acknowledged her with a smile, and the girl returned the gesture. Finally, the elevator arrived and they both stepped in, pressing their respective floor buttons. The doors closed.

The elevator went, steadily, up in silence, and Tammy tensed her stomach, just a little, as she prepared for the elevator to stop at floor 17, for the other woman. It did not stop. The light around the button for floor 17 went out, and the elevator continued its ascent. Tammy and the stranger exchanged glances, before Tammy looked back at the elevator buttons. The elevator then failed to stop at her floor and the light around the button for floor 25 went out. The elevator continued its ascent to floor 26, and stopped. The doors did not open. She looked at the girl and they both groaned at the inconvenience. Being stuck in an elevator, on a hot day, was no better than being crammed into a crowded train.

Tammy picked up the emergency phone inside the elevator and pressed the alarm for twenty seconds. The phone rang. Tammy said to the guard that they were trapped inside Elevator number 5, which was now stationary at floor 26, with the doors closed. She advised that she was heavily pregnant and worried. As the voice on the other end of the phone started to respond, the elevator suddenly dropped... *fast*. As the elevator plummeted and Tammy found herself weightless, trapped inside a tiny box which was falling at warp speed, she screamed bloody murder.

"IT'S FALLING! WE'RE FALLING! WE'RE GOING TO FUCKING *DIE*, OH MY GOD *WE'RE GONNA DIE!*" Tammy screamed out loud into the handset of the phone. Time seemed to slow down, as the elevator fell for what felt like hours. During her rapid descent, Tammy's mind was playing back so many different scenes in her life – mainly scenes of regret, of not seeing her family as often as she should have. She even found herself regretting that she'd never said goodbye to Steve that morning. She was *not* ready to die. *Please do not let my life end like this, oh God. Please…*

The elevator came to a sudden stop, making a "THUD" sound as the feeling of weightlessness came to an alarming halt, throwing Tammy and the other girl to the floor – *hard*. The doors of the elevator opened and Tammy and her partner, still flat on the floor, quickly crawled out of the gap, they both saw. The elevator had come to a stop between floors 16 and 17. As soon as they were both safely in the foyer of floor 16, they turned, in time to see that the elevator had started to fall once more, even though the doors remained open. Tammy's elevator companion slowly got to her feet, and helped Tammy to stand. Once upright, Tammy's feet were unable to move. It was like some ultra-strength adhesive had secured her in place. Her body was completely numb. She'd started shaking uncontrollably and she felt cold. From out of nowhere, a major amount of waterworks were cascading down Tammy's face. Her sobs were loud and inconsolable. Although grateful to be alive, Tammy knew that she had just come closer to death than any other time in her life. Now stranded on floor 16, she had to decide whether to walk the stairs to floor 25, or to walk the stairs to ground floor and go home.

The girl asked Tammy if she needed help. Tammy put her hand protectively on her stomach to make sure her baby had not fallen out, in all of the insanity of what had just happened. With baby bump still in place, she told the girl, in-between sobs, that she needed to go to floor 25. The girl helped her walk up the nine flights of stairs and then to her desk. She asked, once more, if Tammy was okay. Tammy nodded and thanked the girl for her help. She then sat still, holding tightly on to the side of her desk. Her face was completely numb. Tammy could swear that she felt the building moving back and forth – swaying in the breeze.

At 9:00 that morning, Max walked into the office, bright and smiling as always. Tammy did not move. She did not get up to see how he was, what work he had for her, how his weekend had been. She thought about lunch time and how she could not go down in one of those elevators. She still found herself unable to move from her chair.

Tammy closed her eyes, but quickly opened them again. The second she had closed them, she'd found herself, once again, falling – trapped inside a tiny box and screaming. She couldn't go there. Not now. Not ever again. Suddenly finding it hard to breathe, she wished that she could stand and open every window in her office. There was no oxygen inside the building. She was choking. Tammy felt a need to escape from her little office box and fast. She wanted to open a window and jump, just to feel fresh air on her face….

"Are you okay?" Max was standing at her desk. She had not even heard him walk in.

"Something happened," Tammy simply responded, still trying to process what had happened.

Max sat down at her desk, putting all of his paperwork aside, into a pile. It was no longer important to him. "Talk to me. Tell me what happened," Max said, gently.

"It fell," she said, vaguely, still wishing those windows would open. *How can anybody breathe in here? I need air…*

"Tammy, look at me. Please tell me what fell. I can see something is wrong," Max said, seriously, but with a gentleness and patience in his voice.

Tammy then slowly took Max through the details of what had happened in the elevator, just two hours earlier. She told him that she was finding it hard to breathe, or even to stand. *There is no air left. I have to get out of here. I can't breathe!* Tammy started to cry.

Max looked at her, concern written all over his face, and said it would be a good idea for her to take the rest of the day off. He also tried to make her feel better by saying, "You know, it is not the first time one of the elevators has taken a dive. This is a very old building, and the Department just doesn't have the money to…."

"I have to go now. I'm sorry but I cannot breathe in here. I don't know if I can walk. I have to go," Tammy interrupted, looking Max straight in the eyes.

Max nodded and picked up the phone at Tammy's desk, ordering his personal driver to take her home. He then helped

Tammy, who was still shaking like a leaf, into a standing position. As he approached the elevators, one arm around her and the other holding her elbow, she flinched.

"NO! No elevators. No more elevators. Never again," Tammy said, with pure terror shaking her voice so badly, that she found it hard to talk.

Max helped her walk down the stairs. He walked down first, ensuring that, if she fell, she would not fall far and would have "something soft" to land on. She never realised, until this moment, how lucky she was to have such a great boss. Her legs still shaking, Tammy continued her descent down each flight of stairs until they reached the ground floor. Max's personal driver was waiting to meet them in the foyer. Max continued to help Tammy to the car, which was parked in the underground car park, before giving his driver Tammy's home address.

"Take it easy, and take some time. Don't think about work for a while, okay? Just take it easy and ring me if you need anything," Max said, through the window.

By the time the car pulled into her driveway, her back was in all sorts of pain. Twisting, turning, or even the slightest attempt at bending hurt like a bitch. Max's driver got out of the car and helped her to the door. He also unlocked the door for her and helped her into the house. Tammy went to the bedroom and gently lay down. She was sleepy, but afraid to close her eyes. Eventually, she drifted off to sleep, into a land of nightmares so horrific, they made Freddy Krueger's knives look like a fun day out.

Tammy was woken by Steve, who was sitting on the side of the bed.

"Hey, Bubba! You are home early," he said, stating the obvious.

Regardless that she was not in the greatest of moods right now, she was grateful to be woken and pulled out of the nightmares that were eating at her sanity, only moments before.

Tammy did not get up. While lying on the bed, she told Steve that she would not be returning to work for a while. Tammy went on to explain what had happened at work with the elevator, and that she had been driven home by the boss's personal driver because she had problems walking.

"*FUCK!*" he yelled, as he stood up and walked to the window of the bedroom. He then returned to her, sitting beside her on the bed and put his hand gently on her stomach. "Are you okay?" he asked.

Sore. Tired. Freaking out. "Yes, I think I am okay," she responded. Steve went to the cupboard and grabbed a few blankets. He put them over her, took off her shoes, and told her to try to relax and sleep. "I love you, Steve," she said, as she, again, drifted off to sleep.

Once again, trapped inside her elevator nightmare, Tammy started screaming. The elevator was again falling and she screamed and screamed. When she woke, abdominal pain was searing right through her and she held her stomach tight, trying hard to protect the precious cargo that she carried inside of her. Steve came running into the room and said he had rung an ambulance. Tammy started to scream again. *Oh God, somebody please kill me. Make the pain stop, PLEASE MAKE IT STOP!* She tried to breathe and continued to hold her stomach before passing out.

At the hospital, Steve sat by her bed. He wept, as he held her hand. Tammy could not remember being brought to the hospital. She had just woken up, and felt a sudden sadness for her fiancé. Vaguely remembering being in pain, she silently thanked God for taking the pain away. Tammy felt okay, although she once again felt like she was lying on a cloud, surrounded by a fog that encompassed just her and Steve.

"You will be okay, hon," she said, as she put her hand on Steve's wet cheek. "*Shhhh... it's okay,*" she tried to sooth Steve's sadness and tears.

"Our baby is dead," Steve said, bluntly. "You lost our baby." It almost sounded like an accusation.

Tammy closed her eyes and, once again, was sobbing. Inconsolable, she pulled the pillow to her face as the "fog" started to lift. She did not want people looking at her. Tammy did not even want Steve looking at her.

A doctor and two nurses came to her bed, asking Steve to wait outside while they check Tammy over fully and give her the all-clear to go home. But Tammy did not *want* to go home. She had lost their baby. She cursed God. She cursed life. And she wished she had died instead.

Back at home, the tension was high. Tammy felt responsible for losing their baby and Steve was absolutely livid with anything and everything.

"Filthy fucking, dog-cunts. *FUCKING CUNTS!* I am going to fucking kill every fucking last one of the fuckers who did this. I will kill them all, fucking cunts. THEY KILLED OUR BABY! I AM GOING TO FUCKING *KILL* THEM. Your boss, I am going to start with that cunt, gonna fucking kill him and the fucking snotty cunt at front desk. FUCKING CUNTS NEED TO *PAY!*" Steve screamed in fury, while Tammy listened to him, pacing the hallway, cursing and vowing revenge on the world. He then grabbed his keys and stormed out the door, leaving Tammy to cry, silently, in bed.

Steve had taken the next two days away from work, in order to try and make Tammy feel as comfortable as possible, all the while, blaming the world and everybody in it for his problems. She could see, from the way he looked at her, that he also blamed *her* for those problems. Tammy tried to stay out of his way, as much as possible, while ensuring she took her cocktail of drugs (sedative, painkiller, drug for infection). She worried *constantly* that Steve would, in fact, go to her building and try to hurt people but, unfortunately, she had no way to ring there and warn them that there might be problems. Instead, she climbed out of bed and ran herself a very hot bath while Steve was gone. Her back felt extremely tight and sore, and she wanted to relax somehow. A hot bath had helped her in the past so, hopefully, it would work its magic once more.

Tammy climbed out of the bath tub, after soaking for almost an hour. She felt a lot better after a hot soak, but the moment she stood up from the hot water, she was, once again, feeling the pain. Her back was punishing her in a *big* way after the elevator incident, and she knew that she would just have to ride it out.

When the phone rang, Tammy was hoping that it was one of her parents. She really needed a shoulder to lean on, and Steve was most definitely *not* somebody she could turn to. When she answered the phone, she was shocked to find that it was Steve ringing. He was at the police station and needed her to come, pay bail and take him home. When Steve had left earlier, it turned out that he had gone to his own work place, and had beaten the living *shit* out of his boss. *What the hell?* Tammy was told that his co-workers had rung the police for Steve, and an ambulance for the boss. Oh, and Steve was fired for his efforts. *Yes, that is exactly what we need right now. You fucking idiot.* Tammy could not believe how things had gone from being so *good*, to suddenly being so ridiculously bad.

She slowly got dressed (the pain in her back was not helping matters) before driving down to Logan Police Station in Springwood, to spring her fiancé from jail and take him home. After paying his bail, Tammy was also, once again, without a single cent to her name.

Chapter 13

The following week, Max rang and asked Tammy if she was ready to come back to work. She told him what had happened – that she had miscarried, due to the elevator accident, and that her back was constantly in pain. She also advised him that she could not get back into an elevator. Max said that he was putting some Worker's Compensation forms into the post, so that she would continue to be paid, even after all of her sick and holiday leave had been used up. He also said that he would try to call in a few favours, and see if he could find Tammy a job on the ground floor, closer to home, while staying on the same salary. She thanked Max for his help.

Steve was unable to find a job anywhere. His boss had dropped all charges against him, when he found out about the elevator accident and miscarriage. Steve's job, however, had already been filled, and he was told that he would never, in this lifetime, be welcome back. Having been in that job for so many years, and being unqualified to do anything else, Steve had no idea what to do with himself. He'd decided that sitting at home every day, drinking and watching television, was the only solution to his problems. He also quit his job at the martial arts school. Major depression was setting in for both of them, and Tammy knew that it was not healthy for Steve, or his bank balance, to be sitting at home all the time; she no longer had any money to help him financially, once he was, again, drowning in debt.

Maybe it was time Steve started looking at what he could do, and put those skills to work? Tammy thought. He fought very well, loved being in control, loved to bully people, and was good with numbers and basic reading. Although he'd never served in the military, learning the call signs for the alphabet would be quite easy, if he wanted to learn. Tammy looked through Saturday's paper, and pulled out the job section. She scanned through the columns until she'd found listings for Security Guard courses. There was one starting in just over a week and, if they pooled what little bit of money they had together, they could make it happen.

Tammy sat Steve down and showed him the advertisement. She gave her very best sales pitch to Steve, telling him that he would be his own boss, while on the job, that he could put his martial arts skills to use, and that he would look sexy as hell in a Security Guard uniform. This last point brought a smile to Steve's face, and he agreed to sign up for the course. Tammy spent the next week with Steve, training him extensively on some of the terminology which would be used during the course. At the end of that week, she felt that he was ready and, once again, Steve had his confidence back. He attended the three-week course and passed with flying colours.

The next day, Steve took his paperwork and drove to several of the security companies in the south of Brisbane. While he was away, Tammy received a telephone call. She panicked and hoped that Steve had not been arrested for doing something stupid again.

When she answered the phone, the voice on the other end was that of her mother.

"Hi, Tam. I *really* need to talk to you about something, love. It's urgent," Janine said. It sounded serious.

"We can talk about it now, on the phone, if you want," said Tammy, a little bit worried about what might have happened. She was really hoping it was *not* bad news.

"Not on the phone, love. Let's meet up for lunch. I need to talk to you about this, in person," Janine replied.

"Uh, sure. Not a problem. I can meet up anywhere you want, but meeting somewhere local is easiest for me. I'm not feeling too great these days," said Tammy, hoping her mum would agree to meet at a place nearby.

Janine gave details of where they could meet, again insisting that they meet urgently. Tammy waited for Steve to arrive home before leaving. When the Kingswood pulled into the drive, Tammy grabbed her handbag, checked that her wallet and keys were inside, and headed out the door.

On the front porch, she told Steve that she was heading out for a while. Steve asked where she was going and for how long.

"Mum rang. She said she needs to talk to me about something urgent," Tammy responded.

Steve's eyes widened, and a look of *guilt* appeared on his face. *Whatever is going on right now with Mum, why do I suddenly have a sneaking suspicion that it has to do with you?* Tammy glanced at Steve curiously, before asking if he was okay.

"Bubba, I need you to sit down for a minute. There is something that I think I have to tell you," Steve said, slowly, with a look of worry and guilt on his face.

Tammy sat down, completely unprepared for what was about to come next.

Steve confessed, "Umm, I'm pretty sure I know what she wants. She is going to tell you that I have been ringing her a lot." When Tammy didn't respond, Steve continued. "For the past few months or so, I have been ringing your mum, asking if she wants sex."

Tammy's jaw dropped, and she stared at him in total disbelief. "What the *fuck* did you just say to me?"

"Well, I remember you telling me about your ex-boyfriend, when you were a kid, how he left you because he wanted to fuck your mum. So I wanted to see if she would want a fuck…."

"OH MY *GOD!*" Tammy screamed. She stood up, went straight to the car and drove off to meet with her mother. She felt her veins pumping blood so hard through her, that it was almost deafening. Tammy was mixed with a combination of fear, adrenaline and fury at what her *piece of shit* fiancé had been putting her mother through – fuming that he would *ever* do something so disgusting – so *TWISTED* – all this time. Tammy felt absolutely ashamed and horrified that this had been happening, right under her nose, while she had been so sick. *Regardless of what has happened over the past few months, how the hell could I not have known he was doing this?* Tammy continued driving until she found her mum. Feeling responsible for what Steve had done, Tammy could barely look her mother in the eyes.

Janine confirmed what Steve had told Tammy just moments earlier, before she'd left the house to meet her mother. Every single sick thing that he had told her was true. He had been ringing her mother for *months,* like some psychotic, evil, twisted pervert, trying to get her mother to have sex with him. And each and *every* time, Janine had told him to go and fuck himself, before hanging up on him.

"I am so very sorry that he did this to you. I swear to you, I didn't know," Tammy said to her mother, as tears rolled down her cheeks. She wanted to hug her mum. She wanted to beat the living shit out of Steve. She wanted to scream.

"I know," Janine replied, both anger and sadness in her eyes.

Tammy and her mother talked for a short while longer before it was time to go. Janine had to get back to work. Tammy had some anger issues to work out. She sat in her car, in the car park, and closed her eyes, picturing herself beating the shit out of the steel bars and sandbags at her old martial arts studio, but instead of sandbags, Steve's face was there. She'd visualised doing *so many* things to him, to punish him for what he had done. He had already isolated her from her family. Now he had driven an even *greater* wedge between her and her mum. For that, Tammy was going to make him pay, even until it took her until her dying breath.

When Tammy arrived home, Steve was not there. She felt a mixture of anger and relief. Before she knew it, she was cleaning the house. Things that did not even *need* cleaning were being polished from top to bottom. She was too angry to eat. Too angry to sleep. Tammy just needed to clean and work out her aggression before her rat-bastard soon-to-be-ex came home.

She had been cleaning for five hours and had no idea where Steve was. Tammy was tired and contemplated going to have a nap. But first, she would have a shower and wash the sweat and stink off her, which had accumulated over the past few hours, during her cleaning frenzy.

When she stepped out of the shower and dried off, she heard the front door. Steve was finally home. She wrapped the towel around herself and headed for the bedroom to get dressed, still not ready to talk to him. But one single sniff of the air told her all she needed to know. Steve was drunk again. *Another drunk who should have driven his rat-bastard self into a tree.* She fully ignored him and continued to the bedroom.

Steve followed her, grabbing her from behind. Tammy panicked and tried to shrug him away, but he instead ripped off her towel and threw her on to the bed with a crazed look in his eyes.

"Let's make another baby," he yelled, before pinning her down. She screamed for him to get away from her, to get off her, but he held her down tight – one hand on her throat and one hand on her chest – while spreading her legs and forcing himself inside her. Exhausted from trying to fight him off, she stopped struggling, closed her eyes and waited for it to be over. When he finally stopped, she seized the opportunity to escape from his clutches and shoved him off her, sliding out from underneath the monster she no longer knew. As Steve lay on the bed snoring, she looked at him and whispered under her breath, "I hope you die."

The following day, after Steve had left the house to register at more employment agencies, Tammy slowly and sorely climbed out of bed. She wanted to ring the Social Worker she'd met at the LGBT meetings, months earlier. When she reached into her handbag for her wallet, which was where she kept Gay's business card, her wallet and keys were, once again, gone. She went over to the telephone to see if, by some miracle, Steve had left the phone unlocked. *You mongrel bastard!* Tammy was sick of it all – being treated like a prisoner, a slave, and now she had also become his victim in bed. Unable to contact *anybody* by telephone and unable to leave the house, she realised that she truly was alone.

That afternoon, Steve came through the front door with the biggest of smiles. He had great news to share, but Tammy was not in the mood to share in his joy. Regardless, he walked over to her, gave her a very tight hug (which made her hurt all over) before telling her that one of the companies he'd registered with had decided to give him a job. Steve was over the moon at the fact that he was now an *employed* Security Guard. He got to wear a uniform, carry a Maglite, and inflict his evil ways on anybody who he felt was posing a threat or breaking the law, on his watch. *God help us all.* Tammy congratulated him, without even trying to smile, before walking to the front porch to get some fresh air. Unfortunately for her, Steve quickly followed. He sat beside her, lit up a filthy cigar and blew the filth and residue in front of him. The breeze carried the smoke directly into Tammy's face and she coughed.

"Give me back my keys and wallet," Tammy demanded. "They do *not* belong to you."

"Why do you want your keys and wallet? Where do you think you might be going?" Steve asked -- a warning look in his eyes.

"I am tired of being cooped up, Steve! What happens if I am offered another job? What happens if we need groceries? The car is *mine*, dammit!" Tammy was adamant.

"We'll see," he responded, not seeming to care. All that mattered to Steve was that *he* was happy. "Bubba, very soon I will be my very own boss, in my own area, keeping watch on things, making the world a better place…"

Tammy once again started to cough, but this time it had absolutely nothing, whatsoever, to do with the cigar smoke. *You are not even remotely capable of making the world a better place!* She couldn't remember a time between them, anymore, that had brought a smile to her face. The only things that went through her mind, over and over, were the scenes of last night. He was a foul-smelling pig, and she would not lose a wink of sleep if she never saw him again.

One week passed and Steve had his new uniform laid out on the couch. Tammy had ironed it, the previous night, as well as packing his lunch beforehand, so she did not have to get up early. He woke her, anyway, at 4:00 that morning. After all, *somebody* had to make him a nice breakfast on his first day on the job. She got out of bed and cooked him up bacon and eggs on toast with a cup of tea.

Poking her head into the bathroom while Steve was showering, Tammy suggested, "It might be a good idea if you eat breakfast *before* you put your uniform on."

"Yeah, yeah. Whatever," Steve mumbled in response.

Tammy, absolutely exhausted and hurting, climbed back in to bed and fell asleep. Within minutes of her falling back into her dreams, she was shaken awake by Steve, once more. He had spilled egg yolk on his work shirt and his tea had been cold by the time he got to it. *Oh, for fuck sake!* Tammy grabbed his only other work shirt and quickly ran over it with an iron, while the kettle was boiled. She really wished he would grow a pair, and learn how to do this himself. It would be nice if he also *listened* to her once in a while. Her suggestion to Steve about eating *before* putting his work shirt on was not for her *own* benefit. *What a dumbass!*

Approximately 10:00 that morning, Tammy finally got out of bed, once more, made herself breakfast – a piece of toast and a glass of cold water – before taking the chance she'd never dreamed of taking before. After checking her handbag, and finding, once again, that she was without car keys and wallet, Tammy decided it was time to introduce herself to her neighbours. Tucking her handbag under her arm, Tammy stuck her head out of the front door and saw that the neighbour's car was in their driveway. She then closed the front door without locking it.

After climbing the stairs of the house next door, she knocked and waited. In the entire five years that she'd lived with Steve, Tammy had never introduced herself. Although it was not her fault, she still felt bad. An elderly woman with a kind face opened the door.

"Hi. I am Tammy – your next door neighbour. I was hoping to say 'hi' and finally introduce myself to you," Tammy smiled.

"Hello, love. Come on in," her kindly neighbour said. As Tammy walked in the door, the woman said "I'm Maria and this old bastard is Johan." Maria winked, a smile on her face, showing that she was joking. Johan was a giant of a man, but did not seem to have much energy. Maria continued, "Johan doesn't get up and about much. He has emphysema from too much smoking. He's a dumb bastard, but I love him."

Tammy smiled at them both, reintroducing herself. She told them she'd been their neighbour for around five years with Steve, and that she did not get out much anymore.

"Sorry, love, but he's a fucking asshole, that one. I don't know why you put up with it," Maria said, matter-of-factly.

"Yeah. I am sorry if the noise over there disturbs you. And I know that we just met, but I was wondering if... maybe... could I please use your telephone?" Tammy asked, not expecting them to say 'yes' to somebody they'd just met.

"You can't use the phone at the moment. Johan is doing stuff on the internet," Maria said. "Have a seat and take a load off, Tammy. Do you want a coffee?"

Tammy almost gagged at the suggestion. "Coffee? I'll have to definitely pass on that. Can't stand the stuff. I wouldn't mind a cup of tea though, if you *have* tea, that is," she said.

"No worries, love," Maria replied, while her eyes wandered to the fresh bruises on Tammy's arms and neck. "Rotten fucking mongrel, he is," Maria commented again.

While waiting for the kettle to boil, Tammy asked what the internet was. Johan explained that she can ring up other people's computers and talk to them.

"Why not just do that with your phone?" Tammy asked.

"You can't send files with a phone." Johan sounded amused at Tammy's naive questions.

"Well, you can send them with a fax machine, can't you?" Tammy asked, worried that she might come off as a nosy neighbour.

"You can play games on the internet. Games like Chess, Scrabble, and Pinball…"

"PINBALL?" Tammy absolutely *loved* pinball games.

"Of course. I can show you *now*, if you like," Johan offered. Tammy told Johan and Maria that she couldn't stay long. She did not know what time Steve would be coming home, and since she didn't have a key, the house was currently unlocked. Both Johan's and Maria's jaws dropped open, stunned that somebody living in a house for five years would not have a key.

After the introductions and chit-chat, Tammy swallowed her last gulp of hot tea and thanked her neighbours for their newfound friendship. She asked if she could come and visit again sometime.

"You come over any time you want to, love. One of us is usually at home," Maria said, with a smile. "It was lovely to finally meet you," she continued, as she gave Tammy a knowing hug.

Tears started to form in Tammy's eyes. She thanked her neighbours, once again, and headed down the stairs. Just as she got to the front porch, the Kingswood pulled into the driveway. *Shit!* Tammy went inside the house and shut the door. She even considered *locking* it, but thought better of it.

When Steve came through the front door, he stopped in front of her and stared for a moment, saying nothing. Tammy refused to respond to his accusing stare.

"Where were you? I rang and you didn't answer," Steve frowned.

"Didn't hear the phone. Sorry. I was outside trying to figure out what plants to put in the garden," Tammy lied.

"You didn't go for a drive?" he asked, suspiciously.

"With *what* keys, may I ask? The ones you took from my handbag, again? No, I was *here*, just outside," Tammy said, fast losing patience with him.

After accepting her explanation, he nodded before getting a glass of cold water from the kitchen. "I just came home to see if you were okay. I worried when you didn't answer the phone. I love you, Bubba. I hope you know that," Steve said, as Tammy rolled her eyes and said nothing. He then leaned over and gave her a kiss before walking out the door.

The following day, Tammy returned to see Johan and Maria, when Steve was not at home. Once again, she had to leave the front door of their home unlocked, because her keys were, as usual, missing from her handbag. This time, Johan was not on the internet and Tammy was given permission to use the phone. There was just one phone call to make and she dialled the number.

"Logan Police. Sergeant Arthur speaking. How can I help you?" came the male voice on the other end of the phone.

"I was raped," Tammy said quietly into the phone, making sure that her neighbours could not hear her words.

"Did you report to a hospital?" Sergeant Arthur asked.

"No," Tammy said, getting frustrated by the seemingly disinterested voice at the other end of the telephone.

"Can you name or describe your attacker?" asked Sergeant Arthur.

"Yes. He is my fiancé, and..."

"Your fiancé, did you say? Ma'am, if your so-called attacker was your husband or your fiancé, you were *not* raped. Please only contact police, in the future, if there is an emergency," Sergeant Arthur interrupted. "Have a nice day."

"Thank you. Please go *fuck* yourself," Tammy said, as she hung up the phone. With her face numb, tears rolling down her cheeks, she quickly wiped her eyes with her sleeves, before leaving the computer room and making her way back to her neighbour's kitchen. She thanked Johan for the use of their phone.

Maria offered Tammy a cup of tea and a chat, but she really did have to get back home before Steve found out she was gone. After all, it now seemed that *everything* Steve had done to her had been entirely within the law, simply because she accepted a marriage proposal, long ago. *Fuck my life.*

Chapter 14

The week following the phone call to the police, Tammy was at home, mopping the floors when the phone rang. For some reason, the ringing of the phone made her jump. She answered the phone to Max, who seemed a little bit more excited than usual.

"Hey, Tammy! A job has opened up in a ground floor position, if you are interested. It's not far from where you live, and you would be on the same pay level as you are now," Max said.

"Do tell! Where is the job? What would I be doing?" Tammy was full of questions and her day suddenly felt brighter. *It would be brilliant, to not be locked up all day in this place, anymore!* She even found herself smiling, as she fired off question after question to Max.

The job on offer was at Mount Gravatt, right next to Garden City Shopping Centre, which was only a ten-minute drive from Woodridge. She would have a car spot at the front door since there were no trains in that area, and being held up in a long line of peak hour traffic would no longer be a problem. Tammy asked Max when she would be able to go and have a look at the premises.

"You can go today or tomorrow, if you want to. The manager there is expecting you," Max said, with a smile in his voice.

"Today is out of the question. My car is being serviced," Tammy lied. "Tomorrow would be great though! Thank you so much, Max. You really did come through."

When Steve arrived home that night, Tammy told him that she had a job interview the following day at Mount Gravatt, right near the shopping centre.

"What's that got to do with me?" Steve asked.

"Well, for starters, I would need my keys and wallet. Can't really go to my job interview without *those* now, can I?" She wasn't really asking. It was a statement, and hopefully her fiancé would be able to figure it out, without an "English to moron" interpreter.

Steve stared at her, for a moment. Tammy could not work out whether he really *did* need one of those interpreters or if he was about to say or do something stupid. Maybe he was about to do both.

"Yeah. I guess not," he finally responded. Steve reached into his pocket and handed over Tammy's keys. He then went out to the Kingswood to fetch her wallet from the glove compartment of his car.

While Steve was outside, Tammy felt a wave of nausea come over her. By the time he came back into the house, she was in the toilet, heaving up what seemed like every single thing she'd eaten in the past twelve years. Steve sat at the kitchen table and waited for her to return. When she did, he was smiling when he looked at her.

"Is this a good thing or a bad thing?" he asked.

"Fuck my life," Tammy responded, before sitting at the table and resting her forehead on her hands.

Steve giggled, like a mischievous little child, before he stood up and went to the phone. He unlocked it and made an appointment to see his doctor. The appointment was for both of them, and they were able to see him that very same evening.

Tammy and Steve climbed into the Kingswood and Steve drove. Tammy thought he was taking her to the Logan Health Centre, but he drove right past it and headed… where? It almost seemed like he was taking her to Beenleigh, which was a lot further than she would have liked. Steve ended up pulling into a long driveway and parking at a small brick building near Waterford.

"What's this? I have never been here before," Tammy stated, nervously.

With something that almost looked like *sadness,* in his eyes, Steve looked at Tammy, and responded, "Yeah, Bubba. You have."

After they entered the doctor's surgery, she thought she'd recognised the consulting room she was now standing in, but could not remember from when or where. But when the doctor came into the consulting room, it finally hit her. This was the first doctor to treat her, "cash in hand," when Steve had beaten her into her first miscarriage. All of the loathing she'd felt for Steve exploded within her, and she suddenly felt claustrophobic, being here.

"I don't want to be here, Steve! Please, take me to Logan Health Centre or Logan Hospital? *Anywhere,* but here!" Tammy pleaded, but it fell on deaf ears.

One pregnancy test later, plus a prescription for the nausea, Tammy and Steve were back in the Kingswood and on their way back home. Steve was ecstatic and could not stop smiling, but Tammy was borderline suicidal. She was pregnant, yet again. *Someone please kill me now.* This was the very last thing in the world that Tammy wanted or needed. She'd been trying to find a way to get *away* from Steve, not *bond* with him.

The next day, with keys and wallet in her handbag, Tammy drove to Mount Gravatt to take a look at the new office which Max had recommended she be transferred to. On her arrival, Tammy met with the manager, who showed her around the different areas of the office. The building looked almost brand new and there was not a single elevator in sight. Nausea gave her stomach a slight twinge. Tammy asked for a small glass of water, and was shown where the office water-cooler was located. The manager then explained to Tammy that she would be working the front line – the Customer Service counter – dealing with all walk-in clients who needed assistance.

A staff member walked past, carrying a cup of freshly brewed coffee. Without warning, and before she could stop herself, Tammy threw up all over the manager's shoes. She did not know whether to feel anger, regret or relief, but the manager decided that the job vacancy would not be suitable for Tammy, after all.

While waiting for Steve to come home, Tammy vacuumed the carpets and dusted. She knew that Steve would not be upset by the news. He had made it *overly* obvious that he did not want her working anymore. He was the man of the house – the one who wears the badge that says "BOSS" – and his wife-to-be should be at home, doing her womanly chores. This did not bother Tammy so much. She was raised, by her father, to believe that a woman's place is inside the home, while a man's place is outside, doing the hard labour. She did not find it repressing, in any way. To her, it was natural. What she did *not* appreciate was that Steve still thought of her as his possession. She was a lot of things – fed up, pissed off, sick of life – but she was not his now, nor would she ever be.

For the next four months, the house, once again, ran smoothly. Meals were always ready for Steve before he left for work, and when he came home, his uniforms were always ironed, the washing always done, and not a thing was out of place. Regardless, Tammy was absolutely miserable. She missed her family. When Steve came home, one afternoon, Tammy asked if they could go and visit with her dad on the farm. Steve was no fan of Tammy's father, just as Tammy's dad was not a fan of Steve. She missed the farm, the fresh air, and she missed her dad. Surprisingly, Steve agreed to go and visit, on the condition that "nobody starts any shit."

Ralph and Coral were expecting them both, that very same weekend. During the three-hour drive, the Kingswood needed to be refuelled. Steve asked Tammy if she needed to use the bathroom, because they would be stopping at the next service station. Tammy replied that she would wait in the car. The last thing in the world she wanted was the smell of coffee setting her off on a puking spree, for the rest of the journey. She made sure, if nothing else, that she'd packed her nausea medication before she left. She wanted this weekend to be one to remember, but for all the right reasons – and none of those reasons had to do with her puking on her father's shoes.

The last leg of the journey was the road which led to Tammy's father's property. It was a two-kilometre dirt road with pot holes, and was rather narrow. Cows were along the side of the road and horses were in paddocks. The view brought a smile to Tammy's face. She missed this place so much. Although she'd lived in the city for the past eight years, Tammy was still a farm girl at heart. She missed greeting the chickens, turkeys, geese, ducks, horses, pigs and cows each morning. For her, it was a true joy.

Tammy loved nature. As a child, she used to be in charge of the poultry; collecting eggs from the chickens and ducks while making gobbling noises at the turkeys, and being chased by geese if she got too close to their babies. Tammy had also learned to milk a cow when she was quite young, and would sometimes steal some of the cream at the top of the milk with her finger, before taking it into the house in the mornings. She also enjoyed picking mangoes and apples from the multitude of trees around the farm, although she was not such a fan of retrieving bananas from the banana trees, which tended to drop giant goops of sap on her clothes, leaving the most unsightly of stains. But, banana stains aside, those were some of the best days of her childhood.

She turned to tell Steve how amazing and awesome it was to finally be back home, only to see a scowl on Steve's face. He did not like driving his beloved Kingswood through horse or cow shit, nor did he like the fact that his car was now fully covered in dust. *Get over it, jerk. It's just a damn car!* Secretly, she wished that a giant dinosaur would fly overhead and drop a huge shit on his windshield.

Tammy thanked Steve for bringing her to visit her dad and he mumbled something under his breath that Tammy could not understand. Something also told her that, perhaps, it was probably *best* that she didn't know what had come out of his mouth. He was clearly not as happy as *she* was.

Ralph had moved his truck from under the carport, so that Steve could park his car there. That way, if it rained or hailed, the Kingswood would be safe, whereas Ralph's truck could take a beating. A tree could fall on it and it would not cause a single dent. Tammy had a feeling that there would, possibly, be a few pissing contests this weekend, as to whose vehicle was tougher.

Ralph and Coral greeted Tammy and Steve on the front porch, and Steve was handed a beer by Tammy's dad, as a welcome after a long drive. *Wow – manners – have not seen those in a long time!* Steve could actually learn a lot from Ralph but, as Tammy knew, both Steve and her dad were two of the most stubborn people on the planet.

The first thing Tammy noticed, when she walked through the door, was her father's large gun rack. Her dad had one of the most impressive gun collections she'd ever seen. Tammy was taught, at a young age, while growing up on the farm, how to shoot most of those rifles. She was quite the sharp shooter, but was not as much a fan of rifles as she was of hand guns. Ten years ago, when Tammy had shot some tin cans off the paddock fence with Ralph's .22 rifle, the weapon had backfired; it was the very first time in her life that she had ever dared to scream every cuss word in the book – right in front of her dad. For a few minutes, she could hear absolutely nothing. All those cuss words poured out of her mouth and she never heard a single one. But Ralph had heard them all and came running. He knew his daughter was panicking and told Tammy she would be okay. After her hearing had returned, a few hours later, her ears were ringing, but they were back to normal by the end of the day. Tammy made sure not to mention the gun backfiring to her dad ever again, just in case he'd forgotten to punish her for her potty mouth, that day.

When Steve saw Ralph's gun rack on the wall, filled top to bottom with many different rifles of different calibres, his eyes widened with shock, momentarily. Tammy could almost read his thoughts: *Maybe I shouldn't be such a DICK to Tammy's dad, after all.* Tammy's thoughts, however, circled more around the lines of: *Shit – I hope none are loaded!*

Ralph and Coral spent most of the weekend doing normal chores around the farm – cleaning the water trough for the cows and getting fresh water for them, loading fresh hay onto the tractor and taking it over to cows and horses which were waiting for a feed. Tammy wondered where the birds had all gone.

"We got rid of the turkeys and geese, years ago. Still got a few chickens and ducks though. They keep the eggs coming," Ralph explained.

He further went on to tell Tammy that a new baby calf had been born a few days ago, and they had decided to call it '*Tam.*' A tear formed in the corner of Tammy's eye. She felt so very touched to have a baby calf named after her… until Ralph and Coral told her that they would be eating it next year. *Oh, yay!* Tammy thought, sarcastically, her heart slowly sinking.

Throughout the weekend, Tammy made sure to shower Steve with kisses and hugs, making sure that her father saw a happy daughter. Steve did not seem to mind all the attention either, and appreciated, even more, that he was getting free beer. Luckily, he was only offered a couple of beers, each evening. Tammy did not want a drunken Steve anywhere near her or her family, on Ralph's property. Scenes had played out in her mind of what would happen if things turned ugly, like Steve trying to take on Tammy's dad, to prove he was more of a man. She wanted to avoid those scenes, at all costs.

At the end of a wonderful weekend – a weekend where even *handshakes* were exchanged between Ralph and Steve – Tammy and her tired fiancé headed back to Brisbane. She was going to suggest maybe calling in on her mum on the way home, but that thought quickly jumped ship when Janine and Tammy's conversation of months before came flooding back into her head. *A visit from an asshole is the very last thing my mum needs.* Tammy, instead, stayed silent on the journey home, and drifted off to sleep in the car.

Chapter 15

One month after Steve and Tammy had visited Ralph and Coral on the farm, Steve came home after work on a Friday in an extra happy mood.

"I have been moved over to *night* shift, Bubba! Double pay for me!" Steve said, with a smile.

"Congratulations. The money will sure help out here at home." Tammy had been paying Steve's mortgage for the past year, and was glad that he could *finally* take over the payments.

"I am heading out tonight with the boys, to celebrate. Not sure what time I will be home. Don't wait up, okay?" Steve grinned.

"No worries," Tammy said, glad that she would be able to curl up in front of the television on her own, and watch *Late Night with Conan O'Brien* again. Joel Godard cracked her up every single time she watched. Tammy enjoyed the laughs, since she didn't have much of a chance to laugh when Steve was around.

Steve showered, got dressed up and even wore a tie. *A tie for a boys' night out?* Tammy almost felt jealous. She knew that guys didn't wear ties when going out with their friends. But, then again,

Steve has a fiancé with a baby on the way. He wouldn't *dare* cheat, and she knew it.

After kissing her goodbye, Steve and the Kingswood made their way to wherever the hell they were going for the evening. The thought of checking her handbag did not hit Tammy until he had left. *Dammit! You fucking prick!* Steve seriously had trust issues and, for a second, Tammy started to blame herself for these trust issues. After all, she'd made friends with their neighbours and did not even tell him. Steve also (as far as Tammy knew) didn't know about the support group she'd been going to, a couple of years ago. Yeah. He was damaged goods, alright, and it was her fault. When her television show had finished, Tammy shut off all the lights and went to bed.

The following morning, Tammy woke up early, out of habit. *Steve is going to be pissed if his breakfast is not ready when he wakes.* She quietly slipped on her glasses and her slippers before peeking over her shoulder to make sure she had not woken him. What greeted her was… nothing. Steve had not come home. Tammy climbed out of bed again, and tiptoed down the hallway, to see if he had, maybe, come home and passed out in the lounge room. He was not there. She turned on the front light. Steve had most definitely not come home.

Tammy went to the toilet, before going back to bed. *Maybe he is still out with his mates?* With a sigh of relief, Tammy got to do something she'd been unable to do in a very long time – she got to sleep in.

A wave of nausea woke her. She got up, raced to the toilet and threw up. When she looked at her watch, she was stunned. It was 3:00 in the afternoon. She had slept for, almost, the entire day! Tammy again searched the house and front yard. Steve and his Kingswood were still gone. Tammy's wallet and her house/car keys were also still gone. And the phone was locked. After taking her medication and eating a *very* late "breakfast", she sat on the couch and stared at the wall, wondering whether or not she should be panicking.

Not daring to leave the house, just in case Steve came home, Tammy found things to clean. When she had re-cleaned things several times that did not need cleaning, she peeked out at the back yard. The grass was starting to get long. Maybe she could surprise Steve by mowing the lawn? The only problem is that she had not worked a lawnmower since she was eight years old, and her father had started the lawnmower, each and every time. But she was twenty-five years old now. Surely, she could pull the string on a lawnmower and get it started, right? *Wrong.* Tammy's dad obviously had some kind of super strength. The mower had started every single time he had pulled that string when she was little. Sadly for her, however, the string spun around ever-so-slowly, almost seeming to mock her pathetic attempts at getting the mower to start. After five failed attempts, Tammy gave up and tried to think of other things to do.

She took a rock from the garden and used it to wedge the front door open. If she couldn't cut the grass, she could at least water the garden and pull out the weeds. The Snapdragons and Pansies complimented each other beautifully. Tammy smiled at the colourful rainbow which nature had gifted to her, for all of her hard efforts. She had also planted a Bird's Eye Chilli bush, close to the front door, since Steve loved to eat one now and again. Tammy figured that was only because her father ate them like candy. Ralph would watch and laugh when people visited the farm after daring them to chew on one. Tammy's dad was used to eating Bird's Eye Chillies, but she pitied every poor bastard that ever took her father up on his dare. Even *SHE* had done so... once. *Never, ever again.* It took too long to extinguish the volcano lava that had caught fire on her tongue. *Yep, Dad. You are hilarious.*

Snapping out of her daydream of chilli dares, Tammy *again* looked at her watch. It was almost 7:00 at night and still Steve was not home. He had not called. What was going on? She turned off the hose and went inside to wash up. She decided to make Minestrone Soup for dinner. With bread, it was an easy meal and if she made enough, she could quickly heat some up for Steve in their new microwave oven.

Tammy had eaten, before pouring the leftover soup into a large storage bowl and putting it into the fridge. She then did dishes and cleaned up. Maybe she had misunderstood Steve. Was it possible that he started his new job *tonight?* She went and checked his uniforms. One of the uniforms was missing, leaving Tammy to assume that he was, indeed, working. She had simply been wrong about his starting date. Smiling and shaking her head at her own stupidity, she decided to go to bed early for a change.

Sunday morning arrived and Steve was still not home. Tammy had no way to ring anybody and find out if he was okay. She did not even know who his employer was, with his new security job. *Some fiancé, I am! I should have showed more interest and asked!* Pictures danced around inside her head. Had he been at work? *Maybe he went out with the boys again?* Perhaps he had come home, while she was sleeping, and left again? Maybe he was laying somewhere in a ditch, bleeding to death after being mugged? Panicked, Tammy decided to go next door and ask Johan and Maria's advice. She climbed their front stairs, while leaving the front door of her home unlocked, frantic at what could have possibly happened to Steve.

"Tammy! Hello there!" Johan's voice boomed out from the top of the stairs, when the door opened.

"Hi, Johan. I can't come in. Is Maria home?" Tammy asked.

"Not right now. She has gone to see the grand-babies. Is everything okay?" Johan asked.

"Well, I don't really know. Steve went out, two nights ago, to have a boys' night out, and he *still* hasn't come home. I don't know what to do," she explained.

"Really? Hell, THROW A FUCKING *PARTY!* Hopefully he drove himself off a cliff and did everybody a favour, hey?" Johan said, with a grin on his face.

No matter how hard she tried, Tammy could not smile. Yes, it was true that she'd said it to herself, more times than she could count, during their years together, but this was different. She was really worried. She put her hand to her stomach and asked Johan to tell Maria she'd dropped by. Maybe she would come back again a little bit later, once she knew that Steve was okay.

That afternoon, Maria came to Tammy's front door, to see if she was alright. Maria said she'd noticed the Kingswood was not in the driveway, and therefore would not have the displeasure of seeing Steve during her visit. They both sat and had a cup of tea. Tammy was on the verge of tears, still unable to shake the thought that something bad had happened to him.

"We can only live in hope," giggled Maria.

But when Tammy looked up from her cup of tea, she saw in Maria's face that she was not at all joking. Tammy's neighbours had heard the fights. They had seen the bruises. And they knew that Steve was a monster.

"All joking aside, love, you and your little one in there (Maria motioned towards Tammy's stomach) would be much better off without him. You have nothing but love to give, and Steve wouldn't know love if it grew tits and smacked him over the head with them," Maria said, seriously.

Tammy nodded. She knew it was true. But she didn't want to think bad thoughts about a man who could be hurt... or worse. If he had been mugged, they would have taken his wallet. He could be in a morgue and without any identification, leaving the police and hospital not knowing who to call. Tammy felt a panic attack coming on. She was drowning in a sea of helplessness, worried sick for her Steve. When Maria and Tammy had finished their cups of tea,

Tammy escorted Maria to the door and thanked her for coming over to keep her company.

Monday had passed and Steve *still* had not come home. Tammy now spent a lot of time reading books out loud to her unborn child, while trying, very hard, to see through her own tears. Part of her hoped and prayed that Steve had simply left her, but since this was his house, she knew he would not just leave. Something bad had happened, and she was still clueless on what to do.

Tuesday arrived. Tammy sat next to the phone, hoping that it would ring. *If he's alive, he will find a way to let me know.* At lunch time, Tammy decided to try something. She rang the emergency number for police. She almost fell off her chair from shock when it started to ring. *Holy shit, the lock is broken!* She quickly hung up and tried to ring her mum, but a recording came through the phone that the number was not able to be reached due to the phone's lock settings. Letting out a huge sigh, feeling sadness wash over her in waves, she hung up and again rang the emergency number for the police. Tammy was absolutely terrified. What if Steve walked in right now and she was using the phone?

"Emergency assistance. Do you require fire, ambulance or police?" came the male voice, at the other end of the phone.

"Police, please!" Tammy said, urgently. The phone again started to ring on the other end.

"Logan Police. What is your emergency?" a female voice asked.

"My fiancé is missing. He left four days ago and I have not heard from him since. I'm sorry if this is not considered an emergency, but it was the only number I could ring while the phone was locked," Tammy started crying as she spoke to the female voice.

Surprisingly, the voice at the other end of the phone did not get angry that Tammy had rung. She asked for Steve's details – his name, physical description, what he was wearing when he left, what he was driving, whether she knew where he was going on the night that he left. Tammy answered all questions and, when she hung up, she felt a tiny ray of hope that the police would find him. They would find his injured body on the side of the road and they would know it was him from the description she'd given. She had been Steve's "voice" when he was too injured to speak and ask for help.

Two hours after she'd rung the police, Tammy saw the Kingswood pull into the driveway. Her heart leapt with joy and happiness. *You are alive!* He had been able to drive, so he was not hurt. And he was finally home. She could not stop smiling. She quickly checked the kitchen and lounge to make sure everything was clean and in its rightful place, just as Steve walked through the door, wearing his security guard uniform. Tammy raced over to give him the biggest of hugs, welcoming him home, and was greeted with the biggest backhand across the face she had ever felt, knocking her to the ground.

"WHAT DID YOU *DO!?*" Steve screamed, at the top of his lungs.

Wide-eyed, confused and suddenly *terrified* for her baby, Tammy begged Steve to calm down or he will hurt the baby.

"Oh, I have no intention of hurting *the baby*, Bubba," he said, as his work boot came crashing down on top of her right hand. Tammy stifled a scream as the pain suddenly shot up her arm. Steve twisted his boot, after smashing his foot down harder, cracking her wrist and breaking three knuckles. It felt like somebody had taken a razor-sharp kitchen knife and sliced her open from her right ear all the way down to the tips of her fingers. Blood was spilling out of her hand as she begged him to stop.

While keeping his boot firmly in place on Tammy's right hand, he leaned over and screamed at her, "THE POLICE CAME TO MY FUCKING *WORK!* YOU *EMBARRASED* ME! I FUCKING *WARNED* YOU NEVER TO EMBARRASS ME!" His eyes were crazy, his face filled with fury, and when he finally lifted his work boot off her hand, which was now bleeding profusely, she curled up, making sure he did not hurt her baby.

"I didn't... mean to embarrass... you, I swear. When you didn't... come home after... four days, I thought... something had... happened to you and..." Tammy spoke between sobs. The pain was unbearable. Why could Steve not understand that she was scared? She *loved* him. She thought he had needed her help. She lay on the floor, her left hand still held protectively over her stomach, her right hand in pieces, leaving a bloodied mess on the floor.

Steve went to the kitchen to put the kettle on. Tammy expected him to come back with a boiling pot of water to pour over her, or even a sharp kitchen knife to do more damage. Instead, much to Tammy's relief, Steve came back empty handed.

"Get up!" he ordered her.

Tammy tried to sit up, but was unable to put weight on her broken hand, and she was not about to take her other hand away from her stomach. Steve rolled his eyes as he leaned down and lifted her. He carried her to the kitchen and sat her on a chair at the table.

"Do you want a cup of tea?" Steve asked, just like nothing had happened.

Tammy gave him a look of confusion, mixed with a world of blinding pain. She was afraid to answer the question. She held her broken hand as far away from him as she possibly could, since holding it or placing any weight on it was unbearable.

"I'm sorry, but you have no idea how embarrassed I was when the police contacted my employer. Do you know what could have happened? I could have been *fired*, that's what. You almost cost me my job!" Steve said, his tone calmer but still harsh.

"I was scared that you were hurt or even *dead*. You didn't ring and you didn't come home for *four days!*" Tammy cried.

Right then, there was a knock at the door. *Oh God, please don't be Maria or Johan... PLEASE don't be Maria or Johan!* Tammy was unable to move, her mind engulfed in trying to hold the pain in her right hand at bay, somehow. Steve *again* rolled his eyes and stood up. "You just fucking sit there and sulk. *I'll* answer the fucking door, okay?" he said, chiding her.

Tammy could not hear the whole conversation which took place at the front door; "… screams…. complaint… come in…." When

Tammy looked up, two uniformed police officers were standing in the kitchen, looking directly at her.

"Ma'am, we have received a report that screams were coming from this address. Is everything okay, here?" one of the police officers asked.

"Everything is fine. My wife fell and hurt her hand. We are going to the health centre as soon as you both leave, now if you don't mind...." Steve answered.

"Ma'am, are you alright? How did you hurt your hand? Do you need an ambulance?" the second police officer asked, ignoring Steve's statement. He approached Tammy, at the kitchen table.

"I just *told* you she is *fine*, now fuck off out of our house so I can get her the medical attention that she obviously needs!" Steve yelled at the officers.

Tammy glanced at Steve, who stared right back at her with a warning look, before she said, "Thank you. I'm fine. Please just leave." She knew the police would not protect her against her fiancé. They had confirmed that fact, over the phone, when she had rung them after his *previous* attack.

When the police left, Steve closed the door behind them. He returned to the kitchen and sat down beside her, at the kitchen table.

"Thank you, Bubba. You did well. Now, let's get that hand looked at," Steve said to Tammy, before gently helping her to the car.

Once again, Steve and Tammy found themselves nowhere near the health centre. Instead, she was at her treating physician's medical office near Waterford. Tammy requested no painkillers. She did not want her baby to be born a drug addict. Although she hated the idea that Steve had knocked her up, she was more and more falling in love with the lump inside of her. She had not yet met her little bundle of joy – a bundle which seemed to kick up a storm from out of nowhere – but one thing she knew for sure… she would protect her baby – at *all* costs.

Screaming in pain, as the doctor splinted and wrapped her fingers to keep them from moving, Tammy was finally bandaged up and ready to go home. She didn't know if Steve had something *on* this doctor – some kind of blackmail gig – or if the doctor was just a complete waste of space, like her fiancé was. He seemed to know his job, however, and if this was the only choice she had for medical treatment, she would take it.

For the next few weeks, Tammy knew that she would be a completely useless "housewife," with only one functional hand. She prayed that Steve would not make too much of a mess for her to clean up. Part of her started to regret not taking any painkillers. Every time she reached over to the floor to pick up dishes, or pick up clothes that Steve had left behind, she could feel her heart beating in her wrist and her hand. Sure, it hurt a *hell* of a lot, but nowhere near as badly as it did that night. She prayed that it would be fully healed within the next six weeks, which was when her baby was due. It did not take a genius to know that mothers needed *two* hands to properly care for their newborns, and she was determined to be the best mother any child could possibly have.

Chapter 16

Over the next three weeks, the pain in Tammy's hand was becoming more and more bearable. She did not leave the house at all, while making sure she did absolutely *nothing* to provoke Steve. After his *lesson*, Tammy knew that the next time he went for a boys' night out, he may not come home for a week. Instead of worrying, she would ensure that it was, for her, a week of bliss and relaxation.

On 25th December, Tammy felt a kick. And then another. She put her hand on her stomach gently and smiled. No more kicks came. A sudden cramp forced her to double over in pain. She screamed out at the top of her lungs, and Steve came running inside from the shed in the back yard, to see what all the commotion was about. He found Tammy on the floor, crying in pain.

"Baby! Pain! Ambo!" Tammy screamed at Steve.

She needed help *immediately* and she knew it. Now she just needed to make sure that Steve realised how *serious* the situation was. The baby was not due for another three weeks. Steve stared at her like a little lost child and didn't move. Tammy screamed again, as another wave of pain hit her like a sledgehammer. Thinking that she had just urinated on the floor, she looked up, apologised to Steve for her mess, and begged him to ring an ambo.

Steve disappeared from the bedroom in a flash. Wave after wave of pain ripped through Tammy and all thoughts of the pain in her hand had vanished. *I'm losing my baby!* Tammy screamed again, filled with agony and panic, as Steve came running back into the room. He scooped her off the floor, seemingly not caring about the mess she'd left behind, and put her on the bed.

"Help is coming, Bubba. Breathe, okay? Just breathe," Steve said, frantically.

Grateful that he'd called an ambulance, she screamed in pain, yet again. Although the pain was not constant, it kept coming – like waves crashing onto the shore. As soon as it started to ease, it would strike again – *twice* as hard. Tammy closed her eyes and tried to concentrate on breathing. She even tried to find her "happy place," but it seemed to have packed its bags and moved. Again, the pain started to ease. Steve started swearing. When she looked at him, he was dry-heaving as he looked at the floor. Pain struck again and Tammy cried out, praying for it to stop.

Steve quickly left the room. Tammy thought he had gone to throw up, but less than a minute later, he returned to her with her treating physician in tow.

"GET ME A FUCKING AMBULANCE *NOW!*" she screamed at Steve.

With almost all of her energy exhausted, Tammy again tried to focus on her breathing but the pain was ripping her in half. Steve sat at the top of the bed and held both of her hands tightly, staring into her eyes. Tammy could no longer see the doctor, but she heard him telling her to push. She couldn't. It hurt to lay still. It hurt to push. It even hurt to *breathe* at this point. She could not focus, and the room started to spin. *I will die, if it means saving you.* With every single bit of strength she could gather from within her body, she pushed as hard as she could, feeling like she was shitting a giant, heated, spiked mace from her body. She gave one more push before the room went black.

When Tammy woke, she found herself inside her special cloud, weightless. She could not feel anything. She listened to see who else was inside her cloud. *Voices.* She heard them. *Go away and let me sleep!* The voices became quieter and then stopped, as she drifted back to sleep. When she woke again, several hours later, Tammy was still inside her special cloud, but she was no longer without feeling. She felt a dull throbbing pain between her legs. Tammy slowly put her hand to her stomach. Her belly was still big like a water balloon. It hurt a little and it wobbled like a plate of jelly. *I like jelly.* Tammy smiled and closed her eyes.

"Yep. Thanks, doc. seriously, *thank you*," Steve said, from the next room. The closing of the front door jolted her awake.

Tammy tried to get up, but could not. It hurt to try and sit. Her stomach hurt. Her back hurt. Even her girly bits were hurting. Then it all came rushing back to her – the pain, the fear, the doctor.

"Steve!" Tammy called, absolutely terrified of what he was about to tell her. Tears were already free-flowing down her cheeks, and her heart was starting to sink.

When Steve came into the room, he had something in his arms. Tammy looked at his face, wondering what he had bought for her *this* time. She didn't want another teddy bear. She didn't want anything. Nothing would fix this. Tammy frowned through her tears before realising that Steve did not seem, at all, upset. He was actually smiling. *Really* smiling.

"What do you have there?" Tammy asked. She pulled herself up with her elbows, just a little bit, so she would not feel like such a patient. The pain made her grunt.

Steve sat down beside her on the bed, ever so gently. He turned and showed Tammy what had made him smile. Her eyes went wide and her jaw dropped open. A feeling of absolute joy (and disbelief) overcame her. She touched her stomach again. Her jelly-wobbling belly hurt a little bit, but she no longer cared. Steve was holding, in his arms, the tiniest, little baby that Tammy had ever seen in her entire life.

"Our son," Steve said, absolutely beaming, as he looked at the little parcel in his arms.

"Is he okay? Did he come out okay?" Tammy asked, in awe. She could hardly believe this was happening, and wondered to herself if she had the strength to hold him without dropping him.

"Do you want to hold our son, Bubba?" Steve said, looking at Tammy with love in his eyes.

"Is he real?" Tammy wanted to pinch herself, but she already knew the answer. She held out her arms as Steve carefully placed the tiny baby boy into her arms. She no longer worried about dropping him, as she held him close to her, right next to her heart – a heart that was now swelling with love and happiness. "Oh my God, he is real!" she whispered, tears of joy rolling down her cheeks. Tammy gently kissed her son on the forehead.

Steve went out the back to the shed. He brought in a bassinette and placed it next to Tammy on the bed. It was no baby cot, but Steve wanted their son sleeping in the room with them at all times, and the bedroom was far too small for their bed and a cot. Living in a one-bedroom house, a nursery was an impossible dream.

"Did the ambo come yet?" Tammy asked. "Maybe we should be at the hospital?" She was starting to panic. Although she had been taught to change a diaper as a child, having changed her brother, Jack's, soiled diapers on so many occasions, Tammy did not have the first clue about being a mother. She had no idea what she was supposed to do now.

"The doc will be calling in here, each day, with a nurse. Trust me, Bubba. We will be okay," Steve said.

Since Tammy really didn't have a choice, she accepted the fact that medical help would be coming to the house, daily, to check on both her and the baby. While Tammy breastfed her new son, Steve grabbed his keys and ran out to the Kingswood. He brought inside the contents, which had been in the boot of the car for the past week – a baby sling and diapers. Lots and *lots* of disposable diapers. Steve had to make about five trips to the car, and back to the house, in order to bring them all in. This would be a first for her, since she had never before used a disposable diaper.

Tammy had been twelve years old when she'd learned to change her brother's diaper. But, back in those days, the diapers looked nothing like these. Jack's diaper was square white cloth and there would always be a blue liner to go between baby and diaper. Every single day, her mum had washed Jack's diapers, before hanging them on the clothes-line, in the back yard, to dry.

The disposable diapers that were piling up in front of her were nothing like the ones she'd used back then. They were plastic, with side-tabs of sticky-tape, and not a single blue liner was in sight. Tammy wanted, more than anything, to ring her mum, but the thoughts of when Steve had rung Janine, when Tammy had been sick, made her start to burn with anger. Her mum had been through enough *shit,* without having to stand in the same house as Steve. Besides, with the phone locked, it wasn't going to happen, anyway.

A nurse, and the doctor who had delivered Tammy's baby, came each day to the house to give both Tammy and her son a full examination, making sure that both were okay. Steve was told by the doctor that if there were any problems at all, he needed to ring the doctor immediately and, if he was unable get through, to ring an ambulance.

The next few days had Tammy and Steve thinking about names. Tammy told Steve that her whole life, she had promised her father to name her first-born son after him. It was a family tradition which she did not want to break. But Steve *immediately* put his foot down, refusing to have a son called Ralph. Tensions started brewing, fast. Steve finally decided that the baby would be named after *his* father, also using his father's middle name. *Name my baby after a dog murderer? Are you fucking kidding me?* Tammy then suggested naming the baby after Steve's middle name instead, to which they finally agreed.

Within a month, Tammy was exhausted. She wanted to sleep, but her son had other ideas. It was like her baby had been born with a built-in detector, which sensed when his mother's eyelids were almost closed. Although bub slept a lot, he had also sought-out to prove that his lungs were a lot stronger than both Tammy's and Steve's, combined. He could belt out a siren of a scream with the very best of them. Steve was soon regretting his decision of having the baby sleep in the same room as them, but Tammy wouldn't have it any other way. Soon, Steve decided to spend as much time at work as he possibly could, just to avoid the noise. It gave Tammy and her son plenty of bonding time, and she loved every single second of it.

During the day, Tammy had bub with her at all times, as he slept inside his baby sling – a secure wrap which held him snugly in place against his mother's chest, so that she could slowly, but surely, get the housework done. Although her wrist and fingers were no longer so sore, they were also not so easy to move anymore. Regardless, Tammy made sure that the house was clean at all times, so that Steve would not find anything to complain about. There was one thing that she could not do much about, however, and that was bub's crying. When he woke, he cried. When he was hungry, he cried. When his diaper was almost as full of shit as his father constantly was, *more* crying. It led Steve to scream at Tammy on several occasions, to "*Shut that fucking baby up!*"

"Stick one of your tits in his mouth, for fuck sake! Just shut him up!" Steve would yell, so crudely, not caring that half of the street could hear what he'd said.

With Steve now sleeping on the couch full-time, he decided it was time to buy a new couch – a *comfortable* couch – that would give him a good night's sleep, while Tammy slept on the bed next to the bassinette with her baby. It was a routine which Tammy appreciated, more than Steve could ever know.

Towards the end of January, Tammy was woken up with a fright. Steve had walked into the bedroom and thrown a basket full of clean, dry clothes onto the bed. The basket was heavy and landed right on top of her, missing the baby by just centimetres.

"You are at home all fucking day, and you don't even iron my shirts?!" Steve screamed, in anger.

The baby instantly started screaming. Tammy quickly sat up, threw the basket off the bed, and quickly checked that bub was not injured. She then looked at Steve, and said, "I'm leaving you."

"*Leaving* me? No other poor bastard would *have* you. You are fucking *useless!*" Steve said, as he walked off, laughing loudly. He then put on a sleeveless shirt and jeans, grabbed his keys and walked out the door. When he got to the Kingswood, Steve made sure that Tammy could still hear him laughing.

The moment he drove out of the driveway, Tammy quickly climbed out of bed. When she opened her handbag, she was astonished to see that both her wallet and her keys were there. *THANK YOU, GOD!* She quickly got herself dressed, and carried baby and bassinette to the car. That day, she drove to every single real estate office nearby – with the exception of the office she once worked at. By the time she got home, she was smiling.

As soon as Steve walked in the door, Tammy told him to make plans to have Friday off work. He would be helping her move both her and bub into their new apartment.

"You're bluffing," Steve said, calmly.

"This morning, you almost killed the baby with your temper tantrum. Today, I found and paid for, an apartment nearby. You will have your quiet and your space, while bub and I will have each other. Friday, Steve. Help us move or you will never know where we've moved to," Tammy stated, determined to make Steve understand how deadly serious she was.

For the rest of the week, Steve was out during the day. Tammy didn't know, nor did she care, where he was. As long as he was home on Friday, to help with the move, that was all that mattered. By the time Friday arrived, Steve had a trailer hooked up to the back of the Kingswood, and Tammy had packed all that they needed – some food, cutlery, clothing, bathroom items and all of the baby's things – into boxes. Steve carried the boxes to the trailer and Tammy gave him the address on a piece of paper. It was a townhouse in Queens Road, Kingston – just a two-minute drive away.

Tammy secured bub into the car beside her and she drove her VK Commodore out, onto the road, to her new apartment, trusting that Steve would not be far behind. When she arrived at her new address, Tammy breathed in a huge sigh of relief. *Freedom*. She had forgotten what it felt like.

Steve reversed the Kingswood and trailer until it was parked behind her car, directly in front of the new apartment. Without a word, he started bringing boxes into the apartment, not caring where she wanted them. When all boxes had been unloaded, he stopped at the door and finally decided to speak.

"My key?" Steve asked.

Tammy dug into her handbag, pulled out her keys and slid Steve's house key off the key ring. When she handed the key to him, his look was nothing but that of pure confusion.

"I meant for *here*. Where is my key?" he asked.

"I just handed you *your* key. We no longer live together for a reason. This is our address and *that* key I just gave you is for yours. If you want to visit us, use the doorbell like everybody else," Tammy said, before closing the door in his face.

When she unpacked the diapers, baby sling, blankets, Tammy checked that her baby – who she now called A.J. since she was no longer afraid of Steve's reaction – was sleeping, soundly in the bassinette. As quietly as she could, she unpacked the plates and cutlery, quickly wiping them over before putting them into the cupboards. Tammy then dug out some cleaning equipment, and got to work, wiping down cupboards, door handles, sinks, making sure their new home was germ-free.

The first night at the new apartment, Steve knocked, loudly, on the door while, calling out her name. Tammy already knew, without opening the door, that he was drunk. She opened the door a crack without removing the security chain.

"Let me in!" Steve demanded, still bashing on the door. A.J. had been sound asleep for an hour before the entire ruckus, but was now bellowing loudly.

"Thank you *very* much. Now you have woken the baby. Go home. You're drunk," Tammy said to Steve, as she closed and locked the door. She picked A.J. up in her arms and gently lulled him back to sleep. "Don't you worry, little man," Tammy whispered to her son. "Mummy is going to keep you safe from the big, bad monster," and she kissed the top of his head as he drifted back to sleep in her arms.

Unfortunately, every single night became a ritual for Steve. Had he lost his security job? The last time Tammy could remember Steve talking about his job, he was bragging about working nights and getting more money. But his financial problems were no longer hers. She had her own home to take care of. Her own family. Her own priorities. Nothing and *nobody* was more important in this world to Tammy than her tiny baby, A.J., who was already two months old.

Chapter 17

Every time Tammy set eyes on her little man, she felt pure joy coursing through her. She could even feel it in her skin. This beautiful, tiny baby made her life worth living. He made her strong, willing, determined to do anything it took to keep him safe and happy. He slept peacefully during the day, in-between his routine of feeds and diaper changes, but at night, he would always start screaming when he heard Steve bashing on the door. Tammy wished she had her own telephone, so she could call the police, but then again, he was still *technically* her fiancé. The police would not care what Steve did to her.

There was just one thing left for her to do. Tammy unlocked the door, again keeping the chain in place, and handed Steve his engagement ring.

"You used to be a real man. But *now* look at you. I could never marry you, *and* you stink of beer," she said to Steve, before she closed the door. Tammy once again felt that wonderful feeling of freedom sneak up on her. She smiled, as she attended to A.J., and continued to smile until they both drifted off to sleep.

The next morning, Tammy decided to use the telephone box across the road and make a phone call or two. Her first phone call would be to the telephone company. Tammy now wanted – no, *needed* – a phone installed in her apartment. She also thought about applying for a credit card. Although she was not working, she still received a steady income from her employer, and it would help her buy the essentials she needed for her and her baby. After Tammy got A.J. dressed and tucked into his sling, she opened her front door and was horrified at what lay before her eyes. Her car had been spray-painted with SLUT on every door, on the bonnet, on the boot... even on the windshield. Tears of anger stung her eyes. Not a single other car had been touched. She knew it was Steve.

Across the road at the telephone box, she rang Telecom and ordered a phone service (and a phone) for her new address. The operator said that somebody could come out to her address with the new phone, and install it, making sure there were no faults, within the next two working days.

The second phone call was to the police. Tammy reported the act of vandalism on her car, telling them that her very drunk and violent ex had done it. The police asked if she had actually seen him vandalise her car. When she responded that she had been asleep at the time, the police told her that unless she has photographic evidence of him vandalising her car, there was nothing they could do to help her.

"But I *know* it was *him*!" Tammy insisted.

"*Knowing* is not evidence, ma'am. Unless you can provide photog...."

Tammy hung up the phone. Over the years, she'd become accustomed to the Logan Police not caring about what happened to her because Steve had been her fiancé. But even now, he could do whatever he wanted to her, and get away with it.

All of the loud talking had stirred A.J. from his sleep. Tammy crossed the road and headed back to the apartment. A.J. either had a wet bum or an empty tummy, and she couldn't do anything about either of those things, while standing in a telephone box. While changing his diaper, back at the apartment, she baby-talked to him, telling him that the police were useless jerks, just like his daddy. Hopefully, someday, she would have some rights and Steve would no longer control her life.

With her son now sleeping, Tammy headed out the back of her apartment to the tiny, little, *private* back yard. The grass needed cutting. She had brought some basic gardening tools with her to the new apartment when she moved. Tammy didn't actually think she would have a garden to attend to, but the garden tools *did* belong to her and she knew, for a fact, that Steve was never going to put them to good use. She dug the hedge clippers out of the laundry and, walking around on her knees, in the back yard, she clipped the grass until it was a suitable length. It looked pretty ridiculous and she made a mental note to buy herself a hand-mower. No noise. No petrol. It was the perfect mower for a tiny yard of an apartment with a sleeping baby.

That night, after changing A.J.'s diaper, giving him a feed of milk and tucking him in to the bassinette beside her, Tammy drifted off to sleep, waiting for bub's next wake-up cry. It never came.

When Tammy woke the following morning, she felt rested. *Too rested.* She quickly sat up in bed and checked on A.J. in his bassinette. A.J. was lying face down on his little pillow. He was cold to touch and was not moving.

Tammy lifted his lifeless body out of the bassinette and laid him on the bed. His lips were blue and skin was ice cold. *No, God.... NO!!!* Tammy leaned over to feel if he was breathing. Not a single breath left his tiny body. With no phone and no way to get urgent help, Tammy grabbed her baby and ran down the stairs. Not caring whether or not she had her house keys, Tammy ran outside screaming and started to bash on people's doors for help. The second door she bashed on flew open and the woman inside immediately rang an ambulance.

While waiting for the ambulance, Tammy held her baby close to her body, trying to warm him up, hoping that he would suddenly wake up with her touch.

"Don't do this to me, please, God, *don't take my baby away from me!*" Tammy cried.

If only he would wake up. She tried to breathe into his nose and mouth – she would do anything in this world to get her son to breathe again – but each attempt failed. When the ambulance arrived, the paramedics checked for signs of life. They declared her baby "deceased" – a term she could not comprehend. He could not be *deceased.* He had been fine. Last night, when they went to sleep, A.J. was fine. Through her sobs, she looked at the paramedic with pleading eyes.

"He was fine," was all Tammy could say, in response.

She sobbed, as the paramedics took her baby. She couldn't remember anything else that day. The following week was also a blur. Tammy vaguely remembered the telephone person coming to install the phone. She had stared at the phone for a long time. Every part of her body was numb. She was all cried out. Nothing mattered to her anymore. Everything *important* in her life was gone. She didn't go outside, not even to check the mail. All she could do was sit and stare at her new phone. Tammy felt like somebody had reached deep inside her chest, taken hold of her heart, and torn it out in one painful motion. There was nothing left of her soul. Just... *nothingness*. A huge, black, numb, empty void. A bottomless pit of darkness.

Tammy's first clear memory, after that day, was when the telephone actually *rang* for the very first time. The hospital had finished their investigations into the cause of death. SIDS. *Sudden Infant Death Syndrome.*

"Is that another way of telling me you don't know what happened to my son?" Tammy snapped, without meaning to sound bitchy.

"Sudden Infant Death Syndrome – also known as "Cot Death" – is when the baby stops breathing in its sleep, due to the baby's sleeping position. Unless a parent is awake at the *exact* moment the baby stops breathing, there is nothing that can be done...."

"So *I* did this to my baby?" Tammy interrupted. It was not a question. If Tammy had been sitting beside her baby at the exact point when he'd died, if she'd called an ambulance *immediately*... if she'd acted more efficiently, in a bid to resuscitate him *before* the ambulance arrived, A.J. would still be alive. *He is dead because of me. Steve was right. I am useless. I am a pathetic mother. I did this. I did this. I DID THIS! God, please kill me! PLEASE!*

Tammy drove to the health centre. Her sanity was leaving her. She was alone. She missed having somebody there with her and had almost called Steve. But she didn't *miss* Steve. She just missed... she missed A.J., and contemplated swapping her life for his. None of her thoughts were making any sense. She cried and cried, day and night, and she was tired of feeling numb. Tammy hoped that the health centre could help her. She knew that if she continued like this, there would be nothing left of her.

After the crowded waiting room had syphoned through the doctor's surgery, one by one, in the order in which they'd arrived, it was Tammy's turn. The doctor prescribed a strong sedative and wrote a referral to see a psychologist. Tammy was suffering from severe depression. Medication and talking it through with a professional was supposed to make everything good again. She drove home and rang a psychologist, whose office was nearby. Her appointment with the psychologist would be in two weeks. Tammy then went upstairs and took a sedative, before falling into a deep sleep.

Chapter 18

Tammy woke with a fright and sat upright. She thought she'd heard A.J. crying. When she looked on the bed beside her, there was no bassinette. There was no baby. And then reality kicked in. Staring at the bassinette, which was sitting in the corner on the floor of the bedroom, Tammy sobbed.

After going to the bathroom, she put her dressing gown around her and went to the front of the apartment complex to collect the mail, not caring if anybody saw her dressed so badly. *Screw them. If they want to look, then it is their fucking problem. Nosy bastards.* Tammy's mailbox was full of letters, junk mail and the local rag. *The local rag? Huh... delivered a day early.*

When she got back to her apartment, she noticed something she hadn't noticed before. The driver's window of her car had been smashed. She peeked into the car window, but nothing seemed to be taken. *Steve*. Feelings of anger attempted to bubble up inside of her, but all that could produce itself was a feeling of defeat. She was not surprised by the broken window. That was probably her fault, too.

When she went back inside the apartment, Tammy locked and chained the door. She walked to the kitchen bench, unloading all the mail she held in her arms. One at a time, she quickly sorted them.

Bill. Bill. Wrong address. Bill. Previous tenant. Bill... and finally she took the elastic band away from the local newspaper. When she checked the date, Tammy had to rub her eyes and check again.

"*Thursday?*" she said, out loud to herself. "But today is Wednesday! Bloody hell, have I been asleep for two days?"

Unimpressed by her *Sleeping Beauty* impersonation, Tammy grabbed the letter opener and started opening the bills. *Phone, electricity, magazine subscription... huh?* The magazine subscription was an invitation to subscribe, and quickly found itself in the trash.

Tammy decided to go through her phone book of essential people and ring them. She called her parents, before calling her sisters, her aunty and her cousins, as well as Max and Patrick. As empty as she felt, at that moment, without little A.J., Tammy was relieved to be able to talk to her family and colleagues, without worrying about whether the phone was locked or not. It was definitely a strange feeling, being able to talk to her parents without worrying that Steve would walk through the door at any minute; strange indeed, but definitely in a *good* way.

A few days later, Tammy's new credit card arrived in the mail. Her application had been accepted and she could now buy a couch, a television and a video player. She needed to get out of the house, for a change, but the first item on her agenda was to take her car to the Smash Repairs shop, which was only about 500 metres down the road. When she pulled in, she spoke to the owner himself, Rocky, and showed him the damage to her car.

"Poor girl's looking a bit sad, but I reckon we can get a new window into her today or tomorrow. We can also sort out all those scratches on her," Rocky said.

"Scratches?" Tammy replied, confused.

"See right here? Some rotten bugger has keyed your car," Rocky replied, pointing out several places on the car that she had not even noticed.

Tammy shook her head in disgust. She had a feeling, right then, that she would never be free of Steve. "Yeah. How much is it going to set me back?" she asked.

"I'll do it for you for under two hundred... how does that sound?" Rocky asked.

Tammy booked the window to be repaired that day and the paint job to be done at a later date. As long as the car was secure, she would be okay.

The next day, she drove to the railway station and caught a train into the city. Tammy had not been on a train in such a very long time. It was quiet, with very few other passengers on the train in the middle of the day, and she sat in a four-seater, looking out the window for most of the journey. When the train stopped at Park Road Railway Station, she smiled as she looked at Brisbane Prison. Her very first job when she finished college *years* ago had been inside the office of that prison, processing the files of all the incoming inmates. Good times. Next was South Brisbane Railway Station. The Queensland Performing Arts Complex was just behind the railway station. As the train pulled out of South Brisbane

Station, she saw up ahead that they would be crossing Brisbane River. As she looked down at the river, Tammy started to tremble. *We are so far up! What if the bridge falls!*

After the train had crossed the Brisbane River, it immediately approached a long dark tunnel. While inside the tunnel, the train stopped. The lights on the train went out. Tammy screamed. She closed her eyes and continued to scream, before holding her chest. She could not breathe. *Oh my God, I am going to die!* In full panic mode, Tammy was grabbing at her throat, grabbing at the handle of the chair, wondering if this was it. Tears rolled down her face as she still could not breathe. *There is no air in here!*

The lights of the train then switched back on, and the train had started to move again. Next stop was Roma Street Railway Station. Regardless that she wanted to go into the city, Tammy decided that Roma Street would do just fine. *A good, long walk never hurt anybody.* She also decided that she would never, again get on a train.

Tammy caught a taxi to Woodridge Railway Station after finishing her shopping, so that she could collect her car. She had purchased a couch, a small television and a VHS video recorder. The shopping clerk at Myer had offered her a choice between VHS or Beta. Tammy thought the Beta video recorder was too small to sit on the shelf, underneath her new television. All of the items that she'd purchased would be delivered within a week.

While sitting at home underneath the stairs, staring at her apartment, which looked naked without furniture, her heart ached. She wondered if it would be stupid to ring Steve and invite him over. But it was *not Steve* she wanted. She did not miss him. What Tammy missed was *people*. Being around people. Having somebody to talk to at home. She felt the ache of loneliness inside her.

Deciding to do something proactive about her problems, she drove to the real estate agency and asked if she could break the lease. When the property manager asked why she would want to do something so drastic, Tammy explained about the constant vandalism to her car and she showed the repair bills to the property manager. Tammy had noticed that the real estate agency also handled the set of townhouse apartments directly *next door,* on the same street. She asked if any were available. When the property manager advised that two were currently vacant, Tammy asked if it was possible to transfer her lease to the new property, due to what had happened to her car. The new townhouse apartments each had a lock-up garage and *very* tight security. After making a few telephone calls, the property manager agreed to transfer the lease.

On the way home, while sitting at a set of traffic lights, Tammy noticed a pet shop on Kingston Road which she'd never noticed before. It was new and, for reasons she could not understand, when the traffic lights turned green, she indicated *left* and turned into the parking lot. Out the front of the pet shop was a tiny cage, containing a single black kitten. It looked as lonely as she felt. Tammy went inside to ask the pet shop owner how much the kitten would cost.

"Five dollars," the pet shop owner replied.

Without a second thought, Tammy put her money on the counter, before asking what sort of things she would need to own a kitten. The pet shop owner led her around the inside of the store (which was wall-to-wall with fish tanks), and Tammy ended up leaving with a food bowl, water bowl, scratching post, cat toilet, kitty litter, some kitten food and some treats. She also purchased a cat carrier, so that her new kitten would have a comfortable way to travel to its new home.

"What shall we call you then, hmmm?" Tammy asked the little, black, fluffy ball with cute little kitten face attached to the front. "Awwwh, you are so cute, I could just eat you up!" she said, as she held the little bundle of fluff to her chest.

"Mew," replied the black kitten... with no name.

"Oh my *God*, that is too cute! I shall call you Muffin!" Tammy said, cuddling her new little furball.

She put Muffin on the floor, so that he could explore his new home. Tammy was careful to watch where she stepped, as she filled the food bowl with kitten food, the water bowl with water, and the cat toilet with kitty litter. She then picked up the kitten and set him *gently* down onto the kitty litter.

"If you need to pee or shit, this is where you go about your business," Tammy explained, as she held the kitten's tiny front paws and guided them, so that they scratched the kitty litter.

An hour had passed before Tammy remembered the furniture delivery. Playing with the kitten seemed to be, effortlessly, a full-time job, and she loved every minute of it. She went to the phone and quickly rang them with, what *would* be, her new address in two more days. The furniture store agreed to hold off on the furniture delivery until after then, and assured her that it would be delivered to the new address. She also rang Telecom, so that her new telephone and phone number could be transferred when she moved.

That night, while Tammy was *once again* packing up her belongings, there came a knock at her front door. Steve was there, but surprisingly, he was not drunk. He smiled, as she opened the door.

"Hey, Bubba!" he beamed.

"Hey, yourself," Tammy replied.

"I was wondering when you were coming back home? We've got a new dog and...." Steve trailed off. He'd seen the kitten, under the stairs, staring Steve down.

"I *am* home, Steve. We broke up a long time ago, remember? Please, stop coming here," Tammy said, seriously. She'd had as much of his bullshit as she could take.

"You can't have a cat. We have a dog," Steve continued rambling. Tammy stared at him with impatience. There was no more *WE* and Steve knew it.

"Goodnight, Steve," said Tammy, in a bored voice, before closing the door.

Tammy carried Muffin's little scratching post up to the bedroom. She put it directly next to the bed so that he would have a way to climb up on to the bed and cuddle if he wanted to. She quickly found out, however, that kittens do not need scratching posts to climb. Their tiny little sharp claws allowed them to walk up *any* vertical, fabric surface, whether that vertical surface was a bed, curtains, wallpaper, a sofa, or even a human leg wearing pants. The scratching post was just for the kitten to keep those claws fine-tuned. Tammy had to, on several occasions, remind Muffin that her legs were *not* scratching posts and that her toes were not chew toys. *Good grief, could you possibly be any cuter?*

The next morning, Tammy carried several boxes out to her car. She was able to move all of her belongings to the apartment next door in just a few car loads. The final trip, from the old apartment to the new, consisted of her most precious cargo. On the back seat was A.J.'s bassinette, still filled with some of the diapers she'd never used, his pillows, his sling and his blanket. She had been unable to part with them. In the front seat was a not-so-happy Muffin, inside his travel cage. All of Muffin's necessities were in a box in the boot. Tammy took everything inside the new apartment, and spent about half an hour with Muffin, in the second bedroom, getting him used to the new-place smell, before returning the keys to the real estate agency. After returning home, she reversed her car into the lock-up garage and made sure the door of the garage was locked tight.

It did not take long to unpack everything at the new place, but Tammy now had to buy herself a bed since the bed at the old apartment actually came *with* the old apartment. This new apartment was completely unfurnished, except for a refrigerator, and she quickly realised that she would also need to buy a washing machine. Going outside, for *any* unnecessary reason, was not something she wanted to do anymore, and that included carting her clothes to a laundromat on a weekly basis. The whole point of getting a more secure property, was so that she would be secure.

A week after moving, both Tammy and her kitten had bonded nicely and were starting to settle in. Tammy spent countless hours with Muffin and found herself buying new toys for him to play with, as well as finding out that some *unconventional* toys were just as amusing to the ball of fluff. He would chase a piece of string for so long that Tammy's arms felt like they would fall off. If he heard the empty inside cardboard of a toilet roll, he would want to play with *that,* too.

Muffin's happiness warmed her heart. But the pain of losing her baby was just as strong, with Tammy crying herself to sleep, every night. Eventually, she decided to seek spiritual guidance from the church, which had tutored her for so long in how to be a good Catholic. Although she had not converted to Catholicism, this was the only place that she knew she could count on for peace, serenity and love. Tammy had not been on speaking terms with God for almost a month, and maybe it was time to change that.

When Tammy drove down to the Catholic Church in Springwood, part of her wanted to turn around and drive right back out of the car park. This place brought back her memories with Steve. It was something she did not want to rehash. While sitting in her car, contemplating on whether nor not to go inside, she closed her eyes and just let "being there" try to bring her some comfort. She was soon disturbed by a knocking, at the car window. Steve's priest friend was peering in at Tammy and smiling. She wound down her window, before he asked if she would like to come inside.

With that, she grabbed her handbag, locked up the car and walked into the church.

"I have never felt such torment in my life, Father. I don't know how to deal with my baby's death. I can't understand why he was taken from me," Tammy cried, sitting across from the priest at the desk in the rectory.

"I can see your torment, child. But surely you must know the answer?" the priest responded. When Tammy looked at him blankly, the priest went on. "Every child needs his father. You left his father and took the child away. The price you had to pay was to have the child taken away from you by God."

Tammy stopped crying. She was absolutely frozen in her seat. A look of shock and absolute horror had replaced her tears.

"Did you just say that God *killed* my baby to *punish* me?" Tammy asked, her tone demanding an immediate answer. She looked directly into the priest's eyes and waited.

"When you removed the child from his father, you lost your right to be his mother, Tammy. Surely, you can *see* that?" the priest answered, calmly.

"You know what? *FUCK YOU!* And fuck your God! You *seriously* fucked-up, son of a bitch! Do you have any *idea* what that fucking asshole *put* me through before I left? Did he tell you that he nearly killed our son?" Tammy screamed.

The priest, previously calm, now looked furious. He growled at her that she was in the house of the Lord, and no disrespect would be tolerated.

"*DISRESPECT?*" Tammy stormed out of the church, looked up to the sky and screamed at the top of her lungs, "FUCK YOU!"

Cussing the whole way home, she kept asking herself so many questions in order to try and understand what had just happened. *What sort of God kills babies? What sort of God punishes women who leave their partners when they have been bashed so many times? What kind of God would want a baby in the care of a father who almost killed such a tiny person because of a shirt that his mother had failed to iron?* This was not a God she respected. The day God took her son away from her and deserted her, was the day God had shown *HIS* true colours to her. Her faith – a lifetime of trusting a Christian God – had just crumbled around her.

The moment Tammy reversed her car into the garage and locked the garage door, she went inside, lay on her bed, and cried. After about an hour, her crying was interrupted by a tiny little, squeaking "Mew" at the side of the bed. Muffin walked up the side of the bed, lay down beside her, snuggled into her armpit and went to sleep. Tammy kissed the top of the kitten's head and wished that life was as perfect as this tiny little black fluffy ball, which was purring madly, without a care in the world. That was the day that Tammy renounced her faith and walked away from Christianity.

Chapter 19

Three weeks had passed. Tammy had spent as much time as *possible*, continuing to bond with her kitten. Playtime kept her mind busy. She did not regret, for one moment, adding this tiny black ball of fluff to her family. Muffin took away a feeling which had been overwhelming her – the feeling of being completely alone – and when he purred, Tammy smiled. Muffin's happiness and tiny bliss was contagious, in every single way, and Tammy was grateful for that.

Twice per week, Tammy would walk to the supermarket, not far from the top of Queens Road in Kingston. Not only did she buy food for herself, but she would also make sure she'd had enough kitty litter, food and possibly too many new toys for Muffin. She also sought out a vet, to ensure that Muffin was in great health and to make sure he was fully vaccinated. Although he was an indoor-only kitten, it was hot in summer and Tammy would keep the windows and doors open to let the air through the apartment, leaving just the screens between them and the outside world. The screens were secure, however, with the mesh being metal instead of nylon, and each screen required a key in order to open it.

With new couch, television, VHS video recorder, washing machine, bed AND new computer in the apartment, it was time to figure out how the computer worked. Tammy set it up in the second bedroom and plugged it in. It ran on the DOS operating system, which meant absolutely nothing to her. Knowing just one other person who had a computer at home, Tammy drove to Johan and Maria's house and sought out advice. Johan recommended that she install a Windows program (Windows 3.1) with DOS so that she could play some pinball games. He also recommended she get the internet so she could get a swanky new 14.4k dial-up modem. *Ummm... yeah, okay.* All of this was like some foreign language to her, but Johan gave her disks for Windows 3.1 to install. Yeah, this would be fun. Not.

Tammy returned home and reversed the car into the garage, ensuring it was securely locked up as per usual. She then spent the next 4–5 hours trying to figure out Windows 3.1, which eventually led to her just sitting in front of the computer, staring at the screen.

"A computer," Tammy said. "These things are definitely the biggest paperweights ever invented." Tammy looked down to the floor at Muffin, who was now playing, by her feet, with a new toy mouse that she'd bought on the way home from seeing Johan. She continued to stare at the screen, wondering why she'd bought a machine that would probably be phased out within the next year or two.

A loud knock at the door, downstairs, snapped her out of her comatose-like stare at the computer screen. Tammy had not yet had a single visitor to her new home. Only the utility people and those who handled her rent knew where she lived. Her telephone number was still the same. She wanted to make sure that her family were still able to contact her. But *nobody* yet had her address. *Mormons, maybe?* Tammy stood up, almost grateful for the distraction, as she trundled down the stairs. Muffin did his best to keep up with every step she took. When Tammy opened the front door, a blond-haired man was standing there with a worried look on his face.

"I am so very sorry to disturb you, miss, but I have tried door-knocking the other places and nobody answers. My car has broken down out the front and I need to call somebody. Would it be alright if I used your phone?" the stranger asked.

"Well, there is a telephone box just across the road. You can't use that?" Tammy asked, a little impatient at being disturbed from trying to work out her new paperweight problem upstairs.

"I tried but the phone box chewed up all my money. It took every last coin I had. Please, could I ring somebody – a friend – to come and help me out?" the stranger continued.

Tammy felt a bit wary, but without going outside she was unable to verify if her neighbours were home or not. Everybody had locked their cars inside their garage. Although on edge, Tammy *finally* agreed to let the stranger use her phone. She unlocked the screen door and the stranger thanked her as he walked into the apartment. Tammy closed the screen door behind him but did not lock it, knowing that she would be showing him out shortly anyway. She placed the keys on the table at the entry way. Without turning her back to the stranger, Tammy told him that the phone was on the bench in the kitchen, right next to the sink. The stranger thanked her, before pulling a piece of paper from his pants pocket. He looked at the paper and dialled a number.

"Yeah, g'day, mate. It's just me. The car's broken down and need a tow. Mind helping me out? Yeah? Great, thanks, see you then," the stranger said into the phone, before hanging up the receiver.

When he turned around to face Tammy, the stranger smiled and said that his friend would be there in about an hour. He then asked if it would be alright if he waited at her apartment for him, since it looked like it might rain. *What, you can't wait in your car?* Tammy reluctantly agreed to let him wait and offered him a cup of tea, advising that there was no coffee to offer him because she couldn't stand the taste or smell of it.

"Tea would be great, thanks. Black, straight up," the stranger said.

Tammy asked the stranger to have a seat in the living room while she boiled the kettle. As she was filling up the kettle at the sink, it struck her that the stranger had not told the person on the phone where his car had broken down. She plugged the kettle into the wall and pressed the button to let it boil, before slowly turning around.

The stranger stood in the doorway of the kitchen, staring at her while holding a large hunting knife in his hand. Tammy looked the stranger in the eye, while doing all she could to flip through her mental database, trying to figure out how she was going to hurt this intruder so that she would not die tonight. What had Steve taught her back in her martial arts days? *Think, dammit, you stupid bitch!* And then Steve's words hit her: *"Fucking hell. You're useless."*

Tammy's only escape was the back door, but without her keys, she would be unable to open the screen door. Her only other option was to take this bastard down. *Believe in yourself, woman. He is just some douche with a knife.* As fast as she could, Tammy went for his jugular. Twice as fast, he had her on the ground with one punch, followed by another. She tried to grab the knife, but her attacker sat on top of her, pinning her arms to her chest and holding the knife across her throat.

"Feisty, aren't you?" said the attacker, seemingly amused at her attempts to escape him.

This was nothing more than a game to him, but she would fight him to the *death,* if need be. After all, she *once* knew how to take a man down who was twice her size. *Think! Don't die! Don't let him win!*

The attacker then slid the knife down and started to cut her clothes from her body. Tammy tried to get her knee high enough to connect – *hard* – with his balls, but he was sitting on the top of her upper legs and she couldn't get the leverage she needed to take him down. His fighting skills (and douche bag skills) were right up there with Steve's. Still, she continued to fight with every bit of strength she had. *This is your fault, you idiot. You let him in.*

"No!" she screamed – not just at the doubts in her mind but also at her attacker, who now had the upper hand.

He put the knife back up at her neck, right alongside her jugular vein, as he leaned over close to her ear and whispered, "Don't move." He then repositioned himself, putting his entire body weight on top of her, positioning his knees inside hers, as he pried her knees apart. "You are going to enjoy this," he said with a grin, as he forced himself inside of her. Feeling the knife against her throat, Tammy was terrified to move a single inch. Tears ran down her cheeks, as she silently wished Steve was there to stop this intruder from attacking her in her home. When it was over, he stood up and stared at her, his knife still in his hand. Tammy was disgusted with herself. She closed her eyes and covered her face, knowing that he was going to kill her at any moment. She then heard him run out the front door.

Tammy lay on the floor for a long time, crying. Her mind felt numb, unable to form any rational thoughts. Her body hurt. When she finally *did* get up, she immediately grabbed her keys from where she'd left them, by the front door, and locked it. She wished herself dead. *Every single fucking decision you make is wrong!* Tammy knew this was her fault. A smart person would never have opened the door. She threw what was left of her clothes into the trash, slowly climbed the stairs, while completely naked and bruised, and turned on the shower. Tammy made the water as hot as she could bear it. She wanted every single bit of the monster that had just attacked her to be gone. She wanted all the crap in her life to wash down the drain. *Fuck my life!* When she had washed every single part of her body that she could reach, she dried herself off, put on her dressing gown and went to bed.

The next morning, Tammy woke up, expecting to find her purring armpit-loving kitten asleep next to her. When she saw that he wasn't on the bed, she slowly climbed out of bed, flinching at almost every movement she made. It felt like every part of her – every muscle – had been strained the previous night, trying to fight off the man who had raped her.

"Muffin?" Tammy called to her kitten.

There were no kitten noises or movements in the house. She continued calling his name, as she searched every single place that she could think to look, upstairs. Tammy assumed that Muffin was hiding after what had happened, and who could blame him? When the search upstairs came up empty, she continued calling Muffin as she walked down the stairs. As she got to the bottom stair, she saw a very still, tiny, black ball of fluff on the floor.

Tammy ran to her kitten and picked him up. When her hand touched his rib cage, Muffin screamed, still limp in her hands. *Oh my God, that fucking piece of shit hurt you too? YOU FUCKING COWARD!!* Tammy did not bother with a cat cage. She gently tucked the kitten inside her dressing gown, grabbed the keys, and drove straight to the vet.

When she arrived at the surgery, Tammy ran inside the front door with Muffin still safely tucked into her dressing gown. She was absolutely frantic, and begged to urgently see a vet for her kitten who was barely alive. She took Muffin from her dressing gown and placed his tiny, broken body *gently* on the counter. The receptionist immediately paged a vet to come to reception, urgently. Tammy had forgotten about her pain, regardless of her many new bruises. She felt nothing at all, except for concern for the little furry guy on the table – her best friend was this tiny kitten, and she needed him to survive. The vet took Muffin to X-ray. Two of his little ribs were cracked and he was badly bruised. The vet offered to put the kitten to sleep.

"You do whatever you have to in order to make him *okay!*" Tammy found herself yelling at the vet, suddenly wondering where she had heard that sentence before. Those were not *her* words. She apologised for any disrespect, and said she did not care what the cost. If the vet could save Muffin's life, Tammy would pay with the moon, if she had to. Muffin was then admitted to the veterinary surgery as a patient. The vet looked at Tammy and promised that he would do his very best.

Tammy spent every single day, sitting at home, for the next two weeks. During those two weeks, she did not eat much, nor did she get much sleep. Tammy was afraid to leave the apartment, but it was not just because she was afraid to be attacked. She also did not want to be away from the telephone. The vet had promised to keep Tammy updated, and would not end Muffin's life without her consent. She was grateful for this, and was hoping for good news. Something good in her life was *long* overdue, she felt, and if she had to give up every bit of future happiness in order to save her little furry buddy, she would do just that.

The phone finally rang and she answered it before the second ring. Muffin was doing well and was now able to come home, on the condition that he rested. Playtime had to wait for a while. For the first time in two weeks, Tammy was smiling. She was sure that

Muffin had just used up one of his nine lives, but she was so happy that he'd had eight more in reserve. *My tough little guy!* Tammy ran upstairs, got dressed, climbed into the car with her cat carrier (lined with the softest cushion she could find), and headed to the vet's office. She took all of her available cash and her credit card with her, knowing that the bill would not be small, but she didn't care. She let out a huge *GULP* when she was handed the $4,700 bill, but her shock was very short-lived, and replaced with pure joy, at the sound of a very noisy, cranky Muffin, who'd definitely had enough of this place. Tammy paid the bill, and they both made their way to the car.

Arriving back at home, Tammy reversed the car into the garage and again locked *everything*, ensuring that the place was secure. She took Muffin inside and opened up the cat cage, giving him some freedom. Tammy had a feeling that her little fluffy mister was probably tired of being in cages, and his squeak of appreciation proved her right. He slowly, and *cautiously*, walked out of his cat carrier, sniffing the air around him.

"It's okay, my little man. Nobody is ever going to hurt you again," Tammy said, gently as she petted the top of his head with two fingers. *Damn, you have grown!* The last time Tammy had pet Muffin on the head, one finger was just the right size. She then found herself picturing a black cat, the size of a refrigerator, strutting around her apartment, for just a moment. "Ummm... let's not grow *that* much, okay?" Tammy smiled, as she scratched behind his ears.

"MEW!" Muffin responded, before he started purring like a little chainsaw.

Tammy lay down on the couch and watched Muffin, as he walked around the living room, obviously happy to be back at home. When Muffin curled up in a little ball and yawned, before drifting off to sleep, Tammy finally had the strength and courage to ring the police.

An hour later, the Logan Police arrived at her door to take a statement about the attack. Tammy gave them every single detail that she could remember about his face, his height, what he was wearing, the knife, and included the fact that he almost killed her kitten.

"The kitten looks okay to me," one of the officers said, bluntly, looking at the sleeping kitten.

The police went on to tell her that, due to the fact that she had showered, waited a few weeks before she reported anything, and that she had *willingly* let the guy into her apartment to *start* with, there was nothing they could do to help her. They even openly stated that they *couldn't really say* that a rape took place, without any evidence. *Well there's a shock, huh?* Tammy bit her tongue and refrained from saying what was on her mind. It was no surprise to her that the Logan Police were not interested in doing anything that would cause them to work up a sweat.

Each of the police officers handed Tammy a business card. *Thanks, fellas. Might wipe my ass with these later.* After showing them out, and locking both doors securely when they left, she sat on the floor beside Muffin again, scratching his little head. Muffin's chainsaw impersonation started up again and, regardless of the all the shit in her life right now, Tammy found herself smiling at her kitten, grateful that he was doing better.

That afternoon, immediately after Tammy took the garbage and recycling out to the front of the building, she glanced up at the phone box on her way to collect her mail. *What the fuck?* Tammy could *swear* that the man inside the phone box, on the other side of the road – a man whom had just been *peering* at her through the glass at the side – was Steve.

Tammy retrieved the envelopes and local newspaper from her letter box. After *again* looking at the phone box across the street, she turned and ran back to her apartment, locking *both* front doors behind her. She then walked around the apartment with her keys, ensuring that all other windows and doors were also securely locked, including the garage door. *Dammit, was that Steve?* Tammy couldn't be sure. It looked like him. *Exactly* like him, in fact.

While sitting in the living room with Muffin, scratching his little head as he purred, the doorbell rang. Tammy peeked out through the curtains, two metres to the right of the front door. Sure enough, her ex was standing at the door. She opened the main door but left the screen door closed and locked.

"What do you want?" she glared at him.

"Just checking to see if you're alright. I have not seen you in a while, Bubba. Why did you move?" Steve asked, mock innocence on his face.

"I moved because some *fucktard* smashed up my car. Now please explain how you knew my new address?" Tammy asked.

"I asked your old neighbours!" Steve lied.

"Please, just leave me alone, Steve. Go away. Go far, far away," Tammy said, absolutely tired of seeing his face and hearing his bullshit. *Go and play in heavy traffic. There's a good boy!* Tammy closed and locked the front door.

Chapter 20

During her next visit to the grocery store, Tammy visited her real estate agent. She decided to pay that month's rent in cash, and she also wanted to see what other properties were available. Tammy was particularly interested in any properties that accepted a month-to-month lease, instead of locking her into a lease that lasted for at least six months. A property at Eagleby had become available. As it was month-to-month leasing, she immediately applied. The rent was a little bit more than what she had been paying previously, but the past was filled with too many bad memories – her son's death, being raped at knife-point. Tammy needed to start over, yet again.

The following week, she went to the local service station and rented a utility truck, with a large cage on the back. She then contacted her mum and sister, and told them she was moving again.

"I know it's short notice, but can you please spare a hand to help me get some of this furniture onto the ute?" Tammy asked Janine and Lisa. Both were happy to help.

With the utility truck loaded up, and Muffin safely inside his travel cage in the front seat, Tammy drove the utility truck, her mum drove her car and Lisa drove her Volkswagen to the Eagleby address. All were happy with what they saw, with one concern. The car accommodation was nothing more than a lock-up carport. Tammy knew that anybody could jump the fence, into the back yard, and have easy access to her car. But, with any luck, Steve would not know where she was, and Tammy could finally have some peace.

When they all arrived at the new address in Eagleby, Tammy took Muffin into the spare bedroom with his toilet, food and water bowls and his Catnip spray. After filling the food bowl, water bowl and kitty toilet, she then sprayed the lower walls with Catnip, and added a couple of sprays onto the carpet, before leaving the room and closing the door behind her. This way, Muffin could get used to the smell of the new house. It also ensured that nobody would step on the not-so-tiny, black furball, while moving heavy furniture around.

Janine and Lisa helped Tammy move the larger items of furniture into the different rooms, before they all finally sat down and made a cuppa. Sadly, Janine had brought coffee. *Gross, Mum!* But Tammy was grateful for all of the help her mother and sister had given her, so she made no complaints about the stinky coffee on her kitchen table. Well, *almost* no complaints.

"I seriously don't know how you two can drink that crap. It's disgusting. It smells and tastes like shit," Tammy said, as she smiled and sipped her cup of tea.

"I wouldn't know. I haven't tasted shit before," Janine winked at her daughter.

"Oh, ha bloody ha," Tammy said, before all three of them started laughing. It felt good to be with her family again. She felt safe and, for the first time in too long, the smile was not just on her lips, but also reflected in her eyes.

As Janine and Lisa left, Tammy hugged them both at the front of the house and thanked them again for all of their help.

"I have missed you both. Please don't be strangers, okay?" Tammy said, before one more hug. Janine and Lisa then climbed into Lisa's Volkswagen, and Tammy waved as the car disappeared down the street and around the corner.

Returning inside, Tammy locked the entry doors, checked the windows and security screens were all locked, before opening the door to the second bedroom. Muffin was sitting on the window sill, staring out at his new surroundings. When Tammy walked over and scratched the top of his head, he closed his eyes and started purring loudly and happily.

"Strewth! Maybe I shouldn't have put so much Catnip in the room. I hope you're not *stoned*, mister!" Tammy joked, absorbing the secure feeling of their new home.

A month had passed before Tammy decided to take the plunge, delving into the unknown world of the internet. She had never used the internet before – not even at her former work places – and had absolutely no idea of how it worked. Deciding that pinball might fill some of her too-much-free-time, she took a drive to Johan and Maria's place and asked Johan to teach her about the internet. Johan was happy to oblige.

Hearing about ISPs, IPs, dial-up modems, internet addresses, email addresses and hosts, Tammy's mind was swirling. *That was way too much information for something that's supposed to be so simple.* She looked at Johan, blankly.

"I think my brain just exploded," Tammy said. "Not much of that made sense. I'm sorry."

Johan pulled a business card out of his wallet and handed it to Tammy, telling her to ring the phone number on the card, and they would sort everything out for her. As soon as she arrived back home, she took the business card out of her pocket and dialled the number. It was for an Internet Service Provider, and they suggested that Tammy sign up with them, with them taking care of the rest.

Within days, Tammy was sitting in her spare room, listening *intently* to a woman who'd come to her home, hooked up her modem, explained carefully how to dial up the internet, showed her how to go to an internet address, and even showed her how to access her email. *I have email now?* Tammy had never before *heard* of email until a few days ago, when Johan had tried to explain all things internet to her.

"So, why do I have email? Who do I email? I don't actually know anybody with an email," Tammy said, starting to wonder if this all was not just a giant waste of her money.

She wrote down her email address and stuck it to the top of her monitor with sticky tape. If anybody were to ask what her email was, she would easily be able to run in and see it. Tammy thought this would be interesting, indeed, since nobody else she knew *had* email. *Oh wait! Johan has email!* Tammy looked on the back of the business card that Johan had given to her and, sure enough, an email address with his name was written there. She then dialled up the ISP's number, waited for it to connect to the internet (which took about an hour on redial), and then sent Johan and Maria an email, telling them that she is now *officially* an "internet gal."

Tammy spent sometimes a whole day online, trying to figure out how the whole internet thing worked, found out what a search engine was and then started to search for things that would come to mind. She looked for her previous employers. Some were online. Some were not. She searched for some of her old friends. Their names would show in the Telstra pages. Telstra was the new name for Telecom, and they were responsible for all yellow pages, white pages and telephones in Australia, including those inside glass boxes at the side of the road. A month had passed and she wondered why her family never rang her. She had contacted all of them and given her phone number. Tammy thought that, maybe, they were mad at her for moving again, so she decided to ring *them* and find out why they weren't ringing her.

"I try, but you are always on the bloody *phone!*" Ralph said.

Although a little bit cranky that he always got the engaged signal when trying to ring his daughter, he was happy that Tammy had rung, and they talked for some time. Tammy rang her mother and sisters and heard the same answer – the line is always busy. It took a little while for her to put two and two together, and she finally figured out that people cannot ring her when she is on the internet. *Dammit!* From that day onwards, she decided to only do her internet browsing *late at night,* when everybody was asleep. The only problem was that, after a while, the internet became boring.

How the heck was she supposed to stay awake this late at night when she had already done everything that the internet can do during the day? Tammy typed in "chat" and a list of programs came up on her screen. Comic Chat, Pow Wow, mIRC, ICQ... all, of which, she knew nothing about. She decided to download and install them all.

Comic Chat was too fast. If somebody wanted to talk to you, a comic strip would be created and each sentence would create a new comic frame in a voice bubble. It was amazing to watch, but she decided that it was not for *her*. Pow Wow was pretty good, although not many people used it, so eventually, the people who made the program decided to discontinue it. mIRC was difficult to figure out, although Tammy found a list of commands that let her enter chat rooms. She would most *definitely* have to investigate that one further, however, it also seemed to move fast, since so many people would talk at once. It was not a one-on-one chat program.

With Muffin nibbling on her toes and scratching at her socks, she looked at her watch. *Holy crap, is it really 4:00 in the morning?* Where had the time gone? Tammy scooped Muffin up in her arms and they both went into the bedroom. Luckily for her, she did not have to be up early, the next day.

The following afternoon, Tammy received a phone call from Max. She *instantly* got excited, hoping that he was about to offer another job. Instead, he did not sound too happy. Max wanted to know why Tammy had not attended her appointment with the psychologist from weeks ago. He advised that Worker's Compensation was willing to pay for all appointments, if it was going to *help* her. Tammy apologised, and explained that she had to *again* move address, due to circumstances beyond her control, and had honestly forgotten all about it. Max then gave her the phone number and asked her to reschedule. She could explain her circumstances and problems at the appointment. When she rang the psychologist's number, she was able to get an appointment for the following afternoon, due to a cancellation. Nervous, she put on her bravest face and drove to the psychologist's office.

On arrival, Tammy was handed so many papers that she wondered if five or more forests had died, in order to produce all the paperwork she'd been given. *Good grief!* The first page was general information and emergency contacts, as well as employer or insurer who would pay for the appointments. All of the following pages were weird little questionnaires about her depression, anxiety, suicidal thoughts, fears… and Tammy had to circle from 0 through to 10, on the scale of how much she felt each emotion. It took a good hour to complete, but finally she was finished. Tammy handed all of the completed papers to the receptionist, who then thanked her before scheduling her next appointment. *What? I thought a shrink was a face-to-face thing!* Tammy walked to her car and drove home.

That very same afternoon, there was a knock at the door. Tammy cautiously peeked outside and went into full panic mode when she saw that *Steve* was standing outside. *How the FUCK did he find where I lived THIS time?* She told him, through the gap of the door, without removing the safety chain, that she wanted him to leave. He refused.

"Bubba, please! I *have* to talk to you! I haven't done anything to hurt you in a very long time and I already apologised for the times I accidentally hurt you when we were together!" Steve pleaded with her.

"It was *you* who smashed up my car, wasn't it?" Tammy said, angrily. When Steve did not answer, she continued. "Would you mind telling me how you found out my address?" Again, Steve did not answer. "Did you send that fucking asshole to my house to rape me?" Tammy screamed, tears pouring down her cheeks. That got Steve's attention.

"He *raped* you?" Steve roared.

"Oh, so *now* you seem to know what I'm talking about?" Tammy screamed, accusation in her voice. "I should have *known* it was you! *YOU* did this!"

His face, completely red with rage, let slide an angry tear down Steve's cheek. This wasn't the reaction that Tammy expected. Was he angry that she knew he was behind the attack? Was he angry that she was hurt and didn't tell him? Maybe he *didn't* have anything to do with it. Regardless, his look of rage brought back too many memories of their past and she refused to let him into the house. Steve finally realised that Tammy meant business. He walked to the Kingswood, which was parked at the front of her neighbour's house and, tyres screeching, he drove away… *fast*.

As soon as the car was gone, Tammy rang the police. She was scared and wanted protection. When the phone answered, she discussed, at great length, what had happened over the past year. The police officer asked if Steve had recently hurt her and she said that he had not. She was then asked if she had witnessed him committing any crimes or had *proof* of any crimes that he had committed. She again said that she had not.

"He is *STALKING* me! When we were together, he *hurt* me. A lot. I am afraid that he will do it *again*," she explained to the police officer.

"Ma'am, you are no longer *in* a relationship with him. He has not harmed you since you left, and you have no *evidence* that he has committed any crime against you. I'm sorry, but unless he actually *physically* hurts you, the police are unable to help y...."

"You useless *bastards!*" Tammy screamed into the handset before slamming the phone down. What good are the police, if they do not "serve and protect," as they so *often* claim to do in the television advertisements. She would need to get evidence, yet not get hurt. It was an impossible task, and she sure as hell was *not* going back to the monster, just to get evidence against him.

A few nights had passed since Steve's visit. He did not come back, and she hoped that this meant he'd *finally* given up and moved on.

Tammy sat down at the computer and dialled into the internet, while getting a late-night snack. She wanted to settle in and explore the outside world, from the comfort of her home. During a search of her local grocery stores, she found out that some of the larger supermarket chains actually shopped *for* you and delivered the groceries to your door. Tammy thought this was the greatest invention since sliced bread... until she saw the actual delivery costs. *Bloody hell! It would be cheaper to fly around the world than have groceries delivered.* She decided that she would stick with the local grocery stores and bring the groceries home, herself.

Her next item of follow-up was mIRC chatting. She went into a chat room simply called *#chat*, since her imagination was not so great, late at night. Tammy made a few friends that night, and decided to make the chat room a regular thing.

Her computer speakers let out a loud "DING!" and a small window opened. It was a private chat. Her very first mIRC *private* chat, in fact, and she was a little nervous. The user introduced herself as Katrina. *A female. I can talk to a female, no worries.* Tammy and Katrina started to talk and, before long, Tammy found herself smiling at how *easy* it was to talk to Katrina. Then Katrina said something strange.

"I have been trying to track you down for a very long time," Katrina typed. Suddenly Tammy's nerves were jumping hurdles inside of her. *Is she a friend of Steve's?*

"Why have you been trying to track me down? Do I know you?" Tammy asked, almost afraid to know the answer.

"My husband is the one who has been trying to contact you, actually. He saw an advertisement on the internet, and wants to meet you!" Katrina typed.

You're HUSBAND? What advertisement? What the fuck? If Tammy's eyebrows were raised any higher, they would be touching the ceiling. She decided to go all out and ask, "I see. So, you're a crazy person, then?"

Amused by Tammy's bluntness, Katrina explained that she and her husband, Bobby, were separated. *Estranged*, was actually the correct term for it. Yet, even though they were separated, Bobby spent all of his time at her house, on their internet. Katrina wanted him *out* of her house. After all, that is what separation is about.

"I didn't *put* any advertisement. I am *new* to the internet, and am still trying to figure out how to use it!" Tammy typed, feeling very weird about this entire chat.

"Well, somebody did. Bobby liked what he saw, and wants to meet you," Katrina typed.

For a while, Tammy typed nothing. Her mind was reeling. Who had put an advertisement on the internet about her? Why would some *random* guy want to meet her? And why was that same random guy's *wife* trying to set them up? Finally, after a few minutes, Tammy and Katrina started typing again. Tammy was not interested *at all* in meeting new people, but she seemed to click with Katrina, and asked if they could maybe be online friends. Katrina was happy at Tammy's request, and they exchanged telephone numbers so that they could chat during the day.

When Tammy disconnected from the internet, she smiled. Her first new friend since, what felt like, forever. She knew that when she woke the next morning, she would ring Katrina – and she did.

The phone call lasted for over three hours, and it led to a friendship that would last a lifetime.

Chapter 21

A couple of months had passed, and Katrina and Tammy had become best friends, talking on the phone for hours each day. Over their long chats, both on the phone and, finally, in person, Tammy slowly revealed her past with Steve, as well as the death of her child... and the rape. Katrina quickly decided that she did *not* like Steve. *Join the club, matey!* The list of people who loathed Steve was a long one, indeed. In fact, Tammy was sure that Steve was the *only* person who liked Steve.

Tammy and Katrina would get online, sometimes, during the day, and they would both join the *#chat* room in mIRC. A lot of laughs were had, almost every single time they were online. They had become regulars and it was a great way to "waste time" when bored. On average, there were only about fifteen people in the channel at any one time, so the conversation was fairly easy to follow.

One afternoon, when Katrina was not online, Tammy decided to explore what other channels were in the mIRC chat program. She typed the command to list all channels – some of which made her blush, when she saw the names. Others made her want to puke. There were a lot of perverts online who belonged in jail. Once the list of channels had fully loaded, Tammy started reading, from top to bottom. She found a channel called *#Australia*. Tammy dived right in.

The very moment that she joined the channel, several private chat windows opened, all asking her for A/S/L (age, sex, location). *Ummm... how about GO AWAY?* Tammy closed all of the windows that opened. One reopened. It simply asked if she wanted to talk. The first thing the person asked for was a photo. *Not gonna happen, buddy.* Tammy told the stranger that she did not have any photos to exchange. He then sent his photo of himself to her. When she opened it, she screamed. Staring her, right in the face, was a photograph of the very same man who'd raped her at knifepoint.

She immediately disconnected the computer and rang Katrina, crying her eyes out. She could hardly breathe. When she finally calmed down enough to make sense, she told Katrina that the rapist of Kingston had just talk to her, online. She had a photo up on the computer screen. Tammy begged Katrina to come over, straight away. Within fifteen minutes, Katrina's car pulled up at the front of the house. Tammy was still crying when she let Katrina in the door. They made a cup of tea, then went to the computer room.

"Are you *sure* that's him?" Katrina asked, staring at the photo on the screen of a man, sitting on the beach without his shirt on, his face smiling.

"It's him. I remember every fucking detail of his face. It's him. I *swear* it's him!" Tammy cried.

Katrina sat Tammy down and brought a second chair into the computer room from the kitchen. They would give each other strength through this, and Katrina was not about to watch Tammy let this opportunity slip away.

"Sit down and get back online," instructed Katrina, reminding Tammy that the police had demanded evidence of the attack. "You are going to talk to him, but do not tell him who you are, okay?"

Tammy sat down, shaking like a leaf, tears still flowing down her cheeks. She tried, desperately, to get her thoughts into some kind of rational order. While sorting through her brain's meltdown, the first thing she thought to do was save his picture to her hard drive. At least *now,* she had a picture for police.

"Sorry about that," Tammy typed. "I had a visitor and needed to quickly log off, but now I'm back. What would you like to talk about?" she asked. "What is your name? I am Kayla."

"I'm Andrew," came the typed response, before asking Tammy what she looked like. Tammy gave some fake description of being skinny, blonde, tall and smoking hot. Andrew asked if she would like to grab a coffee, some time.

"Sorry, but I work most days and rarely have time. So, are you married?" Tammy asked.

Andrew told her that he was married, but his wife no longer performed in bed. *Yuck. I didn't need to know that.* Tammy asked what he did for a living.

"I am a school teacher. The girls there love me. But only because I work in an all-girl's school! LOL," he typed. Tammy wondered what "LOL" meant and was suddenly terrified for each and every female at Andrew's all-girl's school.

Katrina put her hand on Tammy's arm and Tammy drew every single bit of strength she could from her best friend.

"Have you ever met up with anybody for coffee, before?" Tammy asked Andrew.

"Maybe," he typed. "What part of the city do you live in? I can come to you, if it makes it easier."

Tammy was not about to reveal that she lived in Eagleby. It was at that exact moment that a very crazy idea entered her head. Without telling Katrina, she started typing again.

"I live in Kingston. Queens Road. It's in Logan City. Do you know it?" Tammy asked, as her hands started shaking again. Regardless of her fear, she was determined to do this.

"I know it. I hooked up there once with a girl. Real nice, she was. Real sweet," Andrew typed, making Tammy want to throw up. She paused for a minute or two to catch her breath.

"I have a few people that I work with who live on this street. It would be so funny if it was one of them!" Tammy typed.

"Why don't you name some of the people you work with?" Andrew asked.

Tammy picked some random names out of the air. "Michael, John…"

"FEMALE NAMES! I only like women!" Andrew typed.

"Janelle, Ruth, Tammy, Barbara, Glenda, Trish... just to name a few. Were any of *those* your lucky coffee recipient?" Tammy forced herself to be civil in this little typing exchange.

"TAMMY!" Andrew typed – obviously without thinking.

"You hooked up with Tammy? Was it the same Tammy who lives at the apartments in 127 Queens Road?" Tammy typed.

There was a long pause before he typed again. "It was only once. She wasn't that good, but she *loved* what I did to her," he responded.

Tammy took a deep breath before typing her next sentence. She wanted Katrina to see how he responded to what she was about to type.

"I hope it is not the same girl I work with. Did you wear a condom when you blew her mind?" Tammy typed.

"Of course I did! I was a complete gentleman," Andrew replied.

"Thank God for that! You *know* that she has full-blown AIDS, right?" Tammy patiently watched the screen. Nothing was typed in return for a good five minutes. She then turned to Katrina, only to see that her eyes were wide with shock, and jaw dropped. When Andrew finally returned to the keyboard, Tammy could barely understand anything he typed. His hands were *obviously* shaking very badly, and from what little she *could* understand on the screen, Tammy realised that her rapist had suddenly lost every single bit of power over her, only to become the "*victim*," himself.

Andrew finally admitted to not wearing a condom, that night. He also admitted that he'd never thought about the possibility that this 'Tammy of Kingston' had AIDS, when he'd raped her. All of his thoughts were now solely on himself. He was upset, because now, he would have to tell his *wife* what he'd done. He would have to tell his wife that she may *die* because he'd raped a girl who'd had AIDS. It then occurred to him that he might die too, and would have to endure painful tests over the next two years, to see if he had contracted the AIDS virus. He wasn't ready to die. He was scared. And Tammy, right at that moment, went from being victim to survivor. She felt power over her attacker, for the very first time, and she liked that feeling.

After logging off, Katrina looked at Tammy with concern on her face.

"Have you ever thought that maybe, he might have given *you* a disease or two that night?" Katrina asked.

The next day, Tammy got fully checked by her doctor, who ran many tests, before giving her the all clear, one week later.

Tammy now had a *photograph* of Andrew, along with his email address, his occupation *and* his confession. She quickly saved the log file to her computer, and stored it to a floppy disk. She did not want to lose either of those things. Just because the Logan Police were lazy bastards, didn't mean that *she* should sit still and do nothing. And now, having some knowledge of Andrew's personal life, Katrina and Tammy drove to the school where he'd said he worked and just sat there, filling the whole day with trying to spot him. They also tracked down his home address.

"I have a confession to make to you," Katrina said to Tammy while they were driving home. Tammy pulled over and looked at her friend, trying to prepare herself for how horrible this confession might be. Katrina's face told Tammy that it was serious. "Before that day, when you were talking to Andrew on the computer and I saw how scared you were... I mean, before I *saw* what he typed, I... well, I... didn't actually *believe* that you had been raped. I didn't believe you."

Tammy's heart sank. Her best friend had thought she'd been a liar? Maybe what Steve had said to her, all those years ago, was true. Maybe Tammy really *was* shit. *Useless. Worthless.* She could hear Steve's laughter echoing inside her head, as she heard those words. Tammy drove the rest of the way to her friend's place in silence. As she pulled into the driveway, Katrina apologised for not believing in her, and gave her a hug. Tammy hugged her back, a tear rolling down her cheek, as she drove to her own home to cuddle with Muffin. *At least Muffin knows I am not full of shit.* When Tammy arrived home and walked into the house, she'd found Muffin fast asleep on her bed. Tammy lied down next to him and fell asleep.

The following day, Tammy went through all of the evidence she'd compiled against the man who'd attacked and raped her at knifepoint, inside her own home. She now had photos, the log file from mIRC with his confession, his home address, his place of work, and she was convinced that it would be enough for the police to find her attacker. If not, then they should find another occupation, because they were serving and protecting nobody.

Her first item on today's outing agenda was yet another trip to her real estate agency. Steve knew where she lived – again – and it was, once again, time to move on. Tammy found a house at Bethania, which was less expensive than the house she'd been living in at Eagleby. It was another month-by-month leasing agreement. The house was huge, with large back yard, double lock-up garage out the back, and tall fence all around. All the windows and doors had security screens and it was completely secure. At first, Tammy thought it would be too big for her and Muffin, as it had three bedrooms and way too much space for just one person and a cat, but then she thought about how it would keep her busy with cleaning and dusting. It would also give Muffin a lot of room to play in. Tammy applied for the house and crossed her fingers that she was the successful applicant, as two other families had applied.

After leaving the real estate agency, Tammy drove straight to the Logan Police Station at Springwood with all of the evidence she'd collected, tucked under her arm. She advised the officer at the desk that she wanted to report a rape. The officer led her to a room at the back of the station, and asked her to take a seat. After a few minutes, two other officers entered the room. She recognised them as the same two officers who attended the initial rape complaint many months ago, and who'd mocked her. *You have got to be fucking kidding me!* After all of her hard efforts in doing a job which *they* should have done, Tammy was not about to trust either one of them with all of the evidence that she'd personally collected, with Katrina's help. Instead, she stood up from her chair and simply said, "I *remember* you," before walking out of the police station, the evidence still in her hand.

Tammy returned to her Eagleby home and started to pack her belongings. Whether or not she was *successful* in getting the house in Bethania, she was certainly not going to be staying at the house at Eagleby. While searching the local newspaper for other home listings with real estate agencies, she received a phone call from her own real estate. The Bethania house was hers, if she wanted it. As she had perfect references, a great reputation for looking after each property she'd lived in, as well as *"special circumstances"* listed, the property manager flagged her application as priority. That weekend, Tammy and Muffin moved into their new home, with Katrina and Bobby's help. Their four kids *also* helped with the move, and it brought a smile to Tammy's face to see such a happy family unit.

Once the telephone was connected at the new house, Tammy rang Brisbane City's Police Headquarters. She had given up on the Logan Police ever helping her with something she felt *needed* to be investigated. Brisbane Police Headquarters transferred Tammy's call to the Criminal Investigations Branch (CIB) and, within an hour, two police officers were at her door. One was plain clothed, and the other – a female officer – was in uniform. Tammy invited them both into her new home, and apologised for the mess. The female officer giggled and said if her house was this *"messy,"* she would be ecstatic. Tammy smiled. It was the first time she'd encountered *friendly* police officers, in a very long time.

The male detective had a serious face, and asked if they could discuss what had happened to her, many months ago, when she lived in Kingston. Tammy sat down at the large dining table and the two police officers, Senior Constable Anne and Detective Senior Sergeant Johns, both sat on the other side of the table so that they could face Tammy, as they talked.

With all of her collected evidence on the table in front of her, Tammy went through every detail of what had happened that day – Andrew's story that he had broken down, had no money left for the phone, asked to call a friend, and the sickening details that followed. She told the officers about the treatment she had received for the past several years from the Logan Police in Springwood, including the day that she'd reported the rape. When Tammy started hyperventilating, Senior Constable Anne asked if she'd like to take a small break. Tammy closed her eyes and forced herself to take a few deep breaths, before continuing with her statement.

"When the police had told me that they doubted they could find Andrew, and didn't believe that an attack had taken place, I decided to investigate without them. They were the true definition of 'pigs' in every sense of the word," Tammy said, staring Detective Senior Sergeant Johns straight in the eye.

Both officers glanced at each other before looking back at Tammy, sympathetically. She went on to explain about the chance mIRC conversation which had occurred – a chat in which the odds were a million to one of taking place – and she passed the photo across the table.

"This is him. His name is Andrew. This is the man with the big knife and miniature penis. The man who attacked me that day," she said. Tammy then handed over several pages of a log file – a log which had taken quite some time to print on her new dot matrix printer – and she told the officers that this was a full transcript of the conversation between her and her attacker on mIRC. Andrew hadn't known that he was talking to the girl he'd attacked, and Tammy took full advantage of that fact.

The list of evidence went on and on. Both police officers were impressed by all of the evidence that Tammy was able to gather, with Katrina's help. They told Tammy that they would take the evidence back to police headquarters and go over it carefully. With any luck, Andrew would be arrested. Tammy stood and showed the police officers to the door, thanking them for their time. Just before they left, she had one more question for them.

"Can you please tell me… is it lawful for a man to rape his wife or fiancé in Queensland because they are in a relationship?" Tammy asked.

"It is *never* lawful for a rape to be committed. *Were* you and Andrew in a relationship?" Detective Senior Sergeant Johns asked, in response.

"*Hell, no!* Thank you, again, for your help," Tammy said, her blood starting to boil. All those years ago, she had been led to believe that Steve had been fully entitled to hurt her, rape her, beat her, abuse her and that the police would not lift a finger to help. All of those years, she could have left, but she felt like she had no escape, because the law was on *Steve's* side. *Fuck my life!* Tammy wished the police could have come to her rescue *before* all of this insanity had gotten so far out of control.

When the police car drove away, Tammy closed and locked the doors, before sitting on the couch. Muffin immediately jumped up onto her lap, demanding some head-scratching. Tammy scratched his ears, as tears of anger ran down her cheek. *He fucked with my mind. He fucked with my mother's mind. He disrespected my dad and I stayed with him.* Tammy had never been more ashamed of herself, and the decisions she'd made in her life, than she was at that moment. There had been a way *out* of this hell back then, yet she had no idea until now. Tammy wished that she could re-do her life over, starting from her martial arts training days. Her heart was filled with regret, and she was sorry that she'd stayed with Steve for so long.

Before completely drowning in a sea of self-pity, Tammy decided to pick up her mood by pulling the vacuum cleaner out of the cupboard. *Time to make this place sparkle!* Tammy watched as Muffin bolted into one of the bedrooms. She knew that he didn't like the noise of the vacuum cleaner, but with a house that was fully carpeted (except for kitchen, laundry and toilet), Tammy hoped that he would soon get used to it. After the carpets were done, she packed the vacuum cleaner away and put a load of washing on, before getting out the feather duster.

One thing Tammy had noticed, the day she'd moved in, were the many cobwebs in the corners of the ceiling. As she dusted them away, Muffin ran out and seemed to be having one of his hyper-kitty attacks. Tammy then saw something in his paws... and her skin crawled. She got as close as she dared, then screamed when she saw it. Muffin had captured a giant Huntsman spider, and was wrestling it on the ground, before proceding to *eat* it in front of her. *Seriously? Huntsmen are in this place? SHIT!* Tammy ran to the car, drove to the store, and bought as much *bug spray* as she could possibly fit into her trolley. *Rotten mongrel things. Piss off to the neighbour's house and leave me alone!* Tammy had been absolutely *terrified* of Huntsman spiders since she was tiny. They were absolutely huge – their body and legs spanned 25–30 centimetres across, sometimes, and Tammy always thought they looked like some kind of zombie-spider. Although not poisonous, they *did* bite, as she'd once had the misfortune of finding out. Her father, though – braver than Superman – would walk into a room, see a Huntsman, grab it off the wall with his bare hand and throw it out the door. *Good grief, Dad!* She never understood how he could do it, *without* squealing like a banshee.

With that thought, Tammy sat down and rang her dad, her mum and her sister, so that they would know her new address and phone number. They now also knew that she had Huntsman spiders in her house. Each of them laughed as she told them the horror story of her cat *eating a spider* in front of her. Tammy shuddered at the memory before sitting on the couch with Muffin to watch television. A brand new show was on, called *South Park*. By the end of the episode, she was speechless. *Cartoons are not what they used to be!*

Two weeks had passed, before the two police officers returned to her home. They advised Tammy that Andrew was now in police custody, and that he had asked for Tammy to be charged. Confusion quickly set in. Tammy asked them why her *rapist* wanted *her* to be charged.

"Andrew said that somebody told him you had AIDS, that you *knew* you had it, and that you did not tell him, prior to the sexual assault occurring," said Senior Constable Anne.

Tammy disappeared into the computer room for a moment, before returning with the papers from her doctor, showing that she had a clean bill of health. She reminded the police officers that she had *told* Andrew that his *victim* had AIDS, in order to scare the living *shit* out of him.

"Obviously, poor little Andrew was so scared of catching AIDS, that he shit a few poo-bricks into his diaper-panties, when I told him that *he* might now have it," Tammy stated, a serious look on her face.

Senior Constable Anne giggled and, for the very first time, Tammy saw Detective Senior Sergeant Johns grinning. Both police officers nodded, satisfied with Tammy's explanation, and said that they now fully understood Andrew's phantom-problems. They further advised her, before leaving, that investigations into this case are continuing. Surprisingly, Tammy found herself smiling, pleased that she had instilled the same amount of fear into her *attacker* that he had filled *her* with that day. She was finally taking back her life.

Chapter 22

It had been four months since Tammy had moved to the house in Bethania. The plague of Huntsman spiders were now under control, thanks to her bug spray and her bodyguard (Muffin), who protected her from the big bad spiders. It was also winter, which meant that outdoors was cold, with the indoors being just a tiny bit warmer than outside. Huntsman spiders liked to be warm, so they'd seemingly *all* decided to invade her home.

The phone rang. It was the receptionist at the psychologist's office. Tammy had almost *completely* forgotten about the fun paperwork that she'd filled out, that day. The receptionist advised Tammy that all of the results of her psychological exams had been processed, and asked her to attend an appointment at the end of the week. *Anything to get away from these bloody spiders!* Tammy asked if she had to bring anything with her, before enquiring as to whether she would be talking to another *paper* psychologist or if a real *person* would want to speak to her this time. The receptionist told Tammy that the appointment, on this occasion, would be with the psychologist herself.

Tammy sat, for thirty minutes, in the waiting room, due to the fact that the psychologist's *previous* appointment was going a little bit longer than expected. The receptionist told her that she was the last appointment of the day, so there would be no hurry to get through the session. Looking around, Tammy picked up one of the many out-of-date magazines in the waiting room, and found an old Dolly magazine. She had not read one of those in many years. Each issue came with a new quiz. On opening the magazine, she found a quiz "Are you a good kisser?"

"Nope, I'm crap," she said, quietly, to herself, while rolling her eyes. *Such stupid quizzes!* Tammy felt a wave of relief when the psychologist called her into the office.

The psychologist asked about Tammy's problems. After careful thought, Tammy decided to just address the *small* problems at that time, since the bigger problems were an ongoing police investigation. Tammy told the psychologist about the falling elevator, as well as her abusive ex, who'd been stalking her since she left him. They discussed this for a while, but those discussions came to a quick end, when the psychologist told Tammy that she *needed* to get back into an elevator.

"How about *you* get into an elevator! There is no fucking way in *hell* that I will *ever* get back into a lift!" Tammy yelled. "I would honestly rather be tied to a railway track, and have a fucking train make minced meat out of me, than ever get back into an elevator! No *metal box* is going to decide when I die."

Quiet filled the office for about five minutes, as neither one of them wanted to speak. The psychologist then said they would further discuss it at the next session. She put a file on the small coffee table between them, before pulling several papers from the file. Tammy recognised the papers she'd filled out many weeks before. All of the answers that she'd given that day had *finally* been processed and assessed. Tammy's anxiety levels were shown to be off the charts, and she was diagnosed with Obsessive Compulsive Disorder (OCD), Agoraphobia with Panic Disorder, Post-Traumatic Stress Disorder (PTSD) and Depression. When Tammy questioned the Agoraphobia diagnosis, the psychologist explained that many years ago, Agoraphobia was classified as a fear of open spaces, but was now classified as a fear of fear, or "Avoidance Syndrome." When Tammy responded with a confused look, the psychologist explained, further, that when Tammy finds herself in situations that bring about a Panic Attack – times when Tammy felt such overwhelming fear that she found it hard to *breathe* – Tammy would go out of her way to never be in that situation again. Thus, the "fear of fear," which the psychologist had diagnosed.

A prescription was written for Xanax and Serepax, each to be taken at separate times of the day. Serepax was to be taken at night, to help Tammy sleep without anxiety. Xanax was to be taken in the mornings, so that Tammy could get through each day without being jumpy. *Seriously? What is it with doctors and their compulsion to write prescriptions?* Tammy filled the prescriptions on her way home, but only took the Serepax for the first week. When she woke each morning, after taking it, she felt like a zombie and couldn't focus properly on what she was doing. Tammy knew that she needed all of her faculties working *perfectly,* in order to keep her and Muffin safe.

One week later, Katrina reminded Tammy that Muffin's birthday was coming up. She'd talked to her children about it, and they had all decided to throw a monster-sized party for her brave, black ball of fluff. Tammy looked at Muffin and asked if he would be interested in attending his very first ever birthday party. Muffin looked at Tammy, yawned, and went back to sleep.

"Yep, matey. Let's do it," she responded to Karen on the phone. "Muffin would probably like a spider-shaped cake, but I completely forbid that. How about a Mousie-shaped cake instead?"

Tammy and Katrina spent the next day at the Logan Hyperdome, looking for cake shops that specialise in weird requests. They found a new cake shop that did just that and, luckily for Tammy and Katrina, the specialty cake shop kept a giant laminated book, filled with every single cake shape you could imagine, at the entry of their store. When they couldn't find the right type of cake, Tammy and Katrina approached the counter.

"Her cat is having a birthday," Katrina said, pointing to Tammy. Katrina's gesture reminded Tammy of one of those "I'm with stupid" t-shirts, and she almost took offence.

"We would like to order a cake in the shape of a mousie or a fishie," Tammy said, in a serious tone, hoping these people would not call security for such a stupid request.

"Not a problem, ladies. We cater for many cat birthday parties. How many people will be attending? What colour mousie or fishie would you prefer? And what is the cat's name?" asked the woman behind the counter.

Tammy and Katrina gave Muffin's name, said they did not mind if it was mousie or fishie, but around eight people would be at the party, including four children who loved cake. Tammy then gave her own details and paid for the order. Now for the fun part: to tell the kids that there's be a birthday party to go to on the weekend.

Much fun was had by all, although Muffin did not look too thrilled when Tammy took a photo of him, while wearing a party hat, as his Aunty Katrina held him up to the camera. Katrina and Bobby found a few Huntsman spiders for Muffin to chase while the children enjoyed their cake. Tammy could not remember the last time she'd had so much fun.

When the party ended and the kids were having a nap, Tammy and Katrina dialled into the internet and got online for a little while. An email was waiting from Johan and Maria, telling Tammy that they had moved to a new address in Loganlea. Tammy wrote down their new telephone number and address. One day soon, she wanted to introduce Katrina to her former neighbours and dear friends.

Tammy was eager to see the new house, and took Katrina to meet Johan and Maria two days later. The house was small and was in a great neighbourhood, just down the road from Logan Hospital. When they pulled into the driveway, Tammy knocked on the door. Two little mini fox-terriers came running. Fully grown, the dogs were not much bigger than a Chihuahua. Tammy's heart sank, as thoughts of Snowflake started to flood her brain.

Johan, Maria and Katrina hit it off straight away. Johan now had an oxygen tank with him, taking it everywhere he went, but he was still smoking like a chimney. When he found out that Katrina was also a smoker, he told her that he can get her some very cheap, good quality tobacco, if she wanted to roll her own cigarettes. *Yep. A match made in heaven.* Tammy rolled her eyes. She sat on the couch and spent most of the visit playing with the two small dogs. They were so full of energy and were possibly the friendliest dogs she'd ever met. It was also possible, Tammy thought, that they simply smelled a human who was covered in cat hair, and it was like doggie Christmas to them.

After a whole lot of catching up, Maria told Tammy that they had gifted the old house to their kids because Johan and Maria were now too old for such a big place. Apparently, Steve saw Maria's grandchildren playing in the mango tree which grew in Steve's back yard. The tree was planted right next to the fence line, so at least half of the tree's branches grew into the neighbour's property. After Steve had seen the children playing in the tree, he had yelled at them to get out of his tree, before taking a chainsaw and cutting away each branch that crossed over into the property where the children had been playing. *Once an asshole, always an asshole.* Tammy knew that Steve had not changed one single bit. She asked that they do not discuss him with her any further. She was doing all she could to forget, and tales of his *current* childish exploits would not help her to do that. Maria apologised. Johan then decided to show Tammy his brand new, super-fast dial up modem. It was a 56k and you could download a whole megabyte of data from the internet in just over ten minutes. *Whoa! That IS fast!* Maybe it was time for Tammy to upgrade.

After dropping Katrina home, Tammy headed back to Bethania, only to see a familiar brown Kingswood parked at the front.

"Oh fuck off! *Seriously?*" Tammy exclaimed, as she pulled into the driveway. How the *hell* was he finding out where she lived each time?

When Tammy got out of the car, she glared at Steve who was sitting in the driver's seat of the Kingswood, staring back at her. She did not like the fact that there was *nothing* between them that would protect her, in the event that he might become fist-happy. She opened the side gate and drove her car to the lock-up garage in the back yard. By the time she was closing the garage door, Steve was in the back yard, asking if they could talk. It had been over two years since they had broken up. What part of "*please fuck off and die*" did Steve interpret as "let's make another go of things?"

"Please hear me out, Bubba," Steve pleaded.

"I will listen and then you will leave," Tammy stated, walking back to the side gate. She waited for Steve to follow. When he finally did, she locked the gate, before making her way to the front door. "And no, you are *not* coming inside. I can listen quite comfortably with you outside my house."

"I didn't know he'd *hurt* you like that," Steve started.

"He... who?" Tammy asked, confused.

"I just wanted you to come back home with me. He was just supposed to *scare* you. That's *all*. I didn't know that he would have sex with you," Steve pleaded, a tear rolling down his cheek. Tammy searched her mind, trying to figure out what the hell Steve was talking about, and then it finally hit her.

"YOU FUCKING PIECE OF SHIT!" Tammy screamed. "GET THE *FUCK* OFF MY PROPERTY! DON'T YOU *EVER* FUCKING COME NEAR ME AGAIN. *STAY AWAY FROM ME!*" Tammy slammed the door in his face. She raced into the computer room to get her camera. By the time she got back to the front door, both Steve and the Kingswood had left.

Tammy sat on the couch, rocking back and forth, her knees pulled up to her chest as she hugged herself. *Steve* hired Andrew. He had organised for Andrew to go to her home, attack her and scare her so much that she would run back into Steve's arms for protection. And from memory, Tammy knew that it had almost worked. She remembered that, just for a fleeting moment, she wanted to ring Steve and ask him for help. *You filthy, sick fuck!* Tammy dug out the business cards of the police officers who had arrested Andrew. She rang the number on Detective Senior Sergeant Johns' card. When he answered, Tammy frantically told him what had just happened. The detective told her to calm down and take a deep breath. She was talking too fast for him to follow what she was saying. After taking a few deep breaths, she was able to tell the detective about Steve's visit to her home, just moments earlier, and the conversation that had taken place. Detective Senior Sergeant Johns asked if she had recorded the conversation, or taken a photo of Steve or his car at the property. When Tammy advised that she had been unable to do *either* of those things, the detective told her that he would thoroughly look into any links between the two men.

Tammy knew that it was time to move again. By now, she had the *'moving house'* routine down, pat, but this time, since it was the end of her lease, she decided to find a new real estate. Tammy still had not figured out how Steve kept finding her address, and now it was time to start thinking harder. *Does the real estate office have a leak?* She didn't know, but she was taking no more chances.

Tammy visited several real estate agencies, before finding one that listed a house in Springwood, just around the corner from where Katrina lived. The rent was surprisingly low for a two-storey, three-bedroom house with a lock-up garage. When she questioned the low rent, the real estate agent was honest about the reason.

"In summer, the lower part of the house floods. It is right in a flood zone, so the underneath of the house won't win any prizes in cleanliness. But we can offer you a month-by-month lease in case you have to move, due to flooding," she said.

Tammy knew that, at this rate, she would be lucky to be there for a month. Moving house had almost become a full-time job. After filling out an application and being approved *immediately* (since nobody else wanted to live in a flood zone), Tammy, once again, packed up her belongings, hired a utility truck and moved to her new Springwood home.

Two days after moving in, Tammy asked Katrina to babysit Muffin for a while. She had been invited to Canberra by some friends on mIRC and could *really* do with the break from everything that had been going on. Katrina was happy to help and she knew the kids would love to spend each day playing with the feisty little black cat. Tammy also knew that Muffin had become used to the kids being around, and that he enjoyed play, time just as much as they did.

One week after the move, Tammy was on a discount airline, headed for Canberra. Her fingernails dug into the arm rests for the whole 2-hour flight. Never before, had Tammy been afraid of flying. After retiring from the Australian Navy, Tammy's dad had worked for the airlines for several years. During that time, Tammy had travelled, first class, on almost a weekly basis and, on occasion, was even allowed to sit in the cockpit with the pilots, as they flew the plane. Those were very happy, carefree days of her youth. Her childhood had, indeed, been a good one. But that was a whole lifetime ago. Circumstances and life experiences had changed drastically since then.

Tammy was met at the airport by a group of people that she had been talking to for over a year on mIRC. Although she'd never *met* any of these people in person before, they almost felt like family to her. They did not know her personal crap, nor did they judge her, and they knew how to make her laugh and smile. Tammy needed that so badly.

After a relaxing week in Canberra, she returned to Brisbane with great memories of her new friends. Tammy had also fallen in love with a city, filled with incredible lakes, breath-taking landscapes and beautiful buildings. Canberra had also earned the bragging rights of being the city with the most beautiful sunsets she'd ever seen. With a smile, Tammy knew that she would return to this beautiful city someday.

Back in Brisbane, Katrina picked Tammy up from the airport with some bad news. Muffin had fallen ill while she'd been away, and Katrina had no idea what was wrong with him.

"When I got there one morning, he was just lying on his side. He wasn't moving, but he wasn't dead. I took him straight to the vet," Katrina said, frantically.

"Please tell me he is still alive!" Tammy said, stricken with worry.

"Yeah, mate. He is alive, but we didn't have the money to pay his bill so we took some computer gear of yours to the vet, as a kind of 'down payment.' We explained to the vet that you were away for a week, and that you'd sort it when you came back." Katrina's voice was shaking. She knew how much Tammy loved Muffin. Instead of going home, Tammy asked Katrina to drive straight from the airport to the vet's office.

The vet explained that Muffin had a major urinary blockage. Sharp crystals had built up inside his bladder and had fully blocked him, so his bladder was on the verge of bursting. The vet had used a syringe to remove the urine from Muffin's bladder and had put a catheter in place so the urine could drain, while Muffin was on strong antibiotics to dissolve the crystals.

"How's he doing *now*?" Tammy asked.

"You can take him home in a few days. Your friend, here, said you were interstate and made an interesting payment, so that we would do everything we could to keep him alive. Are you able to replace your computer gear with cash any time soon?" The vet asked.

Tammy pulled out her wallet and paid Muffin's bill *immediately,* before visiting with her sick little man. Muffin growled. He was sore and hated being stuck inside a cage. Although Tammy hated seeing him sick and sore, she knew that this was the best place for him to be.

Back at home, Tammy and Katrina sat down and had a cup of tea. Tammy thanked Katrina for everything she'd done to help Muffin. Part of her blamed herself for not being there, when Muffin got so sick.

"I shouldn't have left him," Tammy said, her voice filled with sadness.

"It would not have changed the outcome, Tammy. You didn't do this to him. It just happened. And it would have happened whether you had been here or not. Besides, Aunty Katrina made sure he was okay, and he is. He will be fine," Katrina said, doing all she could to lighten the mood.

Tammy was lucky to have people in her life that cared so much. For too many years, she'd had to get by in life completely alone. Not anymore.

Two hours later, Tammy received a visit from her two favourite police officers. She smiled and welcomed them into her home, but they both looked grim.

"What is it?" she asked.

Detective Senior Sergeant Johns spoke first. He advised her that he'd found the link between Steve and Andrew – a single cash withdrawal from Steve's bank account, the amount of which was identical to a cash deposit amount into Andrew's bank account. Both were dated the same day. They also discovered that teaching had not been Andrew's only job. He had also been employed as a night time security guard with the same firm that employed Steve.

"When we questioned Steve," Senior Constable Anne said, "he told us that he did not mean for you to get hurt. When he'd realised that he had just confessed his part in the crime, in the presence of two police officers, he stopped talking. Not real bright, that one," she continued.

"Two things now worry us," said Detective Senior Sergeant Johns. "The first thing is that Andrew is *no longer* in custody. He was released, when a Judge decided there was no physical evidence, beyond a photo and some internet log... which could have been created by *anybody*." Tammy felt tears sting her eyes, but said nothing. "Do not worry too much about that, however," the detective continued. "We have *not* told him that the girl he had sexually assaulted doesn't actually have AIDS. I say we let *him* worry about that part of the equation for the next few years. Also, he has been permanently placed on the National Register of Sex Offenders, so he will never work with or near children or women again."

"We need to advise you that, after Steve was arrested, he told me directly, as he was thrown into his well-deserved cage, that if he ever sees you again, no matter where you are, who you are with or what you are doing, he will kill you," Senior Constable Anne said.

Tammy was shocked. Was Steve really *that* stupid? Had he really made a death threat against her, to a uniformed police officer?

"I am sorry, Tammy, but the only advice I can offer you *now*, is to vanish. You need to change your name and disappear, so that neither Steve nor *any* of his friends or associates can find you. You need to do this urgently. It is the only thing, at this stage, that will keep you safe. Do you understand?" Detective Senior Sergeant Johns asked.

Tammy nodded. She had finally reached the end of her lifelines. The detective asked her to only contact himself, or his partner, if ever she needed assistance, regardless of where she moved to. Tammy was not to contact anybody else regarding her name or whereabouts. Detective Senior Sergeant Johns also advised that he would provide an official letter to her, on Queensland Police letterhead, which Tammy would need to present to any company that might demand she use her real name.

She thanked both officers for all the help they'd given her, over those past few months and assured them that she fully understood how serious and urgent the situation was. Tammy notified her mum, dad, sister and close personal friends (Johan, Maria and Katrina) that she had to move *immediately*. Although they were confused, they'd learned to accept that Tammy had been in the habit of changing address regularly, since leaving Steve. She did not offer any of them details about why she had to move. All she would tell them is that it had to happen immediately.

With a house that was now fully-furnished, Tammy had no choice, this time, but to find a removals company with a large truck to come and pack up her things, moving them all in one hit. She managed to find a local company that would do it for $3,000 – a fee which included her furniture staying in the storage container, that was loaded onto the truck until she found a house – and she decided to go with that company. After all, she did not yet have an *actual address* where she was going. Tammy also rang Max, telling him she had to leave urgently, and that she would not be returning. Max pulled a few strings and was able to get every single cent owing to Tammy in superannuation entitlements, long service leave, unused holidays, and anything else he could find. This gave her a total of $25,000 to work with and she was eternally grateful for his help.

Tammy packed up a small amount of clothing, all of Muffin's food, his bowls, toys, toilet, kitty litter, and she drove to the vet. She then explained her situation, regarding the fact that she had to leave Brisbane *immediately*, due to an emergency, and that her leaving would involve a lot of driving. Tammy knew how much Muffin hated car trips, and asked the vet what she could do to keep Muffin calm for the 2,000+ kilometre journey ahead. The vet offered her a needleless syringe filled with water, some sedatives which would fully knock Muffin out for at least eight hours, and advised Tammy to make sure she put a few drops of water on his tongue each hour, to keep him hydrated. After the eight hours, Tammy would need to find a pet-friendly motel where they would camp for the night.

With the car fully packed, Muffin was then drugged up to the eyeballs and fell fast asleep inside his cat carrier, fully unaware of the big journey ahead of them both. Tammy was grateful that Muffin would not have to go through any stress during the trip. Before leaving Brisbane forever, Tammy drove to Katrina's house and gave Katrina and the four children each a big "pop hug" – something Tammy and the kids had invented. It was simply a hug that they pretended was so tight, they would explode, and the hug would end by one of them saying "POP!" Tammy would miss those pop hugs dearly.

Katrina, Bobby and the kids waved goodbye, as Tammy made her way to the Pacific Highway, ready to embark on one of the longest road trips that she would ever make.

Tammy's destination: Canberra.

Chapter 23

It took a little over eight hours of driving to reach the half-way point to Canberra. Muffin had just started to stir in his cage, and Tammy was exhausted from driving such a long distance – just over 1,200 kilometres so far. She pulled the car into a small motel at Taree and paid $60 for a twin share for the night. With Muffin's toilet, water and food set up in the bathroom, Tammy quickly fell asleep on one of the small beds at 9:00 that night. She set the alarm so that she would be woken at 6:00 the following morning. It was enough time to re-sedate her furry travelling companion and clean the room before handing in the key.

Tammy was travelling with $5,000 cash in her wallet, to cover all emergencies for both her and Muffin, along the journey. The rest was safe inside her Suncorp bank account in Queensland. As she did not yet have a place to stay, Tammy decided to speak with management at the Country Comfort Hotel in Tuggeranong, situated on the south side of Canberra. The manager was sympathetic to Tammy's reasons for being in Canberra, and agreed to let her hire a room for both her and Muffin for a couple days. Ever so grateful, Tammy quietly carried a still-fast-asleep black cat and their belongings to the suite. Although the cost was $160 per night, Tammy figured that she would only be here for a few nights, before finding an available house for both her and Muffin to settle into.

Once inside the suite, Muffin snuggled up on the bed and continued sleeping. Tammy headed down to the restaurant to grab a quick bite to eat. Once nourished, she unpacked her things from the car, including her computer, so that she could keep in contact with her friends and family.

On Tammy's second day at the hotel, she noticed that her wallet was missing. She searched everywhere in the room, in the car, *under* the car, any place that the car had been parked… but it was of no use. Her cash, her cheque book and even her driver's licence and credit card were gone. *Fuck!* She frantically asked at the hotel's reception if a wallet had been handed in. With all that ready cash, a credit card and cheque book inside, Tammy knew that there would be a snow storm in hell, before somebody would hand something like *that* in. And she was right. Nobody handed in the wallet. Without it, Tammy could not access any money to eat or to pay her hotel bill and, at $160 per night, she was fast running out of ideas.

Tammy alerted the hotel manager of the situation. The manager pointed her in the direction of ACT Transport so that she could get a new driver's licence. After walking to the site, Tammy took a number and found an available seat. She waited for about ninety minutes before her number was called. Tammy explained that her wallet, with all of her cash, identification, driver's licence and credit card had been stolen. She was a new resident of Canberra and needed a replacement driver's licence.

"Ma'am, without suitable identification, we are unable to provide you with a driver's licence," the woman, behind the counter, advised.

Good Lord, are you stupid? Tammy asked to speak to the manager. When the manager came, Tammy repeated the fact that she'd just moved to Canberra, her wallet had just been stolen, she had checked into an expensive hotel and could not pay the bill because she no longer had access to her money, nor could she legally drive her car because her licence was in the wallet.

"As I am sure my colleague here would have *told* you already, unless you can present us with suitable identification, we cannot issue you with a driver's licence," the manager replied, looking down her nose at Tammy and answering in a snooty tone.

"*Right*. So *please*, Miss Einstein, tell me *exactly* how I can get identification when *all* of my identification and cash have been STOLEN?" Tammy asked, quickly losing all patience.

"You will have to go to the Registrar of Births, Deaths and Marriages in the city and apply for your birth certificate," the manager responded, displaying a total *yawn* of an attitude.

With a sunken heart, Tammy slowly made her way back to the hotel, and advised the hotel manager of the updated situation. The manager pulled out the local phone book and rang the Registrar of Births, Deaths and Marriages. He then passed the handset to Tammy, so that she could explain the situation to them. Once the phone answered, Tammy explained that she had just moved from Queensland to Canberra, that she was staying at a hotel in

Tuggeranong, that her wallet had been stolen, along with *all* of her cash and identification. She then advised that the ACT Transport Department refused to issue her with identification, unless she had a birth certificate to present to them, and asked how she would go about applying for a birth certificate.

"You can only apply for Canberra birth certificates in this office. If you want to apply for *interstate* birth certificates, you will need to present a photographic identification card with your application," the brain-dead zombie on the other end of the phone advised.

Oh come on! I haven't even been here two days, and already my fan is covered in all sorts of shit! Tammy could not apply for a driver's licence without a birth certificate. She could also not apply for a birth certificate without a photographic identification card such as a driver's licence. She was well and truly stuck and, being unable to access the remaining $20,000 in her bank account, she was also rather screwed. Back inside her hotel suite, she hooked up the computer, all the while, wanting to scream bloody murder at the seemingly *stupid* people behind the desks of Canberra government offices.

Tammy contacted Janine, online, and told her what was going on. She was absolutely furious that nobody in Canberra seemed to be interested in helping her with something so serious. After explaining the dilemma of the driver's licence and birth certificate, Tammy's mum offered to apply in *Queensland* to get Tammy's birth certificate, but it would take up to ten days for the application to be processed. Tammy did the maths in her head, and almost fainted after calculating what the cost of the hotel bill would be, after that time. She thanked Janine for the kind offer, but said she would have to find another way.

After telling her Canberra friends of her messy situation, then hearing one after the other tell her, "Sorry, we can't help you," Tammy knew that it really was up to her, and *only* her, to try and sort this mess out. She also quickly discovered who her real friends were. Tammy cursed at the lowlife who'd stolen her wallet. This was the last thing in the world she needed. After pulling up her big-girl panties, Tammy marched back to the ACT Transport Department and waited. She had worked in the government for long enough to know that *nobody* likes a scene, whether it be customer or staff member, and if a scene was the only way that she could fix this, she was ready to bring it on.

Tammy took another number from the ticket machine and waited. This time, she did not have to wait long to be called. When she was called to the window, the officer who had *previously* served her huffed out her chest and approached the staff member who was now serving Tammy. She started to advise that *"this woman"* (indicating towards Tammy) had been in previously and was *clearly* told that ACT Transport could *not* help her. Tammy suddenly got loud. *REALLY* loud.

"Yes, I am sure *EVERYBODY* remembers how absolutely useless you were, when I was in here earlier, but since you failed to solve my problem, without even the slightest bit of empathy, and since I have nothing better to do than *keep* coming back, *DAY AFTER DAY*, after my wallet was stolen, here I am! I am *back*. EITHER *SOMEBODY* HERE CAN HELP ME OR THIS OFFICE

WILL BE MY BED FOR THE NIGHT. MY WALLET WAS STOLEN WITH ALL OF MY MONEY AND IDENTIFICATION AND YOU CAN'T EVEN BE BOTHERED TO *TRY* AND HELP ME? Do you even *HAVE* a brain between those ears? Is there a heart ANYWHERE inside your body? *HELP* ME, DAMN YOU, INSTEAD OF STICKING YOUR NOSE UP AT ME LIKE YOU HAVE A TEN FOOT *POLE* UP YOUR ASSHOLE!" Tammy then took a breath. That was it. Her scene was finished. Now all eyes were on the customer service staff, waiting to see what they would do. It was no surprise when the Australian Federal Police came into the ACT Transport office and asked Tammy to accompany them. *Unbelievable! It just seems to get better and better, doesn't it?*

Having dealt with Queensland's police in Logan City for so many years, she prepared herself for the bullshit, lies and abuse to be thrown in her direction as soon as she was seated. The AFP officer asked her to wait in one of the interrogation rooms, before he disappeared for about thirty minutes. *I saw a scene like this once in Law & Order. Shit. Not good.* Tammy hoped she didn't need to use the bathroom any time soon.

The AFP officer finally returned with several documents in his hand. Tammy felt her eyes stinging. She did not even have money to pay her own bail right now, and was terrified of what the charges were, listed on those papers. *I hope they don't put me in a cell with Big Bertha.* The AFP officer sat down.

"Your name is Tammy. Is that correct?" the AFP officer asked, politely.

"Yes, Sir," Tammy responded.

"Okay, Tammy. Here is what we are going to do," the AFP officer looked her in the eyes. "You moved down here to be with your fiancé. Your fiancé has vouched that you are who you say you are, so you no longer need a birth certificate to pr...."

Her eyes widened in shock. "WHAT THE *FUCK*!! HE IS THE *REASON* I AM IN CANBERRA! *DAMMIT*!!!" Tammy interrupted, panic coursing through her veins. How the hell did Steve know she was here already? Tammy burst into tears and found it suddenly hard to breathe. The police officer handed Tammy a glass of water and gave her a minute to calm down.

When Tammy was finally able to breathe again, the AFP officer said firmly, "Stop talking and *listen* to what I am telling you! I am not *asking* you. I am *telling* you."

Tammy looked at the AFP officer, silently, as another tear slipped down her cheek.

"I made a *lot* of telephone calls to help you. Do you understand me? I have spoken to Queensland Police, to your former employer in Queensland and to a lot of people, down here in Canberra. I am trying to help you out of this unfortunate situation that you have found yourself in, so please, just listen," the AFP officer said, gently.

"Tomorrow, you will go to the ACT Transport Department with this piece of paper. It shows that you are down here with your fiancé and that your fiancé is a resident of Canberra. With this document, you do not need any other proof of who you are. They will take your photo and hand you a new driver's licence. From there, you can use your photographic identification to open a bank account here in Canberra, have your Queensland funds transferred to your new bank account, have your credit card cancelled, and you can pay your hotel bill."

Tammy stared at the AFP officer, totally gobsmacked. Her jaw dropped and she was speechless. Taking another sip of water, her eyes were wide, as a semi-smile started to form on her lips.

"Wait. You did all this to *help* me?" Tammy asked, astonished that any police officer would go to such lengths to help her, when they had never even met her before.

The AFP officer nodded and smiled. He showed Tammy the paper he was able to come up with, so the ACT Transport people would believe her.

"By the way, Tammy, my name is Sergeant Anthony, and it has been a pleasure *helping* you today," the AFP officer said, at the end of their discussion. Tammy's jaw dropped again and she had the sudden urge to stand up and hug him tight.

"Sergeant Anthony," Tammy whispered, "...the Australian Federal Police are *nothing* like the police where I am from – nothing like them at all. You have no idea how *grateful* I am right now to you. *Thank you!*" she smiled, as a whole new set of tears threatened to show themselves. All of her fears were now gone. Tammy was suddenly glad that she had chosen Canberra as her new home.

The next morning at opening time, Tammy was already at the door of the ACT Transport office. The three staff members from the previous day *all* moved away from the counter, when they saw her. Obviously they did not want any more trouble. Tammy's number was the first one called, and a male staff member assisted her. She handed over the paper she'd received from Sergeant Anthony, the day before, simply stating that she needed a new driver's licence. The staff member looked at the document, smiled and nodded.

"This way, Tammy," he said. Sitting in front of the driver's licence camera, Tammy suddenly wished she did not look like a wind-swept motorcycle chick who had not bathed in a week, thanks to the dust storm she'd walked through, that morning. *Oh well, the licence expires in five years. Then I can get a new one.* Well, at least Tammy *hoped* it only lasted for five years. When her name was called, ten minutes later, she checked the expiry date and let out a sigh of relief.

After walking back to the hotel and spending some cuddle time with Muffin, Tammy checked the phone book to see where the closest St George Bank would be. Although she loathed the football team, the colours of the bank almost matched the colours of the Australian Aboriginal flag, and she liked that. When she found out it was just across the road from the ACT Transport office, right in the heart of the Tuggeranong Hyperdome, however, she said a few words under her breath. *Would have been great to know this before I walked all the way back to the hotel!* With so many things to do, Tammy decided to take the car for a drive, and see what else she could get done at the Tuggeranong Hyperdome.

Not only was Tammy able to open her new bank account and send a request to Suncorp Bank, in Queensland, to close off her credit card and transfer her funds to Canberra, she was also able to apply for a new Medicare Card. Suncorp wired $1,000 into Tammy's new St George Bank account almost immediately so she had money for food and her hotel bill. She then set off to find a real estate agency that could offer both her *and Muffin* a new home. The first real estate agency she'd walked into had advised her of a two-bedroom home in Calwell – a suburb situated at the far south of Canberra. There was not only a bus stop 20 metres from the house but also Calwell Shopping Centre would be less than 100 metres from her front door.

"Do they accept pets? I have one cat who is 101% housebroken," Tammy asked.

"They accept both cats and dogs, since the property has a high fence. There is also car accommodation at the house, and storage. Rent is $150 per week," the realtor replied.

Before returning to the hotel, Tammy filled out an application and it was immediately approved. She was now *officially* a Canberra resident, in every sense of the word. She showed the letter from the Queensland Police to the realtor, regarding her name on the lease. The house was now leased to... Lizzie Birdsworth.

Tammy contacted the removals company the following day, and arranged for all of her furniture to be delivered within the week. She also arranged to have telephone, internet, electricity and gas all connected to the house. The only shock Tammy received, when she first saw the house, was that the grass was almost as tall as her armpits. With Muffin indoors, adjusting to the smell of his new home, Tammy walked down to Calwell Shopping Centre and flicked through the pages of the telephone book to find somebody who would cut her grass. When she saw the good rates of a place called *Jim's Mowing*, she rang the number immediately. Her grass was cut the very next day and the bill was slipped into her letter box when the job was done, so as not to disturb her.

For Tammy, it seemed that ever since that *one* person decided to be kind to her – a *police officer* of all people – her life in Canberra was already starting to run smoothly. Well... *Lizzie Birdsworth's* life was running perfectly so far, anyway.

With the money, which had finally come through from Queensland, Tammy was able to pay for one year's rent in advance. This gave her some leeway to find a job, in the new city which she now called home. Having the shopping centre so close to her home was convenient, in every single way. Tammy didn't just buy her *groceries* without using her car, but she was also able to walk to the news agency each day and buy a newspaper. She spent every day, going through the jobs available in Canberra, that she might be qualified to do. *I can't believe how many job vacancies there are in such a small city!* Unfortunately, most of the jobs listed were managerial positions in government and she was most definitely *not* qualified for any of those. The pay was great, but when she had left the Queensland government, Tammy had been a level 4 state government employee, not an executive-level Director.

After two weeks of looking, one advertisement finally caught her eye. A vacancy for a Paralegal was listed in a private, local law firm Tammy had never heard of. After quickly searching through her wardrobe, to see if she could pass for a high end professional, she tore the advertisement out of the paper and rang the number. When asked if she had any experience in law, Tammy advised that she had worked for ten years in the legal field within the Queensland government. The person on the other end of the phone asked that she attend an interview, the following day, at 10:00 in the morning, and was told to bring with her any certifications, references and an updated CV. After hanging up the phone, Tammy did something that she had not done in many years... her happy dance (which lasted for all of five seconds).

Oh shit! I haven't updated my CV in forever! Immediately, she sat her butt down on the computer chair and started typing. Although her work experience within the Queensland government was minimal – Prisoner Processing Officer, Court Recorder, Prosecutions Officer – Tammy knew that this would at least show that she wasn't a job-hopper (somebody who was looking for a new job every single month due to boredom or getting fired). She was a stable employee with ample experience, she was nervous as hell.

On arrival at the legal office in Deakin, Tammy lost count of the amount of other women in the reception area, each awaiting an interview. *Shit. They are younger, prettier and probably a hell of a lot smarter than I am... "You're useless!"* Steve's voice suddenly interrupted her thoughts. Maybe this interview was a stupid idea? *One of them will get it over me anyway....*

"Tammy?" She looked up when her name was called.

"Yes, that's me," Tammy replied, forcing her best smile.

"Please come through to the office," the woman requested.

Tammy followed and her confidence was all but gone, when she saw how fancy the office was. Apart from the one-week stint in real estate, Tammy had never before applied for, or worked in, a job in the private sector. The manager who sat before her was dressed to kill.

"You can relax. There are only seventeen more people to interview after you. I only hope you show more promise than the previous twelve that I have seen this morning," the manager said.

GULP!

Tammy nervously handed over her newly typed CV, presented meticulously in her folder with her awards, courses, references and any other documents that she could think of. The manager read the first page with interest, but then raised an eyebrow when she turned to the second page.

Oh fuck! I bet there is a typing error or something dumb there. Dammit!

The manager looked up at Tammy and asked, "Do you really enjoy archery and pistol shooting?"

"Yes. I was the top archer at school and liked using my father's hunting arrows. I also prefer shooting pistols to shooting rifles. Once a rifle has backfired in your ear, it is no longer your friend," Tammy said, seriously. "I *never* hunt animals, though. Just targets at the range or on the farm."

"I see. And you like martial arts, too?" the manager asked, not looking up from Tammy's CV, but once again smiling.

"Judo, Karate and Kung Fu, yes, but I don't practise anymore," Tammy replied.

After reading through the rest of the pages, noting the awards she had received, as well as voluntary work which she had performed, the manager advised that she was more than impressed with all of the legal experience Tammy had. She was *equally* impressed at the passion she saw, when Tammy talked about her sporting hobbies. The office manager handed Tammy's CV to her assistant and asked her to take a full copy of every page. *Seriously?* Although not wanting to get her hopes too high, Tammy thought that sounded at least a *little bit* promising.

"Thanks for coming in. We'll let you know," said the manager, as she stood. Tammy also stood, shook her hand and then waited in the reception area to have her CV folder returned. The next applicant was then called into the manager's office, and a sudden sinking feeling filled Tammy's heart.

One hour after Tammy arrived home, she received a telephone call. When she answered the phone and listened to what was said, she started shaking. Tammy was now a Paralegal in the private sector, working for a woman who scared the living crap out of her. Her fortune was running high.

Chapter 24

After her first year, living in Canberra, Tammy was easily able to pay another year's rent in advance with her impressive salary. She *loved* coming home to Muffin, and always discussed her day with him. Although Tammy had signed a confidentiality agreement on her very first day as a Paralegal, she was fairly confident that Muffin would not share any of the secrets she'd divulged to him. Between work and her affection for her cat at home, Tammy's heart felt almost full again. She had a purpose in life – something she felt that she'd lost in Brisbane – and her smiles were more abundant.

Two years after she landed the job, Tammy returned home smiling, looking forward to sharing her day with her cat once more. What greeted her was a sight that drove a hot knife right through her heart. One of her front windows was broken. She looked around to the left of the house at the side gate. The gate's lock had been smashed also. The screen to her sliding door had been sliced with a knife and the sliding glass door was smashed. She had been robbed!

She saw that the computer, television and VCR were gone, but Tammy did not give a flying fuck about *any* of those things. Only one thing mattered.

"MUFFIN!" Tammy called. "Muffin? Baby, where are you?" Tammy called his name and looked in every possible place she could think of, worried that her little, black furry man was hurt. Unable to find him, Tammy rang the AFP. Before she hung up the phone, an AFP officer was knocking on her front door. *Bloody hell that was fast!* Tammy opened the door, tears in her eyes, and stated the obvious.

"I have been robbed and my cat is gone!" It was not until Tammy said out loud that Muffin was gone, that she really felt it. She broke down and wept. The pain she felt in her heart was excruciating.

"Ma'am, I live two doors down from this house. It seems that almost everybody's house in the street had been broken into. Luckily for me, it was my day off and I was at home when he broke into my house," the AFP officer said. "The culprit is on his way to the hospital right now. Please provide a list of any items that were taken and any damage that was done. We will take care of it."

"He took my cat," Tammy sobbed.

"We will do all that we can to help find your cat. But right now, we have a van, full of stolen items, which we would like to return to their rightful owners. Please can you look through your house and list, for me, what's missing?" the AFP officer said, gently.

Tammy walked through the house slowly, paying attention to all that should be there but was now gone. She listed, out loud, everything that was missing, as the AFP officer wrote it all down – her computer, scanner, printer, television, video recorder, jewellery... and Muffin. She was able to give the officer a description of each missing item, as well as their make and model. Within half an hour, all of the items stolen were back in her possession. But the one thing that mattered the *most* was still gone. That afternoon, as the AFP officer was leaving, Tammy had her first nervous breakdown.

Unable to remember the next few days, Tammy was brought home in an ambulance. A whole pharmacy worth of medication was put onto the counter of the kitchen – anti-depressants, sedatives, anti-anxiety medication. The hospital had diagnosed her as severely depressed, but deemed her not a suicide risk. Tammy sat, silently, on the lounge chair, and stared at the broken door and screen. She knew that any number of people could have come into her home while she was away, but when she glanced in the direction of the television, she was certain that nobody else had robbed her.

"Muffin?" Tammy called. She curled up on the couch and cried herself to sleep.

Tammy slept through the night. When she woke, she started crying again. It wasn't just the pain of losing her cat, and she knew it. It was the pain of losing A.J. combined with the pain of losing Muffin. That pain had built up, and came crashing down around her. She took the medication on the counter, exactly as prescribed, and started to feel a little more human, after a few hours passed. Once the tears finally stopped, Tammy dialled the real estate regarding the break-in, and advised that she had a police report available for them, for insurance purposes. With their permission, she next contacted O'Brien Glass Repairs and had the window and door replaced with new glass. The real estate advised that somebody would be there within a week to replace the locks and the screen.

The next phone call was to her employer. Once again in tears, she explained what had happened, that her locks were broken and would *remain* broken for possibly the next week. Tammy advised that she had a medical certificate from the hospital, covering her for a full month. Her boss was very understanding and said not to worry; that one of the other Paralegals would fill in for her while she was away. Tammy knew that she was lucky to have a good employer.

Not giving up on Muffin, she went to the side of the house each morning and each afternoon for the next three days, loudly tapping a tin of cat food with a spoon while calling his name. She did not care if it pissed off her neighbours. Only one thing mattered to her right now. She needed Muffin to come home. Her soul felt empty and beaten, like somebody had taken a sledge hammer to it, smashing it until nothing was left. Tammy was tired of crying and feeling numb all over.

Four days after she returned home from the hospital, Tammy dragged herself out of bed, did not bother with breakfast, and once again tapped on a tin at the side of the house for Muffin. Again, her calls were met with silence. Tammy went inside, lay on the couch and stared at the ceiling. Once again, the feeling of numb was starting to consume her and she closed her eyes. Suddenly she heard a noise. With her eyes now wide open, she listened intently. Somebody was trying to come through the side gate! *Right, you bastard. Come inside and make my fucking day!* Tammy jumped up and grabbed a large, sharp knife from the kitchen. She went to the sliding glass door and opened it, as fast as she could. What she saw, *completely* blew her mind. Right before her unbelieving eyes, pushing on the side gate, trying hard to get inside, was *Muffin*!

"OH MY GOD, *MUFFIN, MY LITTLE FURRY MAN!*" Tammy cried.

She pried the gate open slowly as a very raggedy and skinny, black Muffin *limped* over to Tammy. She scooped him up in her arms and took him inside. Muffin had been gone for a full two weeks, and Tammy had no idea if he had eaten *at all* in that time. She pulled out a tin of his cat food and tapped twice on the top, as she would always do at feeding time. Muffin let out a bellowing MIAOW! Tammy interpreted this as "Feed me *now*, woman!" She put the food into his bowl and put the bowl on the floor. He finished it off in no time at all and also had a good drink of water right after. Tammy watched Muffin eat and drink, and could not take her eyes off him. She also could not stop smiling.

Next thing to do was to find a vet who was nearby. There was a large Veterinary Centre not far from her home. She packed Muffin into his cat carrier – this time without any kitty complaints – and she took him straight to the vet. They checked him over thoroughly, x-rayed him, and determined that his leg was not broken. He was, however, very dehydrated and malnourished. They gave Tammy some special food to give him, for the next week, so that his stomach would slowly get used to food again, but this food had ten times the amount of vitamins and nutrients that a *standard* cat food would give. Tammy took all this information in, and paid for

Muffin's special food and vet bill, before they both returned home. As soon as Muffin was safely tucked away in Tammy's bedroom with his food, water and toilet, Tammy nailed a few pieces of wood across the inside of her side gate. If somebody wanted to enter her back yard, in future, they would need to grow wings and fly.

With the screens and locks replaced two days later, Tammy was able to leave the house, knowing that both it *and Muffin* were fully secured, while she was away. Although she could now return to work, she decided to take that final week, in order to keep a close eye on her cat. Tammy was unable to play with Muffin while he was healing, but they *were* able to sit on the couch and watch some television together. She went through the TV guide and found as many programs that she possibly could, which had mice, birds, or any other small animals in them. Each time something small ran or flew across the television screen, Muffin's ears pricked up as he watched.

At the end of one of Muffin's animal programs, a television show came on about religion. Tammy rolled her eyes and was about to shut the television off, but then she saw pictures of Egyptian Gods come onto the screen. Always drawn to anything regarding ancient Egypt, Tammy left the television on and sat down. The show was about Paganism. Gods and Goddesses of the Earth were discussed, as well as the reverence of the cat in ancient Egypt. She looked down and scratched Muffin on his head, right between his ears. He purred loudly.

"Of *course* you were worshipped. You still *are*," Tammy said to Muffin, with a smile.

The following day, Tammy walked down to Calwell Shopping Centre and found a book store. She searched the shelves until she found what she was looking for. There was a whole section in the store dedicated to religions. One book – Egyptian Paganism – found its way into her hand. Tammy purchased it and took it home, determined to read each and every page. By the time she had finished the book, two new television shows had been born – *Buffy the Vampire Slayer* and *Charmed*. Both were television shows that looked nothing like any show she'd ever watched. Tammy decided not to watch the Buffy show. Anything horror was definitely not what she was interested in. But after watching *Charmed* for a few episodes, she started to look into the world of Wicca.

Tammy returned to the book store, and bought some books by Cate Tiernan. The books were simply called "WICCA" and were a series of novels – fifteen in total – about a religion that Tammy was falling more and more in love with. She was now determined to learn anything and everything about this Pagan religion of Wicca.

Back at work, things returned to normal. Although the pains in her back were getting worse, since the elevator accident, she was able to manage it by taking regular breaks. She would finish a letter, stand, walk around the office stretching and touching her toes and then return to her chair to belt out some more correspondence. The Barristers that came to the office on a regular basis were curious, and asked questions about Tammy's elevator accident. It had been several years since it happened, but Tammy did not want to be disrespectful to them, so she answered their questions. One of the Barristers asked if Tammy wanted to take action against her former employer for negligence. *But Max was so nice to me. I could never do that to him!* At first, Tammy made it clear that suing Max would be like stabbing him in the back. It was then explained to her that she would not be suing *Max*. She would be suing the *Queensland Government* for placing their employees in known danger, owing to the fact that Max had openly told her it had happened before, and the government not fixing the problem, due to lack of funds.

"There were no lack of funds. There was just a simple a lack of priorities. If the elevator had malfunctioned and put lives in danger in the *Prime Minister's* office, I can guarantee that it would have been fixed *immediately*, regardless of the cost!" one Barrister said.

Tammy could see their way of thinking, but she also knew how much money they charged for each case. She told them that she could not afford their services – not in this lifetime or the next. One of the Barristers said that he would work with one of the lawyers at the firm and was prepared to do it for her, pro bono. *You would do this for free? Canberra sure is a crazy place!* With that, Tammy agreed to go ahead and sue. Her only reason for doing so, however, was so that nobody else had to have their lives destroyed, with the pain and the claustrophobia that followed her everywhere, after such a horrific experience. Surprisingly, the lawsuit was quick and clean-cut. No problems. No hassles. Within a month, her bank balance was $75,000 fatter. That very same month, the elevator in Mineral House was finally repaired, as the Queensland Government did not want another lawsuit landing in their laps.

The money came just at the right time, because Tammy's streak of good luck in Canberra was about to quickly take a nosedive. At the end of the week, Tammy returned home to find the usual bills, including one from her real estate. She knew that her rent was up-to-date and was not worried about that. Hopefully it was not a bill for the repairs, after the break-in, as the insurer of the house was supposed to take care of those. She pulled out a letter opener, quickly opening the letter from the real estate, first. Tammy began reading, out of curiosity, but was frowning and angry, by the time she reached the end. The owners of the house had decided to put the home on the market. It seemed that they had balked at the fact that their home was damaged, due to crime, and wanted to unload the property onto somebody else. The asking price was $850,000. *Whoa! Pretty steep!* The realtor assured Tammy, however, that if the house *did* sell quickly, the new owner would, more than likely, continue the lease, and nothing would change.

The following Monday afternoon at work, a staff meeting was called. Attendance for all was compulsory. While sitting on a desk in the meeting area, Tammy anxiously awaited the news which had resulted in a staff meeting. Usually it would signify that the owners of the law firm (both based in Queensland) were coming to Canberra, and would be taking everybody out to a very ritzy restaurant. The manager would then openly *mock* the owners of the law firm – one owner who had once been a big name football star and the other owner who had coaxed a nun into trading her habit for a wedding gown. The manager also knew that nobody would dare repeat those words outside of the meeting.

The meeting was brief. The owners of the law firm had been disbarred and were now forbidden to practice law in the ACT. Since all of the clients of the firm were residents of Canberra, the owners had no choice but to close the firm down. The manager told the staff not to worry, however, as both she and her husband had made an offer to the owners, to buy out all client files and start up their own firm. Tammy breathed a sigh of relief, until she heard the punch line.

"We have bought the penthouse offices of a thirty storey building in the city, and you are all welcome to come with us when we move at the end of the month," the manager said.

With that, Tammy handed in her resignation.

Sitting at home, Tammy found herself, once again, looking for a job in the newspaper each day. She was interrupted by a knock at the front door. The postie had a parcel for her, as well as the regular mail. The parcel was a gift from her dad – a little stuffed wolf with a button on the front. When you pressed the button, the wolf let out a huge wolf whistle. Tammy found herself laughing at the corny gift and rang Ralph to thank him. He told her that, when he saw it in the store, he couldn't help but think of his beautiful daughter in Canberra.

"I love you, Dad. I miss you so much," Tammy said, with a smile.

"I love you too, kiddo. We might have to come and visit you soon, I think!" he said.

"I would *love* that! But just hold off for a tiny while, okay? I might have to move shortly so I will let you know when everything has settled a bit. I miss you," Tammy said, again, excited that her dad was thinking about visiting her. She loved that, even from such a big distance, he still thought about her. *If only you lived closer.*

After hanging up the phone, she looked at the envelopes that had been delivered with the parcel. One was from the real estate. She did not expect to hear from them again so soon. Tammy quickly opened the letter, advising that the house had been sold and that the new owner wanted to live in the property. She was given just fourteen days, from the date of the letter, in which to move out.

The next morning, she drove to the real estate office and asked if there were any available rental properties. She showed them the letter from her real estate's sales department, giving her two weeks to vacate. Unfortunately there were no properties available for under $1,000 per week.

Tammy's daily job search now included rental properties, as well as jobs. Unfortunately, her job search came up blank. There were no other legal firms in Canberra which were situated on the ground floor, so Tammy registered her name with some temping agencies – something she had done once before in Queensland. Hopefully she would find something soon. As for her rental property search, she had found several affordable houses available but, since she no longer had a steady job, each application that she put forward was rejected. At the end of the two weeks, she found herself homeless. All of her furniture was put into storage at $100 per week and she lived for three weeks in her car.

She had applied for unemployment benefits, so that she could list a steady income on rental property applications, but since she had $75,000 in savings, her application for unemployment benefit was rejected. *Ahhh, another Catch-22. Canberra seems to be famous for this sort of bullshit.* It brought back all of Tammy's not-so-fond memories of when her wallet was stolen. She decided to contact the Aboriginal Legal Service for advice. After going through her whole situation with one of the officers there, she was put in contact with ACT Housing. Since she was already homeless and only needed a small home, her name shot directly to the top of the priority list and Tammy was shown to a property in Kambah. Situated at the end of a cul-de-sac, it was perfect. Two bedrooms, large living room, decent sized laundry... and so many cobwebs! The property had obviously been empty for a long time. Rent was month-by-month, but she liked to think that her days of having to move to a new address each month were a thing of the past.

Tammy (a.k.a. Lizzie Birdsworth) now had a *new* fake name: Kayla Brady. Just as Lizzie Birdsworth had been her favourite character on the show *Prisoner*, Kayla Brady was her favourite character on another show she had loved for as long as she could remember: *Days of Our Lives*. She arranged for her furniture to be brought out of storage, but she first wanted to get rid of all of the spider webs, clinging to every wall and ceiling. After a two-day cleaning spree, her furniture was delivered, and Muffin was much happier in his new home.

Chapter 25

Three months had passed, and no temporary job assignments had come her way. Tammy even rang the agencies which she had registered with on a weekly basis, hoping that maybe something was there and that they'd just forgotten to call. Each time, she was told that there were simply no vacancies right now. It had started to become quite boring. There were only so many times a person could clean and re-clean such a tiny home.

One afternoon, while watching television, Tammy and Muffin were sitting down in the living room. *Harry's Practice* – a television show that followed the legendary Dr Harry Cooper (veterinarian) around the country – was on the screen, and Tammy decided to do something she'd not thought of before. She contacted the RSPCA in Canberra, and volunteered her time, cleaning out cat cages and giving "cuddle time" to a lot of the cats that were awaiting new homes. She then found herself volunteering with reception duties, due to her fast typing speed of 170 words per minute. After a while, the opportunity to become a Veterinary Assistant presented itself. Although it would not be cheap, it would definitely be worthwhile. Tammy was astonished, when news came back that her application had been accepted.

All theory was online and via correspondence, while all practical study was on the job, at a local animal shelter. Tammy's first time in the operating theatre was nerve-wracking. A poodle was being desexed. To Honey (the vet), it was a routine operation. To Tammy, watching a dog on his back while his *boys* were being removed was gut-wrenching. *Sorry, little buddy. I hope you do not feel too emasculated when it's over.* Her heart went out to the poodle. Suddenly, its heartbeat stopped. *Holy shit!* Honey asked Tammy to take a step back, while she performed CPR on the dog. Tammy's jaw dropped. She'd never seen this side of veterinary medicine before! Honey did chest compressions and mouth-to-nose resuscitation, as Tammy looked on. Within a few minutes, the poodle's heartbeat was back and the dog was breathing normally again. Honey was now dripping with sweat from head to toe. *That was seriously amazing!* When Tammy looked up at Honey, she no longer saw a vet. She saw a hero.

It took three years to work her way through the course. The exams were hard, and on-the-job training was tough. But the rewards were immeasurable. Tammy knew that at the end of the course, she would be a better human mum to her fur-ball, Muffin. Towards the end of the course, an emergency patient was brought in to the surgery. A German-shepherd was on a stretcher, unconscious. An axe was embedded in its skull. Tammy screamed, cursing the monster who would do such a thing. Her thoughts flooded back to Steve's dad, and the dog which had died in his drunken care. *He can't hurt me anymore.* While the emergency vets got busy trying to save the dog which had just been brought in, Tammy reported

Steve's dad to the RSPCA. She then observed the axe, being removed from the dog's head. Incredibly, the dog survived, but he'd lost an eye. It took many months of rehabilitation for the dog – a dog, which the staff had aptly named "*Lucky.*"

Finally, graduation day had arrived. She was no longer interested in working in legal arenas. Her focus was 100% on animal medicine. Now working full-time in the veterinary office with Honey, Tammy was asked to input some files into the computer. It was Friday afternoon and five new arrivals were placed in the patient cages, right next to her computer. Her heart melted when she saw them – five tiny kittens which were scheduled, the following Monday, for desexing. With all medical records successfully input into the computer, Tammy reached into the cage and picked up one kitten at a time, scratching each one on the top of its tiny head. When all five were back inside the cage, she smiled and looked at their little faces.

"Don't you worry. I won't let anything bad happen to you. It is just a tiny little operation, and you won't feel a thing," Tammy said, before closing up shop, and leaving the building to go home.

The following day, Tammy had cleaned the house, and at 1:00 in the afternoon, she sat down on the couch with Muffin and turned on the television. They had been watching television for about an hour when Tammy noticed something very strange in the sky, through the window by the sofa. It had gone from being a perfect cloudless blue to a bright orange. *Pretty!* Tammy fetched her camera from the bedroom and started to take photographs of the amazing sky colour. She would go outside at fifteen minute intervals to take a snapshot, as the orange grew deeper and deeper. After an hour, the sky was no longer orange... it was black. *How the hell is the sky black at 2:30 in the afternoon?* Weird flakes fell from the sky. *What the fuck?* Next came the power blackout. *Everything shut off.*

When Tammy looked into her back yard, she was horrified. One of her trees had caught fire. Her neighbour's house was smoking, but she knew nobody was home. Without a second thought, she ran into the bathroom, Muffin in her arms, and locked him in there with the door closed. She'd put the plug into the bath tub and turned on the water... which also came out black. *OH GOD, NO!!* Before the power had gone out, not a single mention of what was happening had appeared on the television. She laid out all of the soaker hoses in her front yard, across her front porch, and by the outside walls of her house. Digging out an old transistor radio, she put new batteries in and tuned in.

"...and unfortunately it is now too late to evacuate. The firestorm has, so far, destroyed over 300 homes in the southern Canberra region, with Holder, Dunlop and Kambah being the hardest hit. Two people so far have been confirmed dead..."

Her eyes wide and filled with tears, Tammy was in shock. How could they not have alerted the people of Canberra about this? She looked out the front door and Mount Taylor – a mountain just one kilometre away – had a tiny red dot on it. She picked up the phone to call the fire department, but was placed on hold for over ten minutes. By the time they answered, the entire mountain was engulfed in flames. She hung up without speaking, when she noticed two of the trees in her front yard were on fire. Tammy ran outside and grabbed a hose, doing all she could to ensure that her house did not end up being a pile of ashes. With the flames extinguished, she made two more phone calls to make – one to her dad and one to her mum – telling each of them that she loved them. Then the phone line went dead.

All of her neighbours were now standing in the street, at the front of their homes, hosing down *anything* that caught fire. The weird flakes that had arrived earlier – flakes which turned out to be live ashes from a *firestorm* – continued to rain down, as tornadoes of fire twisted throughout the city, devouring everything they touched. Tammy turned the radio back on, turning the volume up to its loudest point, so that she could hear it, while fighting the flames.

"…the body count is now at four. Five hundred houses have so far been lost. All of the former water restrictions have been lifted in Canberra. Save your houses, if you can. Save yourselves…"

Tammy again shut off the radio. She needed to conserve the battery as much as possible. Nobody spoke, as each person focussed on keeping the flames at bay. A thundering roar broke the silence. What sounded like a large jumbo jet, landing at the end of their street, was actually a giant wall of flames... heading right for them. Tammy ran back inside the house and filled up Muffin's cat food container until it was overflowing. She also poured all of her cold drinking water from the fridge into three containers and put them on the floor for her cat. Even if she did not live through this, she wanted to make sure Muffin, at least, had a chance, before rescuers could get to him. On the way back outside, she ripped all of the curtains away from the windows, knowing that it would not take much for them to catch alight.

With temperatures *well* over 45 degrees celsius that night, sleeping had definitely *not* been on the cards. The flames were finally under control, the following afternoon. When the shops finally opened, there was a large line of people waiting outside. As tired as she was, Tammy raced into the store, as soon as the doors opened, and was able to grab a ten litre bottle of drinking water and some batteries. By the time she got to the checkout, the shelves containing water and batteries were now bare. She was grateful for the emergency back-up system that powered the air conditioning in the store. It was blissfully cool, and part of her did not want to leave.

Back at home, she listened to the radio, once again. Seven fire engines had burned in the firestorm, and Kambah Fire Station had burned to the ground. Now that the phone lines were dead, Tammy was unable to contact her family, so they'd know she was okay. *I am sure there is a guardian angel watching over me, somewhere. I just survived a firestorm!* A grateful tear slid down her face.

Tammy's backyard and fence were black. She lost three trees in the blaze and would have lost more, had she not laid the soaker hoses at the walls of her house. The front yard lost all trees except one, which grew right next to the house. She had another soaker hose to thank for that. The grass was dead, as were all of the plants in her garden. When she finally went back inside and opened the bathroom door, Muffin cautiously walked out into the living room and snuggled up beside Tammy. After inspecting all the damage, she thanked her lucky stars that Muffin was still with her.

When the power and phone line had been restored, three days later, Tammy had a whole lot of cleaning to do – hanging curtains, vacuuming, sweeping, as well as cleaning the soot away from all of the windows. When she was done, she turned on the television. The news about the Canberra firestorm seemed to be playing on every single channel. As scenes from the firestorm played out on the screen, Tammy started trembling. Every single picture on the news portrayed so much death and devastation. An aerial shot of the RSPCA was then shown.

"…while staff on duty and some volunteers at the RSPCA were able to release several of the horses, most of the dogs died in their kennels, due to smoke inhalation. Both the cattery and the veterinary building completely burned to the ground. All animals inside both buildings perished," the reporter said, as footage aired on the television.

Don't you worry. I won't let anything bad happen to you. It is just a tiny little operation and you will not feel a thing. Tammy's final words to those five kittens were now playing over and over inside her head.

"I let you die. I broke my promise. I'm so sorry," Tammy said, and curled up into a ball, before sobbing uncontrollably.

The next few months, Tammy's dreams were plagued with images of the kittens burning to death, screaming in the flames, praying that Tammy would come. But she didn't arrive. *I was too busy, selfishly saving myself.* She wondered if Muffin would have been okay, if she'd left him in the bathroom with food, water, soaker hoses wetting the walls of the house... if only she'd gone to Weston, she could have saved those poor, baby kittens. She'd broken her promise, and with that broken promise, every single bit of her confidence had left her once more. *I could have saved them but I didn't.* Tammy could no longer bring herself to work with animals. She was afraid that she would end up killing any animal that was put into her care, and eventually handed in her resignation.

When the RSPCA opened its new cattery one year later, Tammy was first in line to adopt two kittens. Muffin was extremely curious as to what was in the cat carrier, when she got home. He sat at the door of the cat carrier... and stared. He finally growled and walked away, almost as if telling the two new 'intruders' that *he* was the head of the household. Tammy watched with interest. It was her first time seeing Muffin interact with other animals, and she needed to make sure that he would not hurt them.

Being ever so vigilant, she finally opened the door of the cat carrier. Muffin let out another growl. He looked tough and stared at the two little fluff balls as they both came out of the cat carrier at the exact same time. One kitten walked straight up to Muffin and sniffed his face. Muffin hissed. The kitten then bopped Muffin's nose, playfully, with his tiny paw. Affronted, and taken completely off-guard, Muffin ran to the bedroom and hid.

"You both need names," Tammy said, gently. She looked at the orange kitten who had just swatted Muffin's nose. "You have a bit of attitude, just like the computer on the television show *Red Dwarf*.

I think you are a 'Holly.' And you," Tammy looked at Holly's tiny, grey litter-mate, "...you're just adorable. You are *definitely* a 'Bambi.'"

Both kittens started chasing each other around, while sniffing out their new home. Now and then, Tammy would hear a growl come from her bedroom. Muffin was sulking. She giggled, but sincerely hoped that the three of them would soon become good friends. Tammy was overjoyed when, within three months, Muffin and Bambi had become the very best of friends. Holly, however, was a "*Mummy's boy*" and always wanted to sleep on Tammy's lap.

Over the next few months, Tammy was able to do some temping jobs in both medical and legal, in different parts of Canberra. It felt good to be working again, even if the jobs weren't full-time or permanent. Tammy enjoyed the fact that she was at least being *useful*. The cost of maintaining *three* cats at home was considerably higher, and the money she'd received from the lawsuit was almost gone. She'd paid one year's rent in advance, had paid for her own studies to become a Veterinary Nurse, and had bought herself a brand new car.

Tammy had almost forgotten her dad's extremely persuasive negotiation skills. When her father had *finally* come to visit his daughter in Canberra, Ralph, Coral and Tammy visited several garage sales. Ralph scored a few great bargains, including a new dart board for his daughter. The hair-made dart board, brand new in its box, was just $25. Ralph asked to have a look at it.

The owner could not pull it out of the box and simply said to Tammy's dad, "It's brand new in the box, mate! Worth around $100 in the shops. *Seriously* a bargain!" He then went on to tell Ralph that it would not come out of the box because it was stuck.

"Stuck, *my bum*," Ralph said. He asked the owner to pass the dart board to him. While Ralph tried to free the dart board from its box, the whole box tore in two. Tammy's dad let the box fall to the ground. He then took a good, hard look at the dart board. "Not bad. I'll give you $5 for it," Tammy's dad offered. When the owner frowned and didn't answer, Ralph said, "What? It doesn't even come in a box!" Defeated, the owner agreed to the price and Ralph left the garage sale with a smile. He handed Tammy the dart board and said, "Happy Birthday, Tam." *Good grief, Dad!* Tammy thanked her father and smiled, the entire way home.

The following Monday, Ralph and Tammy drove to the Nissan dealership at Woden. Tammy's car definitely had one foot in the grave, and it was time for a new car. She had her heart set on a Nissan Pulsar. After having done much research, she loved the fact that the Nissan Pulsar N16 had won "Small Car of the Year" award for three years running. It also was roomy inside for passengers and the back seats folded down flat – an advantage, if you didn't like driving with a trailer behind your car, after an oversized purchase. Tammy was not interested in any other make or model.

When they arrived at the dealership, there was only one Nissan Pulsar in stock, and it was a showroom car. Listed at $24,000 – a price Tammy was unable to afford – Ralph told the salesman that his daughter wanted to take it for a test drive. With keys in hand, both Ralph and Tammy breathed in the new car smell as soon as they were seated. Tammy was nervous. The last time she'd driven a car with her dad as passenger, he'd been teaching her how to drive. She remembered it like it was yesterday…

She had been sixteen years old and was driving the 'bush basher' along the front of the farm's property line, when her father suddenly screamed out: "STOP! There's someone crossing the road!"

By the time Tammy had applied the brakes and the car had come to an eventual stop, her father looked out the back window, shaking his head, and said, "The poor bastard never stood a chance." Tammy was suddenly shaken up that she'd just killed an imaginary pedestrian.

Back to the present, Ralph told her to stop panicking and just drive. As far as Ralph was concerned, Tammy was a bloody good driver *because* of his teachings. Tammy finally started the car and they were off. Her dad commented several times that the car drove smoothly and cornered beautifully, before going on to say it was definitely worth the asking price. Back at the dealership, Tammy let her father do the talking.

"Yeah, mate, it looks in good nick and all, but it drives like shit. No guts under the bonnet. I think my daughter can do a whole lot better than this," Ralph said, indicating to the car which he, only moments before, was singing the praises of. Tammy remained silent.

Less than one hour later, she was the owner of a brand new Nissan Pulsar N16 – the very same car that she had driven with her father – and the salesman had taken a whopping $6,000 off the original asking price. *Holy crap! Thank you, Dad!* By the time they got back to Tammy's Kambah home, she'd already named her car 'Penny.' *Yep. Penny the Pulsar.* This was a day that Tammy would never forget. When her dad returned to Brisbane a few days later, she was missing him, before his truck had even left the driveway.

Two more years passed. Tammy had been keeping herself busy with as many temporary job assignments as she could handle, but none of them had led to permanent work. She was relieved when her mum and her brother had finally decided to come to Canberra for a visit. Tammy picked Janine and Jack up at the airport, in the Pulsar, and was proud to show her mum and baby brother the beautiful city she'd lived in for the past six years. Being the middle of winter, Janine felt the cold in a big way. It did not help that the indoor heating was not working at Tammy's house.

Tammy suddenly had an idea. She packed her family into the car and drove them to the snow fields for the day. They were all able to hire snow boards, snow shoes, and warm clothing, not far from Kosciusko National Park. Each of them spent that day building snowmen, pelting snowballs at each other and putting their bums on a sled, before sliding down the side of the mountain at warp speed. Tammy's face hurt from smiling so much. It was great to see her family after so many years, and she hoped that they would visit more often in the future.

Six months after Janine and Jack flew back to Brisbane, Katrina decided to take a holiday, in order to 'see how the other half lived.' Tammy had missed her best friend. Katrina spent the weekend playing with Muffin, Bambi and Holly. They also spent some time in the swimming pool Tammy had put in the backyard. Canberra's summers were as hot as the winters were cold, with summers reaching +50 degrees Celsius. Tammy and Katrina spent a lot of time driving around the city, taking advantage of Penny's incredible air conditioning system. They also took advantage of the 24-hour shopping hours at Tuggeranong Hyperdome, before Katrina headed back to Brisbane.

With all these visitors finally coming to see her, Tammy felt, in her heart, that her family were not so far away, after all. While it was true that she could not safely show her face anywhere in Queensland, she was able to move about freely in Canberra, and took advantage of that fact, when visitors came from Queensland to see her. Although years had passed since Tammy had left Queensland, she still very much kept to herself at home. She did not work at any place long enough to make friends, and now, found herself longing for her family and best friend to visit again.

Spending almost every day in the backyard swimming pool, her battery-operated radio playing news and music, poolside, Tammy smiled as she kept herself cool in the water. The swimming pool had a heavy duty mesh netting hanging overhead, securely attached to the aluminium frame of a portable carport. This way, Tammy could stay in the pool for a whole day without worrying about sunburn.

One day, as she was keeping cool in the swimming pool, she saw a giant Huntsman spider eyeing her while she was in the water. Moving so fast that even 'The Flash,' himself, would have been jealous of her speed, Tammy jumped out of the opposite side of the swimming pool from where the Huntsman spider sat. She ran inside the house, as fast as she could. After returning with one can of bug spray in each hand, she proceeded to drown the offending spider, which had interrupted her pool time. The next day, Tammy emptied, dismantled and sold the swimming pool. *No amount of summer heat is worth swimming with a fucking Huntsman!* The next two summers were spent indoors with pedestal fans and a water spray bottle to keep her cool… and luckily there was not a single Huntsman spider in sight.

Chapter 26

Tammy was no longer able to work. The pain in her spine from the elevator accident was now so severe, even with pain killers, anti-inflammatories and physiotherapy, that she could no longer escape it. When Tammy approached Centrelink – Australia's Social Security provider – with Disability Benefits application in hand, along with a full report from her own doctor of several years, who was still amazed that Tammy could actually still *walk*, her claim was, this time, accepted. Fortnightly payments were not much, but they were enough to keep the bills under control.

As Tammy was still able to earn a small amount, each month, she opted to join up with as many mystery shopping companies as possible. Each shopping assignment paid her up to $15 and she would put that money aside, as extra. With the exception of buying groceries or performing mystery shopping assignments, Tammy no longer left her home.

It was almost summer in 2007, when she'd made her way down to Tuggeranong Hyperdome to do some grocery shopping, and look for some small trinkets for her family, as gifts for a holiday she hadn't celebrated since the death of her son. Christmas Day was A.J.'s birthday and it was the day she spent *cherishing* the memories of her baby, every single year, regardless of how short their time was, together.

When she parked her car, she thought she'd seen somebody staring at her from a distance, at the opposite end of the car park. Turning to try and get a better look, she noticed that they had ducked behind a car. *Strange. Some weirdo, I guess.* Tammy shrugged it off, making sure that her car was securely locked before she walked into the shopping centre.

The air conditioning was great, but the crowds were not. Within an hour of arriving at the Tuggeranong Hyperdome, Tammy returned to her car with as many groceries as she'd been able to fit into her trolley, so that she would not have to return for at least another 2–3 weeks. As she leaned into the back of her Nissan Pulsar, packing the shopping bags carefully so that the bread and eggs would remain intact, she jumped when a voice from behind startled her.

"Hello, Bubba."

Every single muscle in her body tensed. When she turned around, Steve was standing less than two feet from her. He wasn't smiling. Tammy looked around to see if anybody was watching or if a security guard or AFP officer was in the vicinity. Unfortunately, although the car park was full of cars, there was nobody around to call out to for help. When she looked at Steve, a half grin had appeared on his face.

"Steve, what are you doi…." Tammy started.

"What am I doing here? With you? So far from home?" Steve interrupted.

Tammy nodded, not taking her eyes off him. *Don't cry. Don't show fear. Be strong.* She took a deep breath and waited for his response.

"I am here to see *you,* my Bubba!" Steve replied. "You *know* that we need to talk."

"I need to put my groceries into the car, Steve. I don't want trouble. Please, no games," Tammy said, quietly, trying her very best to keep him calm. She put the remainder of the grocery bags into the boot and closed the hatch, before turning around once again to face him.

"*Games*?" Steve frowned, and leaned in even closer to Tammy, as a shopper came out of the shopping centre with their own groceries. Tammy turned to look at the shopper, wondering if they could help her, but what she saw was a mother and her baby. *Fuck. Okay, just keep him distracted.* Steve grabbed the back of Tammy's head and kissed her hard, on the mouth. Tammy used every single bit of strength to push him away... and not *vomit*. The look of pure *disgust* on her face was not what Steve had expected.

"We were finished many years ago, Steve. I am *not* your Bubba. I am not your *anything!* I have moved *on* with my life and so should y…!" Tammy tried to be firm, but was interrupted by a sharp backhand to the face, which knocked her to the ground.

"*HEY!*" a man's voice shouted out across the car park.

Steve smiled at Tammy, sitting on the ground with her mouth bleeding. "To be continued," he said, before turning and running into the shopping centre.

Tammy stayed seated, hand holding her face where the back of Steve's hand had connected. With a split lip, her jaw now hurt and was bloody. Tears stung her eyes. A man ran up to her and asked her if she was alright. Tammy said she would be fine, as the man helped her stand up. He picked up the car keys, which had dropped to the ground, and handed them to her. After helping Tammy get into her car, the man took off into the shopping centre after Steve. Tammy started the ignition and drove out of the car park, wondering how he'd found out where she was.

One week had passed since Tammy's encounter with her former fiancé. She'd padlocked the gate at home, so her car could not be stolen. Only the front and back doors were opened, with the steel-barred security screen doors locked at all times. The windows of the house remained locked always. Steve had no way into her home. Tammy was determined to keep her cats, and herself, safe from the monster she'd once almost married.

A storm blew into Canberra. Tammy lay on her bed, staring at the ceiling for the entire night. All she could hear was banging. Was it her ceiling? Had some of the tiles come loose on the roof? Had a tree branch fallen from the giant Eucalyptus tree that towered over the top of her home? *Has he found out where I live?* Two things pumped through her veins – adrenaline and fear. Although it had been nine years since she'd last seen Steve, before last week's encounter, not a single bit of her fear of him had vanished in that time. *Fuck my life.*

The following morning, Tammy rang the Australian Federal Police's phone number, advising that a man, who'd told Queensland Police, almost ten years ago, that he was going to *kill* her, was now in Canberra, hunting her. She referred them to the official letter of Detective Senior Sergeant Johns of Queensland Police, and gave AFP his direct phone number, should they wish to confirm the threat. The AFP suggested that she apply to the courts for an Apprehended Violence Order (AVO), which would instruct him to stay away from her. Just one problem – Tammy had no idea where Steve was living or staying in Canberra and, unless he could be officially served so he could appear in court with her, Steve could not be expected to comply with the order.

Disheartened, Tammy then went to the backyard to try and figure out what the banging noise had been all night. She checked the yard for debris and there was nothing out of place, although she *did* find a Brown Snake nestled underneath her last remaining living tree in the backyard. *I'll get to you, later.* She tugged on the back door, seeing if it would make a similar noise, but it didn't budge. At least her locks were working.

As she followed the walls of the house around to the gate near the car, pushing on each of the storage doors at the back of her house – all of which were silent – Tammy stopped at her bedroom window and gave it a push. It moved. Not just the window, but the entire frame. On closer inspection, she also saw that the screws that typically held the window firmly in place against the brick wall of her home were gone. Almost every single screw had been removed. *Holy shit! Did the storm do this?* Tammy searched the ground below her bedroom window but was unable to see anything except for the dead rosebush stump she'd *someday* have to dig out of the ground. In its place, she would plant a brand new rose bush or maybe even a carnation bush. *Carnations would look much better than roses!* Tammy decided that she would soon pay a visit to the local nursery, to enquire about the best way to grow carnations in Canberra.

Back indoors, Tammy made a phone call to ACT Housing maintenance, telling them that her bedroom window was in urgent need of repair after last night's storm. Luckily, the State Emergency Service was attending to most of the other urgent callouts to people in Canberra, who'd sustained major damage in the storm. Tammy was relieved, when ACT Housing maintenance advised her they would send someone to her home immediately. When the maintenance guy arrived, he was mystified at the disappearance of the screws from the window.

"Is it possible that the *wind* from the storm did this?" Tammy asked.

"Nope. No chance in hell," the maintenance guy replied, while shaking his head. "Somebody has physically *removed* these screws. Was last night the first time you heard the banging?" he asked.

"Yeah," Tammy replied.

"Then whoever stole these screws, did so *very* recently," the maintenance man advised.

He went to his van, and radioed ACT Housing, telling them that he would be at his current location, in Kambah, for some time. Almost all of the window's screws needed to be replaced *immediately*. He further advised that he was surprised the window had been able to sit where it was in the wall, since it was only held in place by three small screws.

One by one, large screws were secured into place by the maintenance man, while Tammy watched. She knew only one person could have done this, but without a single shred of evidence to prove what she knew, there was nothing she could do. After an hour, the maintenance guy climbed down from his ladder, having secured the last of the screws in place. He then pushed on the window, ensuring it was now completely secure, and no longer made a sound.

"I think my ex did this," Tammy said, with tears in her eyes. "He told Queensland Police he would kill me. Now he is in Canberra. I am pretty sure he did this."

The maintenance man looked at Tammy, sympathetically. For a moment, he said nothing, while he looked at the window. He then got an idea that almost blew Tammy's mind.

"You know what?" he said. "Let's make sure he can't do it again, shall we?" Climbing back up the ladder, he drilled each of the screws, one by one, so tight that *all* were now *completely* stripped. No screwdriver would ever be able to loosen them again. Although Tammy had been told, many times, by her dad, when she was a child, to *never* tighten a screw so tight that it strips, she liked what the maintenance man had just done. *If it keeps Steve out of my house, it is definitely a good thing!*

Tammy kept her camera with her, now, at all times. Determination had set in. The very moment she'd laid eyes on a brown Kingswood being parked near her house, or in her driveway, she would be sure to take photos as evidence. The only advantage she had, *this* time around, was that the Australian Federal Police were friendly, and seemed to know exactly what they were doing. They truly went above and beyond the call of duty, to help the people of Canberra – a far cry from the Logan Police in Queensland. Tammy hoped that this would stop Steve from getting the upper hand over her. She'd also started to keep a diary of when things were not right – an idea given to her by Trevor, a stranger on the internet from the other side of the world, who'd become her best friend. Tammy's encounter with Steve in the car park, that day at Tuggeranong Hyperdome, was the first entry. The bedroom window was next.

It was two weeks later when a third entry had to be made in her diary, but she was not sure if it was Steve-related or not. Tammy's hot water system had blown up. For years, it had worked perfectly and she'd topped it up regularly, to ensure she'd always had hot water at the ready. But one day, without warning, she had no hot water for showers, baths, washing clothes or dishes, or for cleaning the house. It was a long weekend when it happened, so although Tammy was able to call the 24-hour emergency number of ACT Housing maintenance, she would have to wait a whole week before anybody could come to repair or replace the hot water system, out the back.

Tammy had just filled and boiled the kettle for the sixth time in a row so she could pour the boiling water to the sink and wash the dishes. While wearing gloves to absorb most of the heat from the water, Tammy jumped when the doorbell rang. Without thinking, Tammy assumed it was her neighbours. She walked to the door and spotted Steve, hands in his pockets, staring at her through the locked security screen door. *At least this time you can't hit me, you bastard!* Tammy told Steve that she would ring the police if he did not leave immediately.

"Just *listen* to me, okay? You don't have to talk if you don't want to. *We* don't have to talk. But I would really like you to listen to what I have to say. *Please*, Bubba," Steve said, a sad look on his face.

"Do you really expect me to listen to *anything* you have to say, after what you did to me at the shopping centre? I mean, what the *fuck?* I am not the same naive moron you once knew. *I* grew up. *ME!* That makes just *one* of us who grew up, Steve," Tammy said, furious with her visitor's audacity.

"We have unfinished business, Bubba," Steve said, a threat in his tone.

"You *told* the police in Queensland that you want me *dead*. After everything you put me through, you said you wanted to *kill* me. Tell me, Steve, *what* unfinished business you think we have left. I can think of *nothing*. As far as I am concerned, all of our business is *over* with," Tammy said, her tears sneaking through.

She was angry, but she did not want him to see her cry. She did not want to give him *that* satisfaction. But it was too late. Steve smiled at her, a mock sympathetic look on his face.

"See? I *know* you still love me. It's not too late, Bubba. We can even have another *baby* if you want. I can *give* you another baby. Just open the door," Steve pleaded.

"I would sooner be dead," Tammy answered, flatly, before slamming the door in his face.

She quickly closed the sliding door at the side of the house and the back door, locking them both. *Fuck! I need a photo!* Her dishwashing gloves now on the kitchen table, Tammy grabbed her camera and opened the front door. To her frustration, Steve was gone.

Two days passed, without any more visits from Steve. Tammy sat at her computer, scanning the internet for a security camera to put at the front of her house. She was determined to get *proof* that he'd been there. But she also knew that a security camera was very expensive. Tammy also had to replace the motion-sensor spotlight at the front of her property which had recently been smashed. As her income consisting solely of the disability pension, however, she was limited in funds.

With the help of Trevor – who'd suggested to Tammy, just a few days earlier, that she put some *oil* on the grass underneath her bedroom window, in case Steve returns – Tammy found many different types of security cameras online. All were out of her price range, and Tammy almost found herself banging her head on the keyboard, while in a video chat with Trevor. They were *both* determined to keep her safe.

Trevor lived in Finland – a place that Tammy had heard of just once or twice in school. She'd not known *where* it was until Conan O'Brien had dedicated a whole episode to such an amazing and beautiful country. *I might have to invest in a lottery ticket, I think.* Tammy was determined to, one day, visit Finland, and see every one of its 280,000 lakes for herself. *Well, a girl is allowed to dream, right?*

The following morning, Tammy had another look for security cameras. She also tried to find some affordable motion-sensor spotlights, to replace the one at her front door. After finding one within her budget, Tammy realised that she had stupidly left her wallet in the car. She peeked out the window of the computer room, making sure there was nobody out there before she unlocked the sliding door, at the side of the house. The very moment she'd taken a step outside, Tammy was grabbed around the throat from behind. Steve had been hiding around the corner, waiting for Tammy to do something stupid – something that would let him win.

Steve turned her around, grabbed her wrists and knocked her backwards off her feet. Tammy was laying on the concrete ramp at the back of her property. Steve was lying on top of her, staring her straight in the eyes.

"You should never have left me," he said, before kissing her hard.

Tammy bit his lip as he kissed her. She would rather be *dead,* than have this monster rape her again. Steve grabbed her hair and slammed her head backwards onto the concrete ramp. Pain shot through her skull. Tammy saw stars and was dizzy. He slammed her head back again and again. The world was spinning, and everything went black.

Chapter 27

Almost a year went by before Tammy had any memory of that day. Almost everything, for the eight months following Steve's attack, was gone from her memory bank completely. There were times when she'd catch a glimpse of things she didn't understand – a quick flash of a picture in her mind, but those flashes were so vague – so foggy. Tammy didn't know what was real or imagined each time it happened, but her head would scream in pain, every single time a flashback-type picture appeared. The pictures only stayed for a fraction of a second but each one would send a surge of panic coursing through her immediately afterwards. Another after-effect of Steve's attack was a constant ringing in Tammy's ears.

Over the months, Tammy was able to piece little bits of the puzzle, that was the past eight months of her life, back together – with Trevor's help. For instance, she discovered that she had bought a return ticket to fly to Finland. *Well that was very brave and bold... and possibly very stupid of me.* Being absolutely terrified of heights and closed in spaces, Tammy had no idea how she would survive being trapped inside a plane for thirty-six hours... *twice!* But sure enough, she had the airline tickets in her email box, dated a few months ago as proof. Tammy was also now the proud owner of her very first passport. When she looked inside, at the photo, she cringed. *What, was I STONED or something? Bloody hell!* She'd seen better photos on prison mug shots.

Tammy had discovered that, in order to pay for the airline ticket, which would take her to the other side of the world and back, she had sold several items on eBay, had cancelled her digital television subscription, as well as cancelling all of her magazine and newspaper subscriptions. She stopped buying any new clothes or shoes, and had saved every single cent from her mystery shopping jobs, saving her almost $4,000 in total. On learning all of this, Tammy gave herself a well-deserved pat on the back.

Although there were a couple of things that Tammy *did* remember – such as the loud crack of her skull, and the searing pain she felt, right before her world had gone black, there were so many things that she could *not* remember. For instance, outside her bedroom window, where the old stump from the rose bush had been, now stood a *brand new* hot water system, which was perched on top of a concrete slab. No matter how hard Tammy tried, she could not remember it being installed. There were no complaints, however. She was going to remove the rose bush stump herself, anyway, and having hot water again was a blessing. Tammy could now get back to doing what she did best; she cleaned the house from top to bottom each day.

Another thing Tammy didn't remember was losing her cats. All three had died at Steve's hands on the day of the attack. She did, however, remember breaking her Christmas Day tradition, that year. Instead of sitting at home, alone, swimming in sad memories of A.J.

and thinking about the precious life that had been so cruelly taken away from her, Tammy took Penny for a drive to the local animal shelter to look at the death-row kitties. Any sick, old or "been there too long" cats were always euthanised, during the week between Christmas and New Year, due to the fact that so many *new* cats and kittens would be brought into the shelter after New Year.

Most animal shelters had many cats to choose from, if people wanted to adopt and save a life. Sadly, however, many people opt for the convenience of buying a kitten or puppy from a pet store, regardless that almost *all* came from puppy farms, or from carelessly un-neutered cats. Years earlier, when Tammy had bought Muffin from a pet store, she hadn't known about the problems animal shelters faced, especially during the festive season. Giving somebody a cat as a Christmas gift was *never* a good idea. Tammy had remembered, on Christmas Day of 2007, not only saving the lives of three young cats – but that those very same cats had saved *her* life as well.

Each day, as the cats played, Tammy would find herself watching them closely. Occasionally, she would smile. All three of the cats were very playful. Tammy decided that the new cats be named after some of her biggest comedic heroes. She had been an avid viewer of *Late Night with Conan O'Brien* for many years now, and *still* made sure not to miss a single episode. Through every bit of pain and hardship she'd endured, over the years, Conan's show was the reason that Tammy was still able to laugh and smile. It had kept her sanity and her sense of humour intact. For this, she would be forever grateful. With that, Tammy decided to name her three new fluff balls Pierre (after Pierre Bernard Jr), Joel (after Joel Godard) and Conan (after Conan O'Brien).

With only a few months to go before she was due to leave for Finland, Tammy went into full scale OCD mode, making a list (in alphabetical order) of everything she would be carrying, in the suitcase, as well as what she would need to take on board. She would pack her suitcase, weigh it, unpack it, decide what wasn't right, then repack it and re-weight it, over and over. Tedious as it was, it ensured Tammy would not be caught out by the scales at the airport. She also made an appointment to see her doctor, so that she could take all of her prescription medication with her to Finland, without being arrested.

While in the surgery with Dr Barbara (who was fondly referred to as B-doc), Tammy discovered that she'd already *seen* her doctor and had done this exact thing… four times, to be exact. B-doc explained that the head injuries Tammy had sustained, almost one year earlier, had caused quite a bit of damage, and that the memory loss, while short-term, was most likely, permanent. B-doc went on to tell Tammy how very important it was, that she receive no more bumps to the head, as the next one may prove to be fatal. The head injuries had also caused damage to her ears and eyes, which is why the Tinnitus followed Tammy around, everywhere she went, both day and night. *Crap!* Without wanting to look *completely* stupid, Tammy took the opportunity to also top up all of her prescriptions, making sure that she would have enough medication for her trip.

Finally, the time came for her to leave. Tammy had arranged for her cats to be fed, watered and cuddled each day, while she was away. She also made it very clear to the cat-sitter that the house was to be securely locked *at all times*, even when the cat-sitter was inside with the cats. Tammy drew up a schedule of morning and afternoon things which needed to be done, and posted it to the linen cupboard door, near the front of the house. She also put full details of the vet's after-hours and office hours numbers, as well as her email address, while she would be in Finland. To some, it might have appeared as overkill. But to Tammy, these things were essential, in order to make sure her cats were still in one piece – and safe – when she returned home.

The bus ride from Canberra to Sydney took close to four hours. When she arrived at the Sydney International Airport, Tammy collected her boarding passes for both Sydney to Bangkok and for Bangkok to Helsinki. Right at that moment, pain once again took hold of her. She advised the airport staff that she was disabled. This was quickly taken care of by airport staff and, much to Tammy's surprise, a wheelchair was waiting for her, not only at boarding time in Canberra, but also when she disembarked from the planes at Bangkok and at Helsinki. Her very first international travel experience was proving to be a lot less difficult than she'd envisaged it would be.

During both flights, Tammy was fully sedated, so that the claustrophobia and panic attacks would not present a problem, on board. She had to be woken every two hours, by the airline hostess, however, so that she could take her ample supply of ginger tablets, to prevent travel sickness. The only other times she was woken during the flight were at meal times, or during take-off or landing.

Once in Helsinki, Tammy was surrounded by signs in a language she'd never seen before. Most of the words almost snapped her tongue in half, when she tried to say them. The Finnish language was not even *remotely* similar to English, in any way, so she simply followed the red arrow, went through customs to declare her medications (the customs officer's jaw dropped when she presented him with the alphabetised list of contents of her suitcase), before making her way to the bus that would take her to her final destination – Tampere.

It was winter in Finland. Tammy thought winter would be a piece of cake, having lived in Canberra for so long, where the average winter temperature had been about -3 degrees. When she walked to the bus stop from the airport, however, she was sure some of her body parts had fallen off during the 20 metre walk. It was -27 degrees and windy. There was ice covering the ground. Every single breath was an effort, and Tammy wondered how her lungs and brain had not frozen.

The bus arrived two hours after she'd arrived in Helsinki, and the trip from the airport to Tampere was a further two hours. All of her medications had worn off and excitement was finally starting to take hold. As the driver spoke in a foreign language over the loudspeaker of the bus, butterflies started doing somersaults inside her stomach. Tammy was *finally* about to meet her best friend in the world, for the very first time, and she was nervous as hell. As the bus pulled into Tampere Bus Station, doubts started slapping her around. *What if Trevor isn't here? What if I get mugged or arrested? How am I supposed to find the hotel? Shit, this trip is the worst idea I ever had!* Negativity pounced on her from all directions as she sat on the bus, watching all the other passengers climb out and retrieve their luggage.

Tammy was the last person left sitting in the bus. She slowly stood up. *Well, this is it.* As she *slowly* descended the stairs at the front of the bus, she looked to her right and there, pushing his bike and wearing the biggest, friendliest smile she'd ever seen, was a very tall, handsome Trevor. All of her fears evaporated on the spot. Although Tammy was unable to remember many things, the one thing she knew and trusted was that nothing and *nobody* could hurt her now. Trevor was the reason she was still alive, and she was grateful, and ever so *blessed,* to finally be meeting her closest friend.

Tammy and Trevor walked to Koskikeskus – the Finnish version of the Tuggeranong Hyperdome – and Tammy was stunned to find that they were the only two people there. She was from a place where the shops were open seven days per week, 24 hours per day. Tammy had never before been inside a deserted shopping centre. She was *further* blown away by the fact that in Finland, all public toilets would cost a minimum of one euro per visit. Tammy suddenly wished she'd been born with a penis, so she could just tie a knot in it when she had to pee.

For about an hour, they sat and discussed the differences in the weather, the shopping hours, the money, and the fact that Finnish people drive on the wrong side of the road. Whilst Tammy had a lot of problems hearing, she was grateful to be able to hear Trevor's amazing accent, as she hung onto his every single word. She then learned the reason the shops in Finland were so *empty* that day. Most people were visiting their fathers around the country. It was Finnish Father's Day on the day she'd arrived. *D'oh!* Trevor apologised, and said he needed to get going to see his parents, but advised Tammy that *another* friend of theirs was due to arrive at any moment, and that he'd meet them *both* back at the hotel in a few hours. Heidi, their friend from further north, had made the trip from Virrat, to meet her Australian friend in Tampere.

Within minutes of Trevor leaving, Heidi walked through the front doors of Koskikeskus with a smile on her face. She tall, with blonde hair which was so long, that it surely would have made Rapunzel jealous. She explained to Tammy that the average height of a Finn was around 195 centimetres. *Shit. Seriously?* A mere 163 centimetres, Tammy knew that most of her three-week visit would comprise of her talking to the knees of her Finnish friends. *So, I guess, this is what a garden gnome feels like.*

At the hotel, Heidi helped Tammy collect her room code (no keys in *this* hotel), before they made their way up the spiral staircase to the top floor. It was there, Tammy discovered that *everything* in Finland was designed for very tall people. The windows were huge and the handles were so high that Tammy had to drag the chair from the table just so she could reach them.

While they talked, excitedly, about the differences between Australia and Finland, Tammy was finding the perfect place for each thing in her suitcase. Suddenly, a knock came at the door. Trevor had arrived. This time, he actually looked a little bit shy. Perhaps it was because it was also the first time he was meeting

Heidi, or maybe it was because he was in a tiny room with two women and a bed. *Don't worry, Trevor. I am not going to attack you, mister!*

Trevor hooked Tammy's laptop up to the hotel's free internet. As he was doing so, Tammy gave herself a guided tour, through the tiny hotel room, looking at the shower, which looked nothing like any shower she had ever seen. There was also a *miniature* shower next to the toilet. Tammy asked Trevor what it was, and how it worked. After turning twenty-eight shades of *embarrassed*, Trevor looked to Heidi for help. Tumbleweeds seemed to roll on by, while crickets chirped in the awkward silence.

"Don't ask *me* how to show you. I don't use them. I am a *guy!*" Trevor finally said, looking utterly *horrified* that I'd dared to ask.

"Oh, it's that's *bidet*," Heidi said, and giggled. "It's to clean your girly bits and your bum. Guys don't use them."

Tammy's jaw dropped to the floor, suddenly horrified at the graphic image, now filling her brain. *Umm, okay. Glad I asked.* She knew that a quick change in subject was definitely in order, since the silence in the room was now at deafening point.

"What shall we do for dinner tonight?" Tammy asked.

"First thing you need to do is get some groceries for the hotel room," Trevor suggested.

Heidi said she had to go and check in with her cousin, since she would be staying with her for a few days. While Heidi was away, Tammy and Trevor crossed the road to a store called SALE. At first, Tammy thought they were advertising some kind of sale. She also thought that the store sold beer because she saw some signs that said ALE. *Maybe I need to learn a bit of Finnish language.* Tammy's comments about ALE and SALE caused a few of the customers to giggle. It turned out that ALE means SALE in English. *Yikes!*

After buying rye bread, milk, Lingonberry Porridge, Karelian pasties and some fruit, Tammy and Trevor made their way back to the hotel and unloaded the food into the fridge, before heading back to Koskikeskus to meet up with Heidi. The trio dined, in style, at the Manhattan Steak House, that night. It was an incredible meal – one which Tammy would never forget.

Over the next three weeks, Trevor and Heidi took Tammy to many different places in Tampere – Näsinneula (a 168 metre tall needle-like building with a revolving restaurant on top), Pyynikin näkötorni (a building almost 100 years old, which gives a full, 360 degree, aerial view of Tampere), Pispala (a suburb with a staircase consisting of 280 stairs from the top of the hill to the very bottom), and Tammy's favourite place – Tammerkoski (a waterfall which created enough electricity to power half of Finland). Tammerkoski was a man-made waterfall, which had been built between Näsijärvi and Pyhäjärvi – two lakes which were joined by a fast-flowing river, and were 18 metres difference in water level height. The number of things Tammy saw, during her stay in Finland, *fully* blew her mind. With each passing day, she fell more and more in love with Finland and was determined to someday return.

Towards the end of her holiday, Tammy encountered her first full freeze. The roads were slippery. The lakes and small puddles had frozen solid and it snowed. Tammy and her cane slipped over constantly. She had no idea, until that moment, how *slippery* walking on snow and ice could be! Trevor suggested that she head to Sokos – a giant department store in the main street of Hämeenkatu – to buy a set of shoe-spikes, so she'd stop falling down. He went on to remind her of how *fragile* her head was. Tammy had never before *heard* of spikes for shoes or walking sticks, but she made her way, *very slowly,* to Sokos, and was able to find a salesperson who spoke English. Once she'd purchased a set of shoe spikes, Tammy then went around the corner to a specialty store, called Piateekki. There, she bought an extremely sharp spike, which the salesperson attached to the bottom of her walking stick. This visit took a little bit longer than that of the previous store, however, as the salesperson at Piateekki did not speak English and was confused when she thought that Tammy had asked for a "nail to put on her condom". *Oh dear.*

The rest of the holiday was slip-free, and Tammy had to pack a bag for Trevor to safeguard until she returned; she knew that the spikes would not be permitted into Australia. Also, liquids such as the leftover dish liquid and various foods would also not be permitted past Australia's border. The very *last* thing Tammy wanted, or needed, was to be the highlight of a show called *Border Security – Australia's Front Line,* which was a program showing the different types of people who'd tried to smuggle drugs or any *other* illegal goods into Australia, or who filled in their customs declaration incorrectly on the plane. Tammy pictured herself trying to hide her face from a camera, while the customs officers asked why she was carrying condom-nails in her suitcase.

The day before Tammy was due to return to Australia, a big problem arose. Terrorists had taken over Bangkok airport. All flights to, from and *via* that destination, were now cancelled. Tammy rang British Airways, and asked them if they could find another way to get her home. They told her it was not their responsibility or their problem, as her *initial* flight would be with Finnair. When Tammy rang to Finnair, they passed the responsibility back to British Airways. Becoming frantic, Tammy then contacted the travel insurance people, hoping that they would offer her a solution, but the only thing they told her was that her policy did not cover acts of terrorism. *No! This is NOT happening, dammit!*

Tammy rang Trevor, crying her eyes out, and updated him on the situation. Trevor told her to calm down, to hang up the phone, and to take a few very deep relaxing breaths. She did just that, and within ten minutes, British Airways had rung Tammy back, apologising profusely for their earlier comments, and instructed her that an alternative flight had been arranged, via London, at *their* expense. *Fuck! Trevor, I don't know what you did, but you are a bloody legend!*

After hugging both Heidi and Trevor farewell, Tammy boarded the bus, which would take her to Helsinki airport from Tampere. Her heart was already aching, due to the fact that she was leaving such a beautiful place, and was now headed back to a place she likened to hell. Staring out of the window of the bus, Tammy cried all the way to the airport. She was already extremely homesick – homesick for a place that she yearned to be her new home; a place called Finland.

Chapter 28

Arriving back at her Kambah residence in Australia, Tammy was glad to see that all three of her cats were happy, healthy and still as playful (and mischievous) as ever. Tammy had caught a taxi from Canberra city, after the long bus ride from Sydney International Airport. The journey back home via London and Singapore was adventurous, but she had decided *never again* to return to London's Heathrow Airport, after the airport security staff had confiscated her camera, deeming her to be a terrorist, after taking too many photographs. It had taken many *hours* to convince security staff that she was *not* a terrorist, nor did she have any links to terrorist-sympathisers. *Never, ever again.*

The cat-sitter gave Tammy a full update on the three weeks she'd been gone, including the fact that there seemed to be a lot of electricity blackouts. Either *that*, or some of the electricity box's fuses needed replacing. *Nice try, assholes.* Tammy said that she'd check it out a little later, since she was absolutely *exhausted* after all the travelling she'd just done, to get home.

"You also had a few visitors who needed to speak with you, but I did as you asked, and kept the door locked. I did not tell them where you were – just that you were unavailable," she said to Tammy, a look of slight concern on her face.

"You did great. Thank you so much for looking after my little furry guys," Tammy replied.

Tammy paid a generous tip to her cat-sitter, before walking her to the door. As soon as she was alone with her cats, Tammy knew that there was just one thing left to do. She checked that all windows and doors were closed and locked, before falling into bed for a well-earned sleep. Once she was in bed, all three cats jumped on top of her, seemingly happy to have their human back home with them. Joel fell asleep on her chest, while Conan and Pierre fell asleep under each of her armpits. *Yay, comfy! Sure hope I don't have to get up to pee in a hurry!* With that thought, Tammy quickly fell asleep, and slept for the rest of the day. She was woken, several hours later, when Joel jumped onto the bed and sat on her head. Trying to talk with a mouth full of Joel's butt hair was *not* one of Tammy's favourite games, so she lifted him off and scratched his head, before feeding the three hungry kitties.

After the cats were fed, Tammy logged onto the internet and checked in with Trevor, advising him that she'd arrived home safely. She also told him about the nonsense with security and her camera at Heath Row Airport.

"Did you get the camera *back?*" Trevor asked, absolutely stunned. "All of your holiday photos are on there!"

"Yeah. I convinced them that the garden gnome with the walking stick was not a terrorist, but rather a stand-by tourist, awaiting her next flight. It was seriously *crazy!*" Tammy replied, nerves still raw from the whole scenario which had, again, replayed itself in her head.

Trevor enquired about any badness which might have happened in Kambah, while she'd been in Finland. Tammy told him everything the cat-sitter had said to her, when she got home.

"Don't go outside at night," Trevor reminded her, "and remember, never open the door!"

Oddly enough, Tammy was reminded of this far more than Trevor knew. Ever since her memory had started working again, the doorbell or knocking would leave Trevor's voice yelling inside her head *"DON'T OPEN THE DOOR!"* She couldn't understand why it was happening, but Trevor explained to her that, many times, when she had opened the front door, she'd been badly injured as a result. This was most likely the reason for the strange, verbal butt-kicking that would play in her mind, when visitors came to the door.

The following day, Tammy knocked on her neighbour's door to see if anybody was home. Although she rarely ever talked to her neighbours, Tammy figured that it was a good time to see if they'd noticed anything strange happening at her home, when she was away. The cat-sitter had visited twice per day, but her neighbours were almost *always* at home, being retirees. When Suzy answered the door, she was surprised to see that *Tammy* was her visitor.

"Hi, Suzy. I am not sure how electricity boxes work. My power keeps going a little mental. Would you mind giving me a couple of pointers?" Tammy asked, not wanting to be outside alone.

Suzy called out to Rex – her husband – and asked him to take a look at Tammy's *"shock-box."* Both Suzy and Rex walked Tammy back to the house. On opening the electricity box, at the side of the house, the very first thing they noticed was a giant *Huntsman* staring back at them.

"Fucking hell!" Tammy screamed, as she hurriedly took about ten steps back.

"B'ah! Don't worry about these things. They are a lot more scared of you than you are of them," Rex pointed out, before reaching into the box to the growling Huntsman, grabbing it in his hand and releasing it into the tree at the front of his house.

"You *crazy* son of a bitch! Now that monster is going to *breed* and make millions *more* of them!" Tammy screamed at Rex, still scared.

Rex chuckled as he checked out the fuses in the electricity box. Tammy was no longer paying attention to anything Rex was doing. Her full focus was now on the tree. The Huntsman spider sat on the branch, staring at her, almost as if to say "Ha! Take *that*, bitch!"

When Rex had determined that all of the fuses were fine, he realised the problem. Somebody had simply flicked the switch, turning them all off. Usually that would only be done by an electrician, at the city's request due to an unpaid bill, but in this case, Tammy knew better. Rex then replaced the last of the fuses, before suggesting that she lock the box, so that nobody can mess about with it. *New lock on the shopping list... CHECK!* Tammy asked Suzy and Rex if there had been anything, which they'd consider weird or strange, happening at her property while she had been away.

"You received a couple of hand-delivered packages, but they vanished just as weirdly as they arrived," Suzy said. "By the way, you might want to keep your cats locked up tight. All the cats around the neighbourhood have been going missing."

Tammy told Suzy that her cats were solely indoor cats. She was, however, considering taking them for walks in the backyard, while on a harness, to see if they would enjoy it.

"Just be careful, Tammy. Our cats get let outside once per day and are pretty smart. They know when to run if somebody comes near them who doesn't seem quite right in the head," warned Rex.

With the electricity now working again, Tammy thanked Suzy and Rex before heading back inside to her cats. She locked the house up *tight*, before driving Penny down to the local hardware store. Tammy decided to buy *two* locks, just in case one wasn't working properly. *All good things are better, when bought in even numbers.* Her OCD was a pain in the ass sometimes. Arriving back home, Tammy cursed as she was reversing the car into the driveway. Her mailbox was gone! *You have got to be fucking kidding me!* Returning to the hardware store, she bought a new mailbox, some street numbers, a 90-degree angle steel bracket, a 30cm x 30cm x 5cm lump of pine and some screws. She then, once again, headed back home.

Turning the car into her street, she saw a white van parked in the driveway of her house. Tammy pulled over at the other end of the street, and watched as two men were having a discussion on her front porch. The driver of the van then hurried back to his vehicle and quickly drove away. Tammy ducked out of view as he drove past, before driving the rest of the way home. The other man on her front porch was still standing there. It was Rex.

Again, Tammy reversed Penny into the driveway. She got out of the car with her purse, keys and new purchases, before asking what was going on.

"That van was parked at the front of your house, a number of times, while you were away. He was leaving you another parcel, so I decided to find out who he was, since he is obviously *not* the postman," Rex growled. "When he couldn't answer my questions, he took his package and left. I don't know *what* his deal is, and I am sorry if I am out of line in coming here to chase him off, but…"

"*No!* Don't apologise for anything at all," Tammy interrupted. "I'm *glad* you did it. I don't want their trash dumped on my doorstep. The White Pages and Yellow Pages are the only two things that should ever be here, since I don't order things, any more, for delivery. I haven't for a long time now."

"Good to know. Have a good afternoon, young Tammy!" Rex said, before returning next door.

When she walked into the house, the cats were scared. Conan was hiding under the couch with Joel, eyes all big and black, and refused to come out. Pierre was under the computer table in the spare room. *What the hell?* After calling them, and trying to coax them out from their hiding places for almost an hour, the cats *finally* relaxed enough to come and get the treats Tammy had for them. She had no idea why her cats were so afraid, and thought it might be because of the angry voices they'd heard at the door, earlier.

Once the cats were calm enough, Tammy got straight to work. She drilled through the hardwood hand railing of her front stairs to attach the steel bracket, making sure it was completely even with her spirit level, before attaching the thick piece of pine to the bracket horizontally, at a 90-degree angle to the hand railing. Once firmly in place, she carefully drilled smaller holes from inside the mail box and attached it securely. The final touches were the numbers on the front and a padlock on the back. *If you bastards want to steal THIS, you'll have to take the whole fucking house with it!* She was really missing the *peace* she'd found in Finland, and decided to start to plan for the next trip.

Over the following six months, Tammy *again* scrimped and saved every single spare cent. She had seen Finland in winter. It would be *amazing* to see it during the summer months. Finally, she'd saved enough money for her return ticket – a ticket which was much cheaper than flying during the festive season. This gave her more spending money. She also booked herself into the same no-frills hotel which she'd stayed at, the previous winter. As a return customer, she would receive a discount. With everything now paid for, Tammy had started on her *new* list of contents for the suitcase, when a loud banging came at the front door.

"*DON'T OPEN THE DOOR!*" Trevor's voice, once again, automatically played inside her head. As Tammy had recently installed a peek-hole, she decided to at least *see* who it was. When she peeked, she was stunned to see a very upset *Rex*, standing at her front door. She opened the door and invited Rex inside.

"What is it?" Tammy asked, gently.

"Our cats are missing," Rex exclaimed. "They went out last night, but didn't come back. They *always* come back."

For the first time ever, Tammy could hear panic and sadness in Rex's voice. He was a very tall and broad-shouldered man, with a rough voice. *Nobody* would dare mess with him, whether in a dark alley or a crowded room. But it was not until now, that Tammy realised how *fragile* Rex could be. He really did love his cats.

"I'm sorry. I hope they come back, and I promise to keep a look out for them," Tammy replied.

Rex nodded and thanked her, before returning to his house. As soon as he left, Tammy locked the security screen door behind him, while locking the main door, as well. Once she was alone with her cats, Tammy started to tremble as she burst into tears, but she had no idea why this news affected her so badly.

The following week, Suzy knocked on Tammy's door to let them know that they found one of the cats. Rex was about 100 metres away, collecting what was left of their tiny cat's body while Tammy and Suzy talked. Suzy told Tammy that Rex was inconsolable, and that both she and Rex didn't hold much hope that her other cat would be coming home. Tammy wanted to ask them why they'd allowed their cats to wander around outdoors, especially after they'd warned Tammy to keep a close eye on *hers,* due to all of the missing cats in the neighbourhood. Instead, she held her tongue. Her heart felt heavy, as she mourned the loss of Suzy and Rex's cats.

Three more months passed and, before Tammy realised it, the time had come to return to Finland and to see her friends, once again. Tammy welcomed the break from all of the insanity, which had continued in the Kambah neighbourhood. She contacted the same cat-sitter she'd used on her previous trip. All instructions were, again, posted onto the door of the linen closet, inclusive of all emergency contacts via email and phone. When Tammy left for the airport, she knew that her cats would be in good hands.

On arrival at Helsinki airport, Tammy was greeted by Heidi, who'd decided to show Tammy around Finland's *capital*, before they both made their way to Tampere – this time by train. Everything was beautiful – the weather, the cleanliness of the streets, the amazing statues. Heidi took Tammy onto a *tram* for the first time in her life. Although it was just a short journey, Tammy struggled to breathe, due to the claustrophobia which overwhelmed her. The trains in Finland were wide, and did not sway from side-to-side, like they did in Australia. They also travelled at over 200 kilometres per hour, so the journey was quick. The tram, however, was extremely narrow, slow and crowded. Tammy told Heidi that she would prefer to do the rest of their Helsinki tour on foot.

Heidi took Tammy to the Helsinki Cathedral – an incredible white building with tall columns around the outside. The building, itself, was at the top of about 100 stairs, each of which were laid out in pyramid-style. Although no longer of Christian faith, Tammy could not help but to be in awe of such amazing architecture.

They then walked down to the harbour, across the road from the Presidential Palace. Tammy knew that *inside* the Presidential Palace resided the most wonderful person in the world – a president that owned her heart – Tarja Halonen. The resemblance between Tarja Halonen and Conan O'Brien was uncanny, and he'd had the pleasure of meeting the president during his special taping of his Finland special, which was televised in 2006. Tammy prayed that someday, she would be able to meet the President too.

Across the road from the Presidential Palace was the market place and Helsinki Harbour. Tammy's jaw dropped, when she saw a ship, the size of a city, which was moored at the harbour. The ship, called *Silja Line,* made frequent journeys between Sweden and Finland.

After buying several souvenirs at the harbour markets, all of which displayed the Finnish flag, Tammy and Heidi began their walk back to Helsinki Railway Station. When they neared the large railway building, Tammy saw two giant green statues which she hadn't noticed, earlier. Both statues were attached to the side of the railway station, and were of two giant men, each holding globes. They were absolutely *magnificent* to look at. Tammy told Heidi that, with the exception of the claustrophobic tram ride, she had thoroughly enjoyed her Helsinki tour.

The train ride to Tampere was over within an hour, and Tammy and Heidi both decided to go halves in the cost of a taxi to the hotel. As soon as the taxi pulled up in the car park, Trevor rode up on his bike. The timing was perfect. Upstairs, at Tammy's hotel room, they each had many things to catch up on, and decided to return to the Manhattan Steak House for dinner, just as they had done on the first night of Tammy's previous visit.

Everything in Finland was a stark contrast to what Tammy had left behind in Australia. Finland's ground was covered in thick, healthy green grass, the gardens were meticulously attended to and all of the fountains, which had been covered during the winter, were now flowing with water, boasting their beauty with every drop. The lakes were no longer frozen. Back in Australia, there was no grass. Almost everything was still dead due, to the endless drought. Most people had only dirt remaining where their front lawn used to be. Due to water restrictions, Australians were not permitted to use hoses to water their lawns or gardens, or to operate any water fountains. Much of Canberra had still not recovered from the firestorm which had hit the city, eight years earlier. The one thing that struck Tammy the most, however, was the summer heat. Although temperatures in Finland were similar to that of Australia's summer, the heat was actually *bearable*. This was possibly because Finland consisted of more water than land. Lakes were everywhere, and were teeming with wildlife, both above and below the water. Fish was a staple food source in almost every Finn's diet, and was extremely affordable.

Tammy was, once again, given a guided tour of Tampere city, *this time* with all of the springtime attractions, including the giant amusement park called Särkänniemi. The amusement park was only open in the warmer months, but Näsinneula – the giant, needle-like tower in the centre of the amusement park – was open all year round. Tammy had seen Näsinneula many times from afar, and it always made her smile. Knowing that she was in Finland again, in her favourite city, the smile never seemed to leave her face.

Two weeks into Tammy's visit, Trevor rang Tammy and asked her to meet him at Särkänniemi. Although not very big on amusement park rides, she agreed to meet Trevor there. This would be the closest she had ever been to Näsinneula and almost immediately, panic started to set in. She did not like going anywhere *near* tall buildings – not since her elevator accident in 1996. It had been thirteen years since that fateful day and, true to her word, she'd never, again, stepped inside an elevator.

When Trevor and Tammy met at the entrance to Särkänniemi, Trevor said something in Finnish to the people at the gate, and they were both waved through. Much to Tammy's horror, Trevor was headed straight for Näsinneula. It turned out that the amusement park rides were about to be the *least* of her worries. Each step which took her closer to Näsinneula, tripled her fear. By the time she was standing at the entrance of the building, she could barely breathe. There was just one way to the top – a high-speed, *express* elevator. No stairs. *No, this is not going to happen!* After Trevor had paid the admission fee for *both* of them, Tammy looked at him, pleadingly. He *knew* how terrified she was of elevators... *and* he knew why.

When the elevator came to the ground floor, Tammy stared, her eyes wide with terror, and she took a step backwards as the doors opened. She then looked at Trevor and shook her head. She was a true coward. Trevor held out his hand to her – something he'd never done before. Trembling with sheer terror, Tammy eventually reached out and took his hand. As soon as their hands connected, she felt something she'd never thought possible, being this close to an elevator. With Trevor holding her hand, she felt *strong*. She felt *safe*. Tammy knew that Trevor would *never* let anything bad happen to her. He would never put her at risk. As Trevor stepped into the elevator, she closed her eyes and followed. When the doors closed, breathing became difficult for her. She squeezed Trevor's hand so tightly, she was *amazed* to see it had not broken into many pieces, when they reached the top.

"You did it!" Trevor said, excited, after they stepped out of the elevator.

Tammy was shaking like a leaf. When she glanced out from the windows of the observation deck, almost 200 metres above the ground, her knees buckled. She needed to sit… and *fast*. Trevor helped Tammy to a table, before disappearing for a few moments. He returned with a juice, and a Finnish pastry for her to eat. *I did it. I did it. Holy fuck, I did it!* Hands shaking madly, she reached down and started to nibble on the pastry, before looking up at Trevor, who had seated himself at the table, across from her. He was *proud* of her. She could see it in his eyes. More importantly, she was proud of *herself*.

There was just one problem… she now had to go back *down* in the elevator, in order to leave. After finally taking in the view, and taking some great photos of their surrounds, Trevor and Tammy walked back to the elevators. To Tammy's horror, the elevator on the left was being repaired. The doors were open and two men were standing on top of the elevator, servicing the cables. *Oh my God, get out of there now before it falls!* Tammy closed her eyes, and Trevor led her to the other elevator before pressing the button.

"It's okay. Elevators in Finland are very well looked after. You won't have any problems here. They are completely safe," Trevor said to Tammy, gently, as the elevator they were travelling in went down to the ground floor. When the doors opened, Tammy jumped out as quickly as she could.

"Hey, *Trevor?* While this has been super *fun* and all, let's never do this again, okay?" Tammy said. She looked at Trevor and attempted her best smile, while sounding ever-so-sarcastic. She had meant every word of it, however. While Tammy was indeed proud of herself for doing it, her heart was pounding way too fast, and she had to sit again, in order to try and calm down a little, before walking back to the hotel.

The weeks went by way too quickly, and Tammy's departure date had crept up on her before she realised it. It was, once again, time to go back to Australia. She decided to go for one more walk around the city, before packing her bags to go home. While doing so, she noticed a man wearing the hockey jersey of her favourite ice hockey team, *Tappara*. Tammy introduced herself to the bushy faced giant, telling him that she was Australia's biggest Tappara fan. He smiled and introduced himself as Mark, before saying a few things about another ice hockey team, *Ilves* – a team that Tammy knew absolutely nothing about. Sadly, Mark had said his comment about Ilves in Finnish and Tammy did not have time for any spontaneous Finnish lessons, although she could guess what *SAATANA* and *HELVETTI* might have meant. One was a font that she used on the computer. The other... well, it didn't sound nice. With no more time to ponder, Tammy needed to hurry back to the hotel and pack.

Trevor walked Tammy to the Tampere bus station. He carried her 20 kilogram suitcase the entire way, from the hotel to the bus. When they'd arrived, sadness came over her, just as it had, the time before. She did not want to be leaving this beautiful place. *Home is where the heart is... and Tampere definitely owns every part of my heart.* Tears flowed down her cheeks, as the bus made its way to Helsinki airport.

"We will meet again," Tammy quietly whispered out the window of the aeroplane, as it was towed out to the runway for take-off.

Chapter 29

Back in Australia, nothing had changed, at all. The problems in Kambah continued. Tammy spent most of her time indoors with her cats, although she *did* make one special trip into the city, to visit the Finnish Embassy. When she pulled into the car park and saw the Finnish flag, flying proudly at the front, she smiled, as memories of her friends and her favourite city started swimming around inside her mind.

The embassy, itself, was like a fortress. It took a while before Tammy actually found the buzzer to press, so she could request entry. The woman who answered had the same accent as her friends in Finland, and it warmed her heart to hear it.

"Yes? How can we help you today?" the voice came through the speaker.

"I would like to talk to you about how it would be possible to move from Australia to Finland... permanently," Tammy responded.

With that, a door opened (almost appearing out of nowhere) and Tammy was invited inside. Her jaw dropped when she stepped through the door. While the *outside* of the building looked like a fortress, the inside looked like a palace! *Oh my God!* Tammy had just seen a painted portrait of President Tarja Halonen on the wall which was no less than two storeys tall. *Every single thing the Finns do is big!*

As Tammy ogled at the picture of one of her all-time favourite people, another woman came and greeted her, inviting her to come into her office. Tammy followed, while the woman (ironically, *also* called Tarja) asked Tammy to take a seat. She eyed the walking stick, before asking Tammy what she would like to know about Finland.

"I have been there twice. Seriously, your country takes my breath away. It is so beautiful!" Tammy said, her face almost aching from smiling so wide.

Tarja blushed and thanked Tammy for her kind words. She was not used to people gushing when talking about Finland, and told Tammy that almost all Finns had a very low opinion of their own country, as they are very humble people. Tammy could not understand this at all. How could *anybody,* living in a place so *wonderful*, not realise how amazing it actually was?

"I would like to move to Finland," Tammy stated.

"Do you have family in Finland?" Tarja asked.

"No, but I do have friends there. My best friend also lives there, and I also support Tappara Ice Hockey team. Janne Ojanen is the best ice hockey play…." Tammy started to ramble.

"Yes, they are a good ice hockey team. Do you speak any Finnish?" Tarja asked.

Tammy thought back to any words she might have heard, and then remembered her encounter with Mark, before she'd left.

"I know *SAATANA* and I know *HELVETTI*. I also know *KIITOS* is what you say to thank somebody for something!" Tammy said, proudly.

The office was silent for a few minutes. *Either she is very impressed or I have seriously pissed her off.* Tammy went on to say that she had a perfect police record in Australia, and was a good person.

"I am sorry, but you will not be able to move to Finland. There are no reasons that would allow you to do so. You could get a working visa, but you have passed the maximum age of thirty, in which to do so," Tarja said, matter-of-factly.

Tears filled Tammy's eyes. She knew that Finland was where her future was supposed to be. Tampere, Trevor, Heidi and even Näsinneula... those things were her *future*. Tammy could not understand what she had possibly said or done wrong, to make this woman *not want* her in Finland.

"So, you are telling me that it is impossible for me to live in Finland?" Tammy asked, just to be sure that she had not misunderstood.

"Yes. It is impossible. You have no family in Finland. You are an invalid. You are too old for working permit. And you only know three Finnish words – two of which are curse words," Tarja replied.

Oh fuck! I KNEW I should have looked those up when I got back! With tears running down her cheeks, Tammy thanked Tarja for her help and went back to the car. She sat, quietly, in the car park for a few minutes, absolutely dumbfounded by what had been said. Tammy knew that she could not put up with the hell in Kambah for much longer. Although Steve was no longer knocking on her door each day, his sister-in-law, *Wendy*, had made a few appearances, trying to convince Tammy that they had become friends – something she was *SURE* was untrue.

Back at home, Tammy got online and told Trevor what had happened at the embassy. He didn't know what to say to her, but did tell her that he knew it would be hard, if she wanted to live in Finland. Their two countries were nothing alike. *I know – why else would I want to be there and not here?* Depressed, Tammy started cleaning the house from top to bottom, while her cats slept. Once the house was sparkling clean, she decided to get busy on a new project – *Tappara*.

Tammy had a MySpace page of her own, but decided that Tappara needed to have one, also. She was the biggest Australian Tappara fan *anywhere,* and had collected many pictures online over the past year or two. Tammy created a page, using as much coding knowledge as she could, to put the page together. She also chose one of her favourite applets, to let the different pictures show within a rotating cube, while the hockey team's club song played. Once she was happy with what she'd created, Tammy contacted another fan – Terry – who was well known as the WORLD's biggest Tappara fan. Terry ran a regular web site blog, discussing all that was amazing about her favourite ice hockey team. She asked Terry's permission to use all of the pictures and the theme music, before she went ahead and made the page public. Terry was thrilled that anybody in Australia had even *heard* of Tampere's ice hockey team, and asked if he could interview her, in order to write a story about her and the page in Tappara's magazine. Almost falling off her chair in shock at such a request, Tammy agreed to the interview.

Roughly one month passed. Fruit baskets and gifts were left on the front porch, with little notes and invitations, attached by Wendy. Each one was thrown to the trash. Trevor had told Tammy, often enough, that Wendy was a lot of things – none of them, good – but she was most definitely *not* Tammy's friend. Wendy was Michael's wife. Michael was Steve's brother. And Tammy was sure that not a single person in that family was even *remotely* sane.

Back at the computer, Tammy's Tappara page had received a friend request on Myspace. When Tammy opened the page of the person making the request, she was stunned. *Ha! It really IS a small world!* The profile picture was of a big, bushy bearded man wearing a Tappara jersey. Tammy immediately clicked *ACCEPT* before sending a personal message to him.

"Mark, I remember you! You talked about Ilves and Saatana and Helvetti, just before I came back to Australia. How are you?" Tammy typed. No answer came back until the following day.

"Yes, Australian Tappara fan. I remember. Did you know they wrote you about in Tappara magazine last week?" Mark asked.

"Wow, that was quick!" Tammy replied, stunned. "They only did the interview a month ago! So you are a Tappara fan?" Tammy asked. *D'oh! Of course he is, you bloody idiot!!* "Never mind, of course you are, hehehe. I approved your friend request to the page."

"Did you see me?" Mark asked.

"Umm... see you where?" Tammy suddenly felt like she had missed something in the conversation.

"I am in your MySpace banner, holding up one of the big letters of T-A-P-P-A-R-A. That is me, next to one of my best friends. We are big Tappara fans!" Mark typed.

"Holy crap! That is brilliant! You look awesome!" Tammy replied, now looking at Mark in the picture. "Hey, if you are on Skype, do you want to exchange details?"

With that, Mark and Tammy became instant friends, both on MySpace and Skype. Tammy often found herself talking to Trevor and Mark, both at the same time, although not in the same conversation. While all of them were major Tappara fans, Mark and Trevor didn't have anything else in common, except that they were Finnish. Trevor was a computer genius, Tammy's guardian angel and best friend. Mark was a Tappara fan who loved to talk about ice hockey, ice hockey and even more ice hockey.

Two weeks after adding Mark to Skype, Tammy was in a video chat with him for the very first time. Mark was in a high-rise hotel, with Näsijärvi in the background. The room where he was staying was absolutely beautiful, but he looked completely miserable. Tammy asked Mark why he was so sad.

"I broke up with my fiancée a few months back. At the moment, I am in the hotel, which was a gift from my mum and my grandma, for our honeymoon. It was non-refundable. I hate being here," Mark said, sounding so lost. "I will be here on my own for one whole week. Just me, lake views and a television. All of this, I could be doing at home. It is boring."

"Yeah. I know all about boring. I am at home almost always. We could Skype chat each day, if you like. Then it would not be so boring," Tammy suggested. "Are there any Tappara games coming up soon?"

"No. The season finished, even before you went back to Australia, that day!" Mark said, surprised that Tammy did not know.

"But you were wearing your *Tappara* jersey, that day," Tammy pointed out.

"Of course I was! Tappara is the *best* team! Tappara on terästä!" Mark said, breaking off into a world of song about Tappara, for the next fifteen minutes.

Whoa! Definitely addicted, this guy! When Mark finished his vocal dedication to Tappara, Tammy stood at her seat and applauded. Although he lived and breathed Tappara the way that Tammy lived and breathed Finland, she was appreciative that he, at least, had a good singing voice to go with it.

Mark and Tammy video chatted for many hours each day, which made Mark's week alone, not-so-lonely after all. They enjoyed talking to each other, and when Mark returned home, they continued their daily chats, even when he was visiting with his mum and his grandma. Tammy would hear them all talking Finnish to each other, and she didn't understand a single word. Mark would also hear the commotion which occasionally came from Australia when Tammy was online, and he did not like what he heard.

One day in October, Tammy had yet another encounter with Wendy. They got into a screaming match at the front door, and Tammy forgot that she had an active video chat going in the next room, until *after* she'd finished screaming obscenities, and slammed the front door so hard that it almost came off its hinges. She stood there for about a minute, muttering under her breath about how much Wendy stunk up the planet, before she remembered her chat with Mark. *Oh shit!* When she went running back to the computer room, Mark's jaw was on the floor. He asked what was going on, and Tammy went through the full story about her ex, her hiding, her memory loss, the cats in the neighbourhood going missing for many months, and her *constantly* being harassed by her ex's sister-in-law. Tammy absolutely hated her life.

"Hmmm...," Mark started, and Tammy could see that he was deep in thought. "Both of our lives suck beyond words," Mark said, stating the obvious. "We have been talking every single day now for a few months. You know all my secrets. I now know yours. And you have even seen inside of my underpants, one time, when I dropped the laptop on the floor, when I was talking on Skype video chat in toilet."

Yes. Thank you so much for reminding me of that. Gross! "Yes, all true," Tammy said.

"So, want to get married?" Mark asked. Tammy stared at him in total disbelief, wondering if he was actually serious. Silence filled the air, until: "Look, your life sucks. My life sucks. Individually, our lives suck. But together... well, when I am talking to you, my life doesn't suck," Mark said.

"Plus we also both love Tappara, *and* we both love Finland," Tammy finally replied.

"Do you think you would want to marry me?" Mark asked, again.

He is nothing like Steve. Plus, he can sing! A thousand thoughts went through Tammy's mind, before she finally smiled her biggest, happiest smile and shouted "YES!" She quickly updated her status, both on MySpace and Facebook, as *"ENGAGED,"* and tagged Mark in the update. Mark was excited about his Australian fiancée. Well at least he *was...* until he got the update notification request.

"Umm... I haven't told my Mum yet," Mark said, looking at the screen with a worried face. "Oh, what the heck!" he continued, before accepting the update notification request. His status *also* changed to *"ENGAGED,"* before Mark's mother called him into the kitchen. She didn't sound happy, and Tammy had a feeling that Mark's mother knew, a little bit *too* quickly, about the status change. "Sorry, but I have to go now. See you tomorrow!" Mark said, waving to the screen. Tammy waved back.

After closing the window, Trevor came online to say hello. *Did I really just get engaged?* Lost in her thoughts, Tammy finally noticed the new chat window.

"Hey there, Mr T. I have news," Tammy said to her best friend.

"Yeah?" Trevor said.

"I just got engaged!" Tammy said, still trying to let it sink in.

"What? Who did you get engaged to? Wendy?" Trevor asked, mockingly.

"No. I got engaged to Mark," Tammy said, simply. "And I am still stunned. And yes, he is nothing like Steve, and he likes Tappara and he loves Finland and he...."

"Calm down," Trevor said. "Is this *real*?"

"It's real. I'm getting married," Tammy replied, finally smiling. She could not wait until tomorrow, to talk to Mark again. As soon as they actually made official plans regarding a wedding, Tammy would tell her family.

The following day, Mark came online. He told Tammy that his mother was furious about the engagement, but his grandma liked Tammy's laugh. It was loud and it was real. On hearing this, Tammy already liked Mark's grandma. But she knew that getting his mother to trust her – especially with Mark being her only child – was going to be a very big, uphill battle. *Bring it on!* Mark was definitely somebody worth fighting for.

With both Mark and Tammy having to fill out lots of paperwork for international marriage permissions in their own countries, they got busy *immediately*, ensuring that everything would be done properly. Once the paperwork was officially stamped with each country's seal, they could finally set a date.

"How about 14th February?" Mark suggested. "Oh wait, that is full already. Crap!"

"It's okay. Are there *any* dates free in February?" Tammy asked.

The only available date on the Magistrate's calendar was 10th February, so they grabbed it. Each of them would need at least one witness at the ceremony. Mark would be inviting his grandmother and his best friend. His mother decided not to attend. Tammy invited Terry and Trevor to be her witnesses. Terry accepted, but Trevor declined, breaking her heart.

Three weeks before leaving for Finland, Tammy developed a severe tonsillitis infection, landing her in hospital. She had not been able to drink anything in almost a week, and was extremely dehydrated. Sitting in the emergency room for seven hours, her throat in agony, she was unable to make any noise as her throat was so constricted. Doctors and nurses ran past, this way and that, and she watched as patients were treated and discharged. She was now at the stage where she could barely breathe. Then she heard a baby screaming. The baby had been attacked by the family dog, and although that baby was unable to say many words, Tammy could hear her, pleading with the doctor, not to touch her. Tears ran down Tammy's cheeks as her eyes grew heavy. She was tired.

A nurse suddenly stopped in front of Tammy, before screaming for the doctor to come quickly. The stress of hearing the baby's pleas had caused Tammy's nose to start bleeding. And the liquid running down her cheeks was not water. She was crying, yes, but white and yellow pus were all that her eyes could produce. Her dehydration was at a life-threatening level. Tammy was admitted to the hospital, and three bags of saline were fed through her veins, via IV drip. It was not until the *third* bag was almost empty, that Tammy finally needed to pee. The following morning, she was also able to eat again, but only soft foods. The final complication… she was now Deaf.

By the time her doctor had returned from holidays, one week later, a very small amount of hearing had returned to her left ear. B-doc examined Tammy's ears and throat, before drawing a diagram of what had happened to her ears, regarding acidic mucous from the tonsillitis, which led to scarring of the tube which ran between her ears and throat. She also advised Tammy that this could also be more aftermath of the attack that day, which had come back to haunt her. Tammy was told that her hearing may or may not return, but at this stage, it was not looking hopeful.

On 16th January, Tammy *again* arranged for her cats to be fully looked after and spoiled, while she was away. It was time to head back to Finland – her very last visit as a tourist. When she arrived at Helsinki airport, after going through customs, she made her way to the arrivals area. Mark was seated on a bench, staring at his phone.

She walked right up to her beau, suitcase in tow, and said, "Hey, mister."

Mark blushed and smiled. The very first thing Tammy noticed about him was that he'd actually shaved! Her fiancé had sacrificed his beard for this meeting, and she wasn't sure whether or not she should thank him, or be saddened by all that newly-homeless hair. Mark went back to looking at his phone. It was then, that Tammy realised Mark was texting back and forth with his mother. *Oh boy. This is going to be a lot harder than I thought. Please tell me his mother doesn't also make all of his decisions for him.* With three weeks to go until the wedding, Tammy was soon going to know *all there was* to know about her fiancé, and his family.

After the bus ride to Tampere, Tammy slipped twice – once, in front of a bus – as well as falling into a snow pile. By the time she *finally* met Mark's mum, Sunny, and his grandma, Amelia, Tammy looked like Frosty the Snowman's long lost cousin. She was *literally* covered, from head to toe, with snow... and had dropped her video camera into a snow pile. It took a few days before the video camera worked again, such was life. She decided to kick herself in the butt *later* for it, when there were no witnesses.

Tammy and Mark hit it off *famously,* during those three weeks, but Tammy started to get cold feet, two days before the wedding. She went for a walk around town on her own, after an argument with Mark about a chocolate bar, and found herself walking along one of the streets towards Näsinneula. She'd seen the Heating Plant on the lake, and walked in that direction, admiring how it constantly changed colours. Before she knew it, she was lost. Tammy pulled the little GPS out of her pocket, so that she could find her way home, but the memory card had fallen out. The GPS was not going to help her tonight. She was also far too humiliated over their silly argument to call Mark. When it started to snow again, Tammy was shivering from the cold. She rang the only number she could think of. When Trevor answered the phone, Tammy was crying. She was lost.

"Look around, and tell me everything you see, right now," Trevor said, urgently, knowing how cold it was outside.

Tammy described the tall buildings which surrounding her, a gate (or maybe it was a fence), a tunnel, and she could see the Heating Plant and a road, but she was stuck inside a yard full of snow, and couldn't get over the gate. *How the hell did I end up here?* She wondered if her time was up and if she would freeze to death tonight but, within minutes of hanging up the phone to Trevor, a voice called out to her.

"*There* you are," Trevor said, calm and relieved.

He handed Tammy some sultanas to get her blood sugar up and raise her body temperature. Tammy told him about the stupid argument she'd had with Mark, and how she'd gone for a walk to clear her head, before ending up lost. She was attracted to the colours in the Heating Plant. Trevor took her there, and she was able to take some incredible photos. He then walked her to the bus stop, before ringing Mark to let him know that Tammy was okay, and that she was now coming home.

"You will be okay," said Trevor, looking into her eyes. "*Everything* will be okay, now."

And she believed him.

Chapter 30

The day of the wedding had finally arrived. Tammy was nervous, but was able to maintain her calm and confident outer-shell. Mark's face was bushy again, and Tammy asked if he could, at least, trim it. He decided to make a deal. If she allowed him to wear his *Tappara* jersey for the wedding, he would shave the hippy hairs away. *Oh dear.* With not much time to spare, Tammy finally agreed. Mark disappeared into the bathroom, re-appearing a short time later with toilet paper pieces stuck to his face. *Yeah, that is exactly the look I was hoping for, on my wedding day.* Shaking her head, she tidied Mark's face up before they headed to the car. It was -16 degrees outside and, just as they arrived at the car, Tammy asked Mark if he'd remembered to bring the rings.

"Rings? What rings?" Mark asked, honestly confused.

"Seriously? *Seriously!* You do not have *rings* on the morning of our *wedding?*" Tammy snapped.

Mark shook his head, "No."

Their first stop, that morning, was to a jeweller, after Tammy put her foot down and said, "No rings, no marriage. It is that simple." She was not joking and, Mark knew it.

Finally, they both *nervously* made their way to the Magistrate's office. Tammy wore her wedding dress underneath her thick snowsuit and snow boots. When they arrived at the Magistrate's chapel, Tammy quickly ducked into the toilets and stripped off the snow gear. Mark's face showed that he was happy, when she walked back into the chapel wearing a wedding dress and high heels. *Even with these bloody heels, I am still a short arse!* Tammy was feeling butterflies, *boot-stomping* the waltz inside her stomach. She looked over and saw Mark's two witnesses – his grandmother and his best friend. Tammy's witness was also present, and she thanked Terry for coming. She handed him the video camera and asked if he could possibly capture the event on camera, to which he happily agreed.

Mark stood by Tammy's side, in front of the Magistrate, who then asked, in Finnish, if Mark wanted to be Tammy's lawfully wedded husband. Mark responded in English: "I DO!" The Minister then asked Tammy, in English, if she wanted to take Mark to be her lawfully wedded husband. In Finnish, Tammy responded "TAHDON! (I DO!)," and, they'd fully confused the Magistrate by language-switching. Both Tammy and Mark were nervous, and giggled when they realised what they'd just said. After the marriage certificates (one in English for Tammy, and one in Finnish for Mark) had been signed and issued, it was then time to prepare for the honeymoon.

For Tammy, a honeymoon in Canberra for three months was boring. But for Mark, this would be his first trip to Australia, and he was excited. Being used to Finnish winters, Mark decided to mainly pack clothes he'd wear in summer. This made sense, except for the fact that in Finland, all buildings were *heated* indoors. It was a basic human right to be warm. But in Australia, one had to be financially well-off to afford heating inside their home. At Tammy's house, if the outside temperature was -5 degrees, it meant that the temperature indoors was *usually* around -2 degrees.

While watching television, on the first night in Canberra, Mark's only words, through chattering teeth, were, "*Fuck*, here's cold!" He had socks and slippers on his feet, a beanie on his head, and 2–3 blankets over the top of him, as he shivered.

The honeymoon took place in Australia for two reasons. Firstly, it was Mark's chance to experience an exotic country, which he'd dreamed of visiting, his entire life. Secondly, it would give both Tammy and Mark a chance to figure out where they would want to spend the rest of their lives – in Australia or in Finland. It took less than a week for Mark and Tammy *both* to decide that *Finland* would be their home, after the honeymoon ended.

Tammy's family, in Queensland, planned a family reunion. The timing was crucial for them, as it would be the very *last* time they'd ever see Tammy. It would also be the *only* chance they'd have to welcome the new addition to their family, which proved to be very interesting, especially since Tammy had not returned to Queensland in fifteen years. Penny made the journey, up north, a comfortable one. The air-conditioning kept them warm or cool, depending on the air temperature outside. Tammy and Mark spent a week with Ralph and Coral. Both were amazed at how *tall* their new son-in-law was, while Ralph had many problems understanding Mark's Finnish accent. Mark also didn't understand much of what Ralph and Coral were saying either, since they *apparently* had strong Australian accents, themselves.

At the end of the week, Ralph and Coral headed down to the Gold Coast for a Navy Reunion with Ralph's old sailor mates, while Tammy and Mark headed to the family reunion. Almost all of Tammy's family had skin as black as midnight. Whenever a person in Australia heard Tammy's surname, it was immediately linked that of the Australian Aboriginal Gubbi Gubbi tribe in Queensland. Everybody at the reunion shared the same surname. This now included Mark, who'd chosen to take his wife's name when they married. As each relative met him, Mark would introduce himself by his first and new last name. Each person he met almost fainted. Here was a giant of a man, skin almost fluorescent-white, amongst his new family of short Blackfellas. By the time the reunion ended, several hours later, however, everybody had become well-acquainted with the newest member of their clan. Mark touched many hearts that day, and was heartily welcomed into the family.

Back in Canberra, Tammy showed Mark the most beautiful sights of Canberra. He also saw more than his share of kangaroos and koalas. He tried many new foods, and fell in love with the Aussie meat pie, as well as lamb shanks and kangaroo steaks. Most of his meals, however, were cooked at home by his wife. Mark was in charge of answering the door, and accompanied his wife, at all times, when she had to go outside, whether it was to the store or just to the backyard. He was her husband – her protector.

Then the time had finally arrived. It was time to close up shop. Tammy hired a giant skip to go in front of her house, and she carefully went through everything she owned, deciding what was rubbish and what was not. Most of what she'd owned would go to charity. Each box of her own items would cost $400 to send to Finland by post. In total, she posted ten boxes to Finland, most of which included antiques, cat toys, shoes and some clothes. She also packed her Altar Tools into boxes, her giant Amethyst crystal bowl, DVDs which could not be purchased overseas... the list went on and on.

Tammy also had to get her *three cats* ready for the journey. All three were microchipped, and a company which specialised in sending pets internationally – Dogtainers – were hired to get her three furballs to Finland *safely*, with all paperwork required for customs in both countries.

When almost everything was sent, with the exception of what would be going with them in their suitcases, Tammy decided to hold an open-house, indoor garage sale. People came in *droves*, when they heard about the garage sale, all wanting to scoop up a bargain. In those two days, Tammy managed to raise around $7,000, which was a mind-blowing effort. Although it had been pouring rain, people were grateful to be able to look at everything in dry comfort. The tools and Tammy's Harry Potter collection went first, followed by everything in her kitchen. By the end of the weekend, just a few items of furniture remained. A truck arrived, on Monday morning, to pick up the furniture, while *another* truck came to take away the skip. The cats went to the vet's office, in preparation for their flight, and it was almost time to go. Just one thing was left: Penny.

Two days before their flight was due to leave, Tammy and Mark drove to a car yard, in Fyshwick, which had been recommended to them. They had tried to sell the car privately, but only one person had responded to the advertisement – a New South Wales police officer, Shane, who had refused to offer her more than $1,000. Tammy scoffed. *Are all state policemen total assholes?* Her car was worth a lot more and she knew it, as it had all of its papers, and she'd been the only owner. Penny was in mint condition, and had never missed a service. When Tammy said she would *not* take $1,000, Shane *literally* laughed at her, and said, "If you can do better, be my guest." With that, he left. *Snobby bastard, you are! Please give me your business card, so I can wipe my butt with yours, too.* What a jerk.

Back in Fyshwick, Tammy and Mark entered the car yard, after parking her beloved car out the front. Tammy had removed her personalised plates from Penny, and had re-attached government-issued registration plates. While they sat inside, the car yard owner went out and appraised the car. When he came back inside, his offer was ready.

"We can give you $6,000 for the car," the car yard owner said.

"Deal," said Tammy. They had no time to barter or mess around. While it was very sad for her, to be selling a car that her father had helped her choose, she also felt joy that a bully like Shane would *not* be getting the car. As soon as cash had changed hands, Tammy and Mark walked to the bus stop and, once on the bus, Tammy happily rang Shane and told him that the car was just sold for $6,000.

"Bullshit. You're *bluffing*," said the bullying Shane. "You *promised* it to *me!*" he screamed into the phone.

"Nah. Your exact words, I believe, were, *if you can do better, be my guest.* So I *took* your challenge, did better, and now the car is sold. Thank you, and have a lovely day," Tammy said, with a smile.

"You fucking *bitch!*" Shane screamed into the phone. *Oh, such a gentleman.*

"Thank you," Tammy said, before hanging up the phone. She found it rather *uncanny* how similar Shane and Steve were, in personality.

Back in Kambah, the house was completely empty. Tammy offered all of her remaining cat furniture to Suzy and Rex, next door. Rex had still not recovered from losing his cats, but he thanked her anyway, and said that they will have more cats in the future.

Tammy asked ACT Housing's manager to meet them at the property on the Friday – three days before their flight was due to leave. The manager didn't show up, so Tammy left the keys on the bench inside, after taking photos of every single room inside the house, which had been professionally cleaned and was immaculate. She then took photos of the front and back yards, which were perfectly mown and manicured. Tammy and Mark then left for the bus station, each with a full suitcase and a carry-on bag, excited to be starting their new lives... *together.*

Aided by a wheelchair for Tammy, both she and Mark were taken through each airport in record time, due to the fact that Tammy was already sedated with pain medication, travel-sickness medication and sedatives, and was almost *asleep* in the wheelchair. Mark carried Tammy's walking stick, so it would not be lost.

On arrival at Helsinki airport, Sunny and Amelia both waited for Tammy and Mark to arrive. The car was parked nearby. Tammy and Mark went through customs, as per the usual thing, but as the customs officer recognised her from her *other* trips (referring to her as *the Tappara fan from Australia*), he simply waved them through.

When they'd all met up in the arrivals lounge, Tammy unlocked her bag so that she could change the SIM card over. The sight which greeted her left her utterly *speechless*. The very last thing Tammy had packed into her suitcase was an almost-full box of Splenda – a powdered white sugar that Australians used in their tea. That box had actually *burst* in transit, leaving everything in her suitcase covered in a fine, white powder. Mark and Tammy looked at each other, eyes wide, *both* grateful that their suitcase had *not* been opened at customs. They would have certainly had a whole lot of explaining to do!

For the first week in Finland, Tammy and Mark lived in Nokia, at Mark's grandmother's house, while Mark's grandma lived with Sunny in Tampere. Once a suitable apartment was found, after the cats had safely arrived in Finland, they would then finally move to a new address.

All three cats arrived in Finland in one piece, but were a little shaken at having been with so many strangers. It did not take long for them to calm down, however. They slept in the car, for the entire journey from Helsinki to Nokia. That evening, Mark spent some quality time in the Sauna. Out of habit, he left the Sauna window *open* before going to bed. The next morning, all three cats were gone.

Mark was absolutely beside himself with grief, apologising profusely. Tammy was frantic. She had *not* just gone through the past (what felt like) hundred years of insanity, just to lose all three cats in one day! When they opened the front door, Joel and Pierre were standing there, looking scared. Mark carried them back inside. Tammy then went through the neighbourhood, searching and *praying* that Conan would be found. When she'd asked a neighbour, the neighbour suggested that perhaps a fox had taken Conan. *Oh yes, thank you for making this so much fucking harder!*

After walking quite some distance, falling into a ditch and spraining her ankle, Tammy then sat on the back porch of the Nokia townhouse, calling Conan's name over and over, crying her eyes out. After about four hours, Tammy heard something oddly familiar. Was it Conan's cry? She stopped crying and listened, but no noise came. Again, she called out to Conan. It took about a minute, before she heard it again. "Meeew," came Conan's distinct cry. It was faint and Tammy could not figure out where it was coming from.

"MARK! MARK, COME HERE QUICKLY! *MARK!*" Tammy shouted.

When Mark came to the back door, she asked him to be quiet and listen. Tammy then called Conan's name again. This time, Mark and Tammy *both* heard Conan's cry.

"Can you find him? I don't know where the noise is coming from," Tammy said, quietly. Mark walked around to the back of the neighbour's place, listening, as Tammy continued to call Conan's name. Finally, he found Conan, trapped under the wood slats of the neighbour's back porch. They had no idea how he'd gotten himself in there, but they knew there was only one way to get him out. Mark used his bare hands, and lifted up one of the wood slats. Conan willingly let Mark pick him up and take him back home to his human mum. Tammy knew Conan wasn't about to run off again, any time soon.

One week later, Tammy, Mark, and all three cats moved into their new apartment, in Tampere. Tammy was still Deaf, in her right ear, and had minimal hearing in her left. This did not impede her ability to clean the house, however, and she spent the next few days sorting everything out, inside their home, finding the perfect place for every little thing. Once the house was set up, they only needed to buy two things – a bed and a washing machine. Both were done easily, and with minimal fuss. One thing Tammy *quickly* found out, was that everything costed a whole lot *less* in Finland, than it cost in Australia.

Regardless of her new setting, at the back of her mind, Tammy *still* worried that Steve would eventually find her. She knew he wanted her dead, but now, she lived in a place he could not access. With a criminal record, there was no way he'd be able to get into the country, nor get past Mark – *or Trevor* – to get to her. The Finnish police were alerted to the severity of the situation, as was the Magistrate's office. Tammy was able to legally change her name for free, but this could be done only *once*. Knowing it was her only opportunity to stay hidden, she took full advantage of that offer, and now officially lives under a new name... in her new forever-home.

Epilogue

Tammy spent the following five years at school, learning the Finnish language, full-time. Not only did she want to be able to communicate with people in her new country; she also wanted to immerse herself in the culture, and needed to be proficient in Finnish, in order to become a Finnish citizen.

During her second year of schooling in Finland in 2011, Tammy received a concussion, when snow and ice slipped from the roof of a seven-storey building, landing directly on top of her. Tammy spent two days at home calling out to one of her dead cats, wondering why he would not come when called, before she was taken to the hospital. Many people die each year, in Finland, when snow and ice fall from the trees or rooftops in winter. Regardless, Tammy had once again survived. Her guardian angel was still watching over her.

* * *

Until writing this book, Tammy had not known that her family had *often* tried to ring her, during the time she'd lived with Steve. She asked them all why they contacted her only two or three times in six years, only to find that each time they had rung her, Steve would tell them that Tammy was not at home.

With everything that had happened to Tammy in Australia, she has no plans to return to her native country. The laws of Australia do not protect Aboriginal women, especially those who are in danger from their spouses. For the rest of her life, Tammy will be running from a man who simply couldn't let go. She now puts all of her faith in her husband, her best friend and the Finnish authorities, to keep her safe.

Studying a foreign language when almost Deaf is difficult – near-*impossible*, actually – but Tammy persevered, and achieved a passing grade in reading, writing and speaking. Although failing the listening part of the exam, Tammy was able to submit her citizenship application, with an accompanying medical certificate regarding her deafness. She is now an Indigenous Australian with Finnish citizenship.

Mark spent those same five years at school, learning to become a builder and a security guard. Although these were the same two occupations of Tammy's previous fiancé, she knows that Mark and Steve are nothing alike, nor will they *ever* be. Mark has stood by her through it all.

On 23rd November 2014, Tammy lost the remainder of her hearing and was diagnosed as profoundly Deaf. Although she is able to speak both English and Finnish, she can no longer communicate with her best friend or family without the use of a keyboard. The city of Tampere advised Tammy and Mark that they could learn Finnish Sign Language, at a cost of 4,000€, in Helsinki, if they wished. Without that kind of money lying around, the only other option was to wait many months, before the city could provide them with a Finnish Sign Language teacher. Going for months, without communicating, was a sure way to end a marriage.

Tammy and Mark opted, *instead*, to study *American* Sign Language, thanks to the guided tutelage of Dr Bill Vicars of Sacramento State University, USA. All lessons, and tuition, were provided, free of charge, by Dr Bill Vicars, who has devoted *countless* selfless hours to Tammy and Mark, teaching them both how to communicate using ASL, thanks to his American Sign Language University website at http://www.Lifeprint.com. Dr Vicars continues to be a trusted friend to Tammy, to this very day.

Tammy and Mark have been happily married for seven years, now... and counting, with both destroying every single obstacle that tries to divide and conquer them. When Tammy became fully Deaf, Mark did not have to think twice, when offered sign language lessons through Dr Vicars.

Since living in Finland, Tammy has learned of the many differences between her native country and her new home country. On the good side of things, Finland is serious about saving the planet, offers schooling (including University studies) for free, offers free health care, free indoor-heating in winter, and every home has high-speed internet ...also for free.

On the downside, Tampere city refuses to provide Tammy with an interpreter, because her knowledge of Finnish language is below par. Her requests to have a Speech-to-Text interpreter, in Finland, have been constantly denied, time and again, since Tammy lost all hearing, regardless of the laws which state that Deaf, blind and disabled people of Finland are not to be discriminated against, in any way.

On 7th May 2015, Tammy was diagnosed as legally blind. Her loss of hearing and eyesight were both a direct result of the head injuries inflicted by Steve, with both exacerbated *even further* after the concussion she sustained in 2011.

In April of 2016, the mystery of how Steve had kept tabs on Tammy's constant whereabouts was solved. Tammy's trust in befriending people from the internet has been irreversibly shattered.

Regardless of the hurdles, which have been *constantly* thrown her way in Finland, Tammy has been able to remain hopeful, with the help of her family, Dr Vicars, The Finnish Association of the Deaf and the Finnish Deaf-Blind Society. She also believes that the Goddess has given her strength, when she needed it the most, and that her guardian angel (A.J.) is watching over her.

* * *

Thank you so much for reading Tammy's – *my* story. I have written this book in the third person, so as to try and distance myself from these memories directly, while reliving and writing about them. As hard as this book was to write, I am hopeful that men out there will read it, absorb it and treat their special someone like gold. Men need to think of what they would do if *another* man treated his sister, daughter, mother or grandmother in an abusive way, before deciding how to treat the women in their lives.

I am equally hopeful that women out there will know when to walk away from a relationship which turns violent. I pray that any of you, who have read my story, will gain strength from it, and will never give up. Regardless of how helpless you may feel, you are stronger than you realise.

When every single door in your life seems to close around you, grab a sledge hammer and make your *own* door. Remember, you are in charge of your own destiny.

Connect with Rosie Malezer

Thank you for reading my story. Should you wish to contact me, here are my social media coordinates:

Follow me on Twitter:
http:/www.twitter.com/rosiemalezer

Follow me on Facebook:
https://www.facebook.com/rosiemalezer

Subscribe to my blog:
https://rosiemalezer.wordpress.com

See my books on Amazon:
http://www.amazon.com/Rosie-Malezer/e/B00YSHBHFS